Timber-Frame Houses

Fine Homebuilding®
GREAT HOUSES

Timber-Frame Houses

The Taunton Press

Cover photo: Robert Chase
Back-cover photos: top left, Tom Collicott;
top right, Tafi Brown; bottom left, Sandy Bennett

© 1992 by The Taunton Press, Inc.

First printing: November 1992
Printed in the United States of America

A Fine Homebuilding Book

Fine Homebuilding® is a trademark of The Taunton Press, Inc., registered in the
U.S. Patent and Trademark Office.

The Taunton Press, 63 South Main Street, Box 5506,
Newtown, CT 06470-5506

Library of Congress Cataloging-in-Publication Data

Timber-frame houses.
    p.   cm.
   "Collection of 31articles from the first 10 years of Fine
homebuilding" – Introd.
   "Fine homebuilding, great houses."
   "A Fine homebuilding book" – T.p. verso.
   Includes index.
   ISBN 1-56158-047-3
   1. Wooden-frame houses – Design and construction   I. Fine homebuilding.
TH4818.W6T56   1992   92-32046
690' .837 – dc20   CIP

Contents

Introduction

The ancient craft of timber framing has enjoyed a remarkable revival in recent years. And no wonder—contemporary timber framers have been able to maintain the beauty and durability of their complex craft while meeting modern needs and using new construction techniques.

Over the past century, the evolution of wood-frame construction has been driven by the search for greater efficiencies more suitable to large-scale construction projects. One result is that the beauty has been taken out of the framing. Modern stud frames are hidden in the walls, where hundreds of 2x sticks are joined by nails. Timber framing, on the other hand, celebrates and flaunts the wood frame, as well as the joinery that holds it all together. And that, perhaps above all else, is what makes it so appealing to modern home owners.

Fine Homebuilding magazine helped popularize modern timber framing and was a catalyst for its revival. This collection of 31 articles from the first 10 years of *Fine Homebuilding* includes articles by leading teachers and practitioners of the craft, including Tedd Benson (author of *The Timber-Frame Home* and coauthor of *Building the Timber Frame House*), Jack Sobon (coauthor of *Timber Frame Construction*), Ed Levin, Alex Wade, Jeff Arvin, George Nash and many others.

This volume provides a thorough introduction to modern timber framing. Articles cover the history and evolution of timber framing and its various influences (Japanese, European and American). The tools and techniques of traditional mortise-and-tenon joinery are discussed alongside innovations in foam-core (stress-skin) panels. Also included are stories describing the construction of replicas of architectural classics as well as inspiring designs featuring open, modern floor plans and passive-solar techniques. Additional articles cover sizing and handling large beams and hybrid designs combining timber and 2x framing. Together, these articles will inspire and inform readers seeking to understand and to practice this 2,000-year-old architectural style.

—The Editors

An Introduction to Timber Framing

Learning this traditional method
begins with the mortise-and-tenon joint

by Tedd Benson

The standards of work in timber-frame structures aren't new; we have inherited them from a 2,000-year-old tradition of craftsmanship. The evolution of this building method (which throughout much of history was just about all there was to carpentry) resulted from pursuing a very simple goal: to put together better and stronger buildings. The proof of the success of this development can be found in the barns, houses, churches, temples and cathedrals that have become architectural treasures in all parts of the world. It wasn't until the advent of nails, joinery hardware and dimensioned lumber that true timber framing went into decline.

In reviving the craft today, we pay careful attention to the lessons and the standards evinced by these old buildings. Indeed, the thrill of practicing timber framing today lies in knowing that there is much left to learn, and in believing that each improvement brings us closer to the day when we can feel we are no longer journeymen. At the same time, we are working toward continued refinement and development. Timber-frame buildings are finding renewed acceptance for many reasons, but the integrity of the structure and the rewards to the craftsman and home owner are preserved only when high standards are maintained.

In our own shop we have learned this obvious truth the hard way—good timber frames happen only as a result of good joinery. Precise work is as important in timber framing as it is in cabinetry, so joint-making is the first thing an aspiring timber-framer needs to learn.

Mortise and tenon—This joint is practically the definition of a timber frame. Most of the joints that go into a frame are variations on the basic mortise-and-tenon joint. Once you've mastered the skills for making this joint, you should be able to execute just about any other joint in the frame. And since there are several hundred joints in the average timber frame, speed and precision are equally important.

The joint we will be working on is the shouldered mortise-and-tenon (above). It's a good example of a slightly modified mortise-and-tenon. We use this type of joint where major girts or connector beams join a post. The full width of the horizontal timber is held by the bottom shoulder on the post, and this extra bearing surface makes the joint far stronger than a straight mortise-and-tenon.

Squaring up—Before you can lay out the joint, the timber must be square at the joint area. Each face of the joint must be square if you're going to achieve a precise fit. One way to square and flatten timbers is to run them through a large thickness planer. With pine,

From *Fine Homebuilding* magazine (December 1982) 12:22-26

What makes a good framing chisel?

The framing chisel is to the timber framer what the racket is to the tennis player: You can't play the game without it. Since every phase of timber framing requires work with the chisel, you will want to own the best possible tool. A good chisel will not make you a good timber framer, but like a good racket, it will immediately improve your game and make you much happier as you learn. Those of us who work with timbers a lot look for the perfect chisel the way that King Arthur's knights used to search for the Holy Grail. It's just that elusive.

Let me describe the perfect framing chisel, sometimes called a firmer chisel or a beamer's chisel. The blade should be stout and strong, but not too long because it's difficult to control the cutting edge if your hand is a foot away. The blade should be 6 in. to 8 in. long, $\frac{3}{8}$ in. thick at the shoulder, and $\frac{3}{16}$ in. thick at the bevel. The steel must have a Rockwell hardness in the range of 60 (C) if it's going to hold a good edge, especially in oak or other hardwoods. The back of the blade must be honed perfectly flat if it's to cut true. To reduce friction and to enable the cutting edge to get into tight places, it's better if the side edges are bevel ground. The handle itself should be hickory or ash, and it should be fitted with a steel ring just below its striking surface. To prevent the handle from splitting, it should fit into a socket rather than over a tang. You'd order the tool as a bevel-edged socket framing chisel. Old or new, I have yet to see an unmodified tool that fits this description. The chisel you will get will probably be a compromise.

If you are lucky enough to find an old framing chisel that is still in good condition, buy it. Most of these are socket types (the old-timers were very practical) and you might well find one of the better-known brands like Buck, Witherby or White. Be careful, though. Many of these old chisels have lost their temper or have been used as a pry bar once too often.

If you're buying a new chisel, you'll probably have to choose between a Marples (heavy-duty tang), Sorby (heavy-duty tang), or Greenlee, and several brands of Japanese temple carpenter's chisels. Almost everyone in our shop uses either Marples or Sorby chisels. They have excellent blades and are nicely balanced. Most of us have modified them by having the edges beveled at a local machine shop. All of us are frustrated by the frequency with which we have to replace split handles.

The most disappointing chisel in the group is the Greenlee. Though they do have sockets for the handles, my experience with them shows that their blades are poorly ground, and their backs are anything but flat. We've cut at least 1 in. off the tip and completely reground the back of several Greenlees to make them useful. On some, the tang is slightly off center, which makes the tool feel very unbalanced.

The newest tool on the market is the Sorby framing chisel, which is made specially for Lee Valley Tools. It's a well-made tool and is rugged enough to take demanding use. Its problems are that it is still a tang chisel, and with a length of more than 19 in., it's just too long for fine work. With such a long tool, the timber being worked must be very low so you can strike the chisel at a comfortable level. Still, it is pleasing to see a tool that is so well made, and if you don't work your beams up on sawhorses like we do, it might be just right.

We are just becoming familiar with Japanese chisels. These tools fulfill most of the requirements I mentioned earlier, and with their laminated steel blades, they have a harder cutting edge than any Western chisels. The problems are that the blade is quite short (about 3½ in.) and the metal at the socket seems to be made from softer steel, which can bend too easily. These chisels work very well as long as they're not struck, so we use them for paring.

Most chisels are bought with a factory bevel of between 25° and 30°. This angle is fine for mortising softwoods such as pine, spruce, fir or hemlock. For work in hardwood, it's better to change the angle to between 35° and 40°. Too blunt a bevel angle will crush the wood fibers in softwoods, while too shallow an angle can cause the chisel to chip if you're working in hardwood.

In either case, the honing angle should be about 5° greater than the angle of the bevel. This makes the cutting edge stronger by eliminating the feathering at the tip. It also allows you to touch up the edge quickly since there is so little surface area on the honed edge.

For honing, we use two stones: a soft and a hard Arkansas. Though we've started to experiment with Japanese waterstones in the shop, the Arkansas stones are the ones we take to the site. There are a few jigs available that clamp to the chisel, guiding it across the stone to maintain a consistent honing angle, but we haven't found much use for them. If you spend enough time using your chisel, you should be able to hone by eye, and by feel. Be sure to back off (hone the back of the blade) only on the finer stone. After a chisel has been honed four or five times, we regrind the basic bevel.

The slick—This tool is just a chisel with a wide blade and a long handle that is not meant to be struck with a mallet; it's designed to be pushed by hand. The slick is used for paring large surfaces, and it's especially good for slicing across the grain to finish the sides of mortises and tenons. Of course a chisel can be used for final paring as well, but most professional timber framers prefer a slick because its wide blade makes for quick, accurate work on broad surfaces, and its long handle provides extra leverage and control.

Since this tool is used only for paring, its bevel should be ground to a shallow angle—about 20° to 25°. There aren't many brands of slicks. Most people in our shop use the slick sold by Woodcraft; it's well made and moderately priced. However, for the quality of steel, light weight and balance, I would have to say that the best are made by the Japanese. If I can save enough money, I'll buy one.
—T.B.

Squaring up. Using a flat outside face of the timber as a reference, check the other three faces around the joint area for square. The surest way to do this is to use a framing square and a combination square together, as shown at left. A small plane is fine for trimming high spots, and a tolerance of 1/32 in. is acceptable.

Mortise layout

S₁ A E G B
C
F H D
S₂

3¼ in.   1½ in.
3¼ in.
1 in.
8 in.

to make all layout lines with a sharp pencil and light touch, but be sure to scribe the joint before cutting it, using a sharp awl along the grain and a utility knife across the grain. The advantage of the scribed or scored line is that it cuts the surface fibers of the wood and gives you a notch into which you can set your chisel.

Measure to the top of the mortise (the height of the tenon) and scribe line CD. Now, from the outside face of the timber, measure to the outside edge of the mortise and make two marks that can be connected by using the framing square as a straightedge. Scribing with the grain is difficult in a coarse-grained wood, so take care that lines don't wander. This gives you line EF. Measure from E and F the width of the mortise and make line GH. Then make a line down the exact center of the mortise to guide the drill bit. Mark this centerline at both ends of the mortise, measuring in half the diameter of the drill bit plus 1/16 in. from AB and CD. This extra 1/16 in. gives room for error and lets you to work up to the line with your chisel.

The mortise is now ready for drilling, but you should lay out the shoulder first. With the blade of the square held on the mortise side of the timber, scribe a line exactly 1 in. down from A and B to S₁ and S₂. Connect S₁ to C and S₂ to D.

The goal of drilling is to remove wood quickly, roughly excavating the mortise to its full depth and staying away from the scribed edges of the joint. We use power tools for this part of the job. I think that as we work toward the revival of the craft of timber framing in the 20th century, we should use the tools, techniques and knowledge that are available in our age. Throughout the history of timber framing, as the tools improved and as the knowledge about wood became more complete, the joints became more sophisticated and stronger; buildings became better.

C.A. Hewett, the English building historian, documents tremendous changes that took place in the evolution of timber framing as the tools became more highly evolved and easier to use. When it was a great struggle to drill one hole to remove the wood for a mortise, only one hole was drilled and the mortise was therefore approximately square and contained no housing or shouldering that might have improved its strength. It was simply too difficult to remove the wood. In the 11th century, there was a marked improvement in the quality of the mortises, which seems to have been tied to the ability to drill holes more easily. As a result, the joints became more elongated, using more of the surface area of the pieces being joined.

It is in gross wood removal that we have the greatest advantage over our predecessors. With power tools we can remove wood extremely quickly and therefore make strong, beautiful joints more efficiently than ever.

Use a drill bit that is at least 1/8 in. smaller than

hemlock, fir and other softwoods, this works well. But with oak, we've had no luck. There just doesn't seem to be a planer that has enough power to get the job done without driving the operator nuts. Therefore, we take a big power hand planer to the timber for rough squaring (we've had good results with the 6⅛-in. wide Makita 1805B), and then finish the job around the joint area with a hand plane.

Use a straight, flat outside face of the timber as a reference to square up the other three faces. The outside face is least likely to be worked or otherwise altered when you cut the joint. If there is no outside face (as on an interior post), then square up from a designated side to keep all the adjacent faces perpendicular, and opposite faces parallel. Interior beams such as floor joists and summer beams should always be squared from the top face. Use a framing square to check the joint area as you trim each face with a plane. By resting a combination square on the blade of your framing square, as shown in the photo above, you can check three faces of the timber at once.

The mortise—With the timber square to a tolerance of 1/32 in., you're ready to lay out the joint. Whether you measure from the side of

the timber or from its center depends on the relationship between the timbers that are being joined. For example, both timbers might need to be flush with an outside face, as is the case with a post and girt. Or you may have an interior timber that is smaller in section and needs to be centered on a post or beam.

There are a number of ways to do layout. Except for very repetitive details, I favor methods that require the worker to keep thinking about how timbers relate to each other in the frame. Too many templates or marking shortcuts can lead to the belief that layout is an automatic process. When you fall into this pit, strange things begin to happen—the wrong template is used; the marking gauge doesn't get reset; you forget that this is the one layout that is different because of a sizing adjustment (a timber slightly larger or smaller than its blueprinted dimensions)—and you can't just throw timbers away when you make errors like these. For most of our work, we use the framing square. It's a simple tool that can be used to lay out any joint as long as you think while you use it.

With the blade of the square held against a side of the timber, scribe or draw the shoulder line at the bottom of the mortise (line AB in the drawing above). At this point you may choose the width of the mortise, so you can work up to the finished surface with your chisel. If you're using a portable electric drill and you don't have a positive stop, file a mark into the drill bit to gauge your depth. In our frames, major tenons are usually 3¾ in. long, so we drill to a depth of 4 in. Bore the holes at either end of the mortise first, as shown in the photo at right. Then, using the centerline as a guide, bore a series of overlapping holes.

Now you're ready to work with the chisel. Use a good framing chisel (see p. 9) with a blade slightly narrower than the width of the mortise. Just as boring the mortise was part of the rough work, your first work with the chisel also involves removing lots of waste. So don't spend a lot of time being fussy when it isn't necessary. Get the waste wood out quickly so you'll have the time and concentration to be precise as you work toward the line of the finished mortise.

Roughing-out should take you to between ⅛ in. and 1/16 in. of the line. Strike your chisel with heavy blows from the mallet and hog off reasonably large slices of wood (photo below left), but be careful in this rough stage not to attempt too large a bite. Make sure that you are in control, not the grain of the wood. Attempting to take out too much wood usually results in back-chiseling (going beyond true) or in a stuck chisel. Make your cuts across the grain before turning the chisel with the grain so you don't run the risk of splitting the wood. This will also break pieces of wood loose more easily. A corner chisel can be used at this stage, but don't take the whole corner out at once; let the chisel drift toward the center of the mortise.

Tap the chisel more lightly as you get closer to the line. Finally, you can pare the remaining slices off by pushing the chisel or a slick with your hand (photo below right). As you work, keep checking the inside of the mortise with a combination square to make sure that the walls are straight and square.

When the mortise is complete, it's time to cut the shoulder. Set the blade of your circular saw 1/16 in. less than the depth of the finished shoulder—15/16 in. in this case. We use worm-drive saws because their extra power makes a difference in oak. When you cut across the shoulder (line AB), stay about 1/16 in. shy of the line. Then set the saw at full depth and turn the timber to each side for the two side cuts into the shoulder (S₁C and S₂D). Again, stay away from the line by about 1/16 in. You can break out the two waste pieces on either side of the completed mortise quite easily by driving a chisel into the kerf at line CD.

Staying away from the lines on these cuts means that the joint is actually finished with a chisel and a slick. The theory is the same as for the mortise—do the rough wood removal rapidly with power tools and then work up to the line with more control.

Making the tenon—Begin once again by squaring the timber at the joint area, working from a designated face as you did when you laid out the mortise timber. If necessary, square off the end of the timber so that the end of the

Drilling the mortise. The bit diameter should be about ⅛ in. less than the width of the mortise. Set the bit point on the mortise centerline, drill the two outside holes first (above) and make a series of overlapping holes to open the slot.

Cleanout. Next come wood removal, left, and paring to the line, below. Strong blows with the mallet help the framing chisel to slice out large pieces of waste to within about 1/16 in. of the line. Then more careful paring removes this last narrow section of waste.

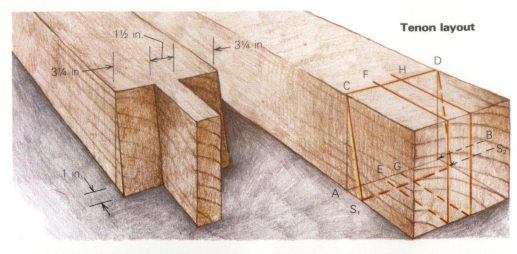

Tenon layout

1½ in.

3¼ in.

3¼ in.

1 in.

C F H D

B
S₂

E G

A
S₁

tenon will be square. Then measure 3¾ in. (or ¼ in. less than the depth of your mortise) back from this edge and square a line all the way around the timber.

Now you are ready to lay out the beveled shoulder of the tenon to match the angled cheek of the mortise. Mark its 1-in. depth from the squared line (AB in the drawing at left) at the bottom of the timber. This will give you line S_1S_2. Connect S_1 and S_2 with points at C and D, which correspond to the measurements used to mark the cheeks of the mortise. Remember that although the timber dimension may vary, you have to keep the measurements constant. Complete the layout by marking both sides and the end of the tenon, as shown in the drawing. To ensure that the tenon will be perpendicular to its shoulders and properly aligned with its mortise, use a single outside face of the timber as a measuring edge.

Cut along the beveled shoulder lines (CS_1 and DS_2) first. Set the saw depth to leave $\frac{1}{16}$ in. of waste outside the tenon line, and stay about the same distance from the shoulder line when you make the cut. Make the next cuts—four in all—from the end of the timber, sawing in on the top and bottom of the tenon with the blade at full depth. Again, stay shy of the line. Then use these saw kerfs and the twin vertical lines on the end of the timber to guide the blade as you make drop cuts on either side of the tenon (photo far left). Now you can remove the waste wood by driving the chisel into the kerfs at the end of the timber. This completes the rough wood removal.

Working with the tenon on its side, chisel to the beveled shoulder line first. Start by establishing the line with a series of shallow chisel cuts and then work the rest of the surface to this edge (photo left). It's always a good idea to cut across the grain like this before cutting with the grain to remove wood. It doesn't hurt to back-chisel about $\frac{1}{32}$ in. from the edge to ensure a tight edge joint and to compensate for possible shrinkage near the surface of the wood. Check the accuracy of your work with a combination square.

Pare the surface of the tenon to the line with a slick (photo bottom left) or a rabbeting plane. You can use calipers to check the tenon thickness, or sight beneath the blade of your combination square by eye. To finish, bevel the end of the tenon slightly so that it will start easily in the mortise.

The last step is assembly and pegging. When the timbers meet, the tenon will fit tightly into its mortise, the beam will rest squarely on the full surface of the shoulder, all face edges will meet precisely, and both timbers will be in proper alignment with the rest of the timber frame. We usually use a come-along and rope to pull joints tight and square; then we hold them that way until the hardwood pegs are driven. For this shouldered mortise and tenon, we'll drill out a pair of 1-in. dia. holes 2 in. from the top and bottom of the mortise and 1¼ in. from the beveled face on the post. □

Roughing out the tenon. Shoulder and side cuts have already been made to within $\frac{1}{16}$ in. of the joint line. The drop cuts at the end of the tenon, shown above, are the last ones to be made, using the kerfs from the side cuts and the penciled joint lines as guides.

Paring to the line. Set the chisel edge in the razored scribe line and make shallow finish cuts all the way across the face of the shoulder (right). Below, the easiest way to complete the tenon is with a slick. Work the blade across the grain until the surface is flat and true.

Tedd Benson's timber-framing company is based in Alstead, N.H.

Earthquake-Country Timber Frame

Satisfying the building code and traditional sensibilities

by Jeff Arvin

Seismic suitability has been a stumbling block for people wishing to build with heavy timbers and wooden joinery in earthquake zones. Although engineers familiar with timber framing consider the flexibility and shock absorption of joined timbers ideal attributes in earthquake country, local codes rarely cover such building. Often, if codes permit timber-frame construction, officials require through-bolted gusset plates or steel strapping—a compromise that conflicts with the spirit and aesthetics of timber joinery. Recently, however, for a job in the California foothills, we found a solution that not only met, but exceeded earthquake codes, and used no added steel or supplemental connectors.

I teach timber framing in workshops all over

For protection against earthquake damage, the timber frame shown in the photo above has six bents, two more than a typical frame of this size. These reduce spans and increase load capacities. Also, every intersection of post and beam is braced (right) to increase shear resistance and to reduce stress on the connections. Still more braces were added after the raising to reinforce the post-to-sill connections.

Top photo: Sandy Bennett; Bottom photo: Jeff Arvin

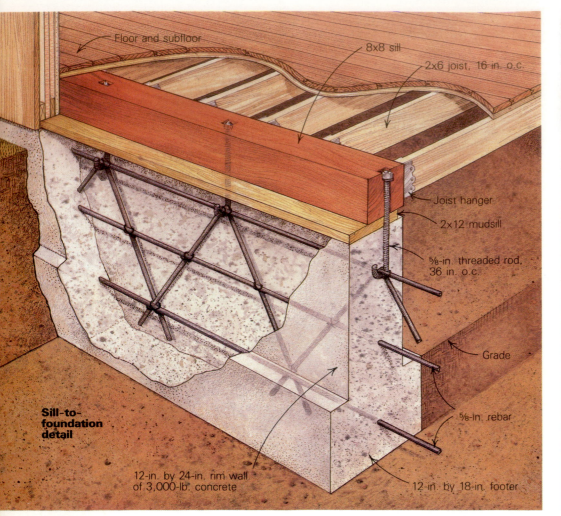

Floor and subfloor

8x8 sill

2x6 joist, 16 in. o.c.

Joist hanger

2x12 mudsill

⅝-in. threaded rod, 36 in. o.c.

Grade

⅝-in. rebar

Sill-to-foundation detail

12-in. by 24-in. rim wall of 3,000-lb. concrete

12-in. by 18-in. footer

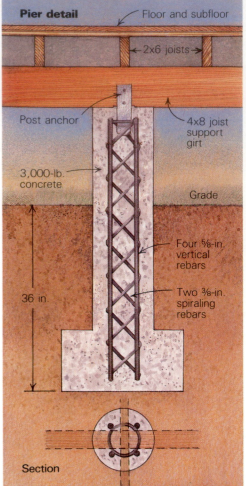

Pier detail

Floor and subfloor

2x6 joists

Post anchor

4x8 joist support girt

3,000-lb. concrete

Grade

Four ⅝-in. vertical rebars

36 in.

Two ⅜-in. spiraling rebars

Section

---

the country for Riverbend Timber Framing (P.O. Box 26, Blissfield, Mich. 49228). So when I got a call from former students Paul Beatty and Debra Lawlor asking if we could conduct a workshop, with the students cutting and raising the frame for their proposed home, I was excited by the prospect of a week in California. But at the same time I was concerned about running afoul of earthquake codes.

When I told Paul about these concerns, his reply was surprising. "Don't worry," he said. "Wait until you see the blueprints; I've got it all worked out." Over the preceding 18 months, Paul had thoroughly researched seismic engineering and had come up with creative solutions to some sticky problems. The design also was approved by a professional engineer and had the blessings of the building department. The solution affected all the major structural elements of the house design—the foundation, the first-floor deck and, of course, the timber frame.

Foundation and sill—Paul maintains that improving the seismic resistance of wood-frame homes is neither expensive nor difficult. The foundation itself and the foundation-to-sill connection are the primary concern. To begin with, all of the foundation and pier work was done with 3,000-lb. concrete. Also, Paul replaced the customary ½-in. J-bolts on 6-ft. centers with ⅝-in. threaded rods 36 in. o. c., which he cut and bent with a standard rebar bending and cutting tool. He hung Vs of ⅝-in. rebar on each rod to provide a firm anchor in the concrete. Three

horizontal bars were wired to these Vs (drawing, above left). The 8x8 sills provide sound purchase for the threaded rods and a traditional base for the timber frame.

Within the 24-ft. by 50-ft. perimeter foundation walls there are twelve 12-in. dia. concrete piers, in three rows of four. The piers were reinforced with spiral rebar bent at the site around a a limbed cedar tree set deep in the ground. With a big screw eye at the base holding one end, Paul began parallel to the ground and pushed the rebar around the tree trunk, rising gradually to the top. A full circle at the top made it easy to wire on vertical rebar. A left and a right spiral meshed with a little cussing. Four vertical ⅝-in. rebar lengths were wired to this assembly (drawing, above right). It has been shown that columns that have been reinforced with opposing-helix rebar will fracture but won't fall apart in earthquakes, and will keep the structure from collapsing. These modifications to the foundation added about $500 to the cost.

An 8x8 floor girder running parallel to the ridge sits atop the center row of piers and is held in place by post anchors embedded in their tops. Six feet on either side of center, rows of piers support 4x8 girders, 5½ in. lower in elevation. Floor joists (2x6s, 16 in. o. c.) resting in joist hangers at the 8x8 girder and the sill are supported at midspan by an intermediate girder. By reducing the maximum span to 6 ft., the deck can withstand the increased compressive loading created in an earthquake. Over the joists, ¾-in. plywood was glued and nailed.

The frame—In a platform or balloon-frame building, studs carry the loads of the structure to the foundation. But in a timber frame like this one, 18 posts carry the load that would take 300 studs in a conventional frame. And since the loads of the structure are concentrated on a relatively small number of pieces, the stresses on the connections (that is, the wood-to-wood joinery) are similarly amplified—100 nails are replaced by a single through-pegged mortise-and-tenon joint. So it made sense for us to find a way to reduce stress on the joints.

To do this, Paul planned to increase the vertical loading capability and lateral shear resistance of the entire frame (sidebar, facing page). The choice was between using exceptionally large pieces with exceptionally large joints, or using more pieces in the frame to lessen the stresses affecting each joint.

Paul decided to decrease the spans between the bents, and so was able to retain typical timber sizes (8x8, 8x10, 8x12) and joinery specifications. The result is a 24-ft. by 50-ft. structure built with a six-bent, five-bay format (top photo, previous page). The maximum span is 12 ft. within the bents and 10 ft. between bents. This reduces the loads on individual pieces.

By comparison, if we had been building this structure on our home territory in the Midwest, it would have had four bents and three bays. For the California house, the cost for the additional timbers was just a fraction of the overall budget for the project, and the workshop students provided the added labor. Paul and Debra consider

Drawings: Gary Williamson

Earthquakes and the Richter scale

by Paul Beatty

Even though we don't live in a primary seismic zone, I believe it is foolish to ignore the possibility of a severe earthquake. The 1983 devastation of many houses in Morgan Hill and Coalinga, Calif., convinced me to guard against such an "unlikely possibility."

Earthquakes are generated by shifting of the tectonic plates that make up the earth's surface. If a plate's edges are smooth, it will slowly slide past its neighbor (this is known as fault creep). But if a plate's edges are rough, they tend to lock against the adjoining plates. As the plate begins to rotate, stress builds along its edges. When the edges fail in shear, the "elastic recoil" generates a quake.

Many faults exhibit periodicity—that is, they build and release energy in 20 to 200-year cycles. Faults that accrue force the longest generate the most energy. As a result, and somewhat ironically, some of the worst quakes originate in faults thought to be dormant or inactive. For example, in the early 1800s, it's estimated that Missouri sustained a quake of 8-plus on the Richter scale (based on historical notes). This behavior builds my case for caution, but makes cost-benefit analysis muddier.

Earthquake force is measured by the Richter scale, named for Charles Richter, who devised it in 1938. Each point on the scale corresponds to a tenfold increase in ground shaking. Normal conditions are described as 1 gravity (or 1G) vertical loading and 0.2G lateral shear loading (this is the basis for ICBO building codes). At 5 on the Richter scale, concern for the structural integrity of a building begins.

Once an earthquake reaches Richter-7 magnitude (about .2G), wood-frame dwellings may exceed their limits of shear resistance. Failure frequently occurs at the sill, resulting in the house sliding off its foundation or fracturing its foundation walls. In the great earthquakes, forces of 1.25G may occur, with wall failure and roof collapse the frequent results. Fortunately, only a few quakes each year reach Richter-8 magnitude. As a result foundation reinforcement may be all that is cost effective. But, if one lives near an active fault or has a fondness for lots of big timber (as I do), more can be done to avoid failure at the next weakest point—the frame.

By using the G factors present in great quakes, I made some working generalities. First, by more than doubling the structure's ability to withstand vertical loading, the frame's G rating should increase from 1G (as required by code) to 2G (or the G force present at R-8). Secondly, by multiplying the shear strength by five, the frame should withstand the 1G shear force present in a great quake (.2G code value x 5 = 1G).

The first generality can be met with huge cross-section timbers, or closer spacing of bents in the timber frame. In my house, I chose to place bents on 10-ft. centers and use 8x8 posts with 8x10 girts. This yields a strength 225% greater than normal vertical loading requirements.

The second generality (1G resistance to lateral shear) can be met by increasing the size and amount of diagonal bracing. In the context of the timber frame, down braces from post to sill improve strength and shear resistance at that critical point. Bracing all around a bay ensures that any motion will yield compression loads at several points.

In my house I decided to use arched braces cut out of 4x10 stock. This allowed a much larger tenon on the end of the brace. The gentle curve cut into the brace cured the bulky look of the 4x10.

My initial static calculations suggested this frame would tolerate R-8-plus with little structural damage. I've since done a finite-element computer analysis that substantiates my earlier figures.

Richter himself described 8.5 as the "maximum credible quake." I hope my home is never tested to this limit, but I'm sure it would stand nonetheless. □

Paul Beatty is an emergency-room physician in Mokelumne Hill, Calif.

---

that the extra cost was a small price to pay for the added security.

All of the posts are tied, either to the sill or to the center girder, with through-pegged mortise-and-tenon joints. And while this is the typical method for post-to-sill connections in timber frames, adding the extra bents to the frame means decreased stress at these junctures.

Extra braces—The racking stresses exerted on a building by the wind are very similar to those exerted during an earthquake. To increase racking resistance and to reduce stress on the joinery, this West Coast frame borrowed a technique from Midwestern barn building—wind braces in mass quantities.

Historically, diagonal bracing was achieved in many different ways. The English cruck frames used curved trees to brace entire bents. Colonial frames in North America borrowed the knee-brace idea from ship builders, and used them primarily in corners to stiffen frames. However, in the farm country of the Midwest, where the barns were much larger than Colonial structures, the combination of open country and buildings that present large surfaces to the wind ("the broad side of a barn") meant that simply bracing the corners would not be enough. Barn builders in the Midwest began adding braces with a vengeance. Many old barns have diagonal bracing at every intersection of post and beam, particularly along perimeter walls.

Following their lead, we braced every intersection of post and beam and post and sill along the perimeter walls—118 braces in all, creating 118 rigid triangles that dramatically reduce stress on beam-to-post joints (the post-to-sill braces were added after the frame was raised). We also thoroughly braced the central core of the frame. The braces were cut from 4-in. by 10-in. by 4-in. blanks with an arch for decorative effect (bottom photo, p. 13). These larger-than-normal blanks were needed to accommodate the curve, but also allowed for bigger, stronger tenons. Finally, stealing a lick from stud construction, Paul is planning to build his north-south interior walls with 2x6 bracing let into the studs. The structure *will* be stable.

Working in West Coast timber country helped us over one remaining hurdle. I know of other framers who have been faced with project delays and additional expense because they used site-milled timbers, and a building official required structure ratings for them. We used commercially milled, structure-rated timbers—#1 and #2 grade Douglas fir. This allowed us to present known quantities to the inspector.

Cutting and raising—The actual cutting of the frame went superbly. The core group of students numbered twelve, and others were in and out during the week.

The Douglas fir turned out to be an ally. It was delightful to pare a tenon to its final shape with a chisel or slick. Although it didn't chop as cleanly as oak (in spite of regrinding our chisels to 25°), bits and blades stayed sharp three times longer than when working with oak. And the timbers were easy to lug around. Four stout people could carry a 24-ft. 8x10. It would take at least twelve to move a similar piece of oak.

Everything fell into place at raising time. As the cutting neared completion and the first bent was assembled on the deck, I estimated the bent's weight—1,800 lb., 1,400 if we removed the rafters. A quick count identified 20 available bodies, most of which looked capable of lifting a 70-lb. allotment. My partner, Sandy Bennett, and I decided that we could raise this bent by hand. The group agreed, and we raised that rascal at sundown.

In the morning a block-and-tackle appeared, and it gave everybody the confidence to raise the entire structure by hand. We added extra temporary bracing to the first bent and guyed it off to three nearby trees and Paul's old International Travel-All. With the aid of the block-and-tackle, the second bent went up, rafters and all, without incident. Using ropes and scaffolding, we found that it was easy to work the connecting pieces, missing rafters for the first bent, joists and purlins into place. After the third bent went up, we called off the crane.

Eighteen months of research and design and seven intense days of cutting and raising (completed without error or injury) were capped off with a pine bough and a party that went well into the night. □

Jeff Arvin directs the timber-frame workshop program at Riverbend Timber Framing, Inc. in Blissfield, Mich.

A Tudor Timber Frame

In this remodeled house, only the bricks remain the same

by Eric Rekdahl and Joe Wilkinson

The road from Oakland, California, to nearby Lafayette passes through a tunnel known locally as "the oven door." On the west side of the ridge separating the cities, the air temperature is moderated by the Pacific Ocean, while to the east it regularly hovers around a 100° in the summer. But Lafayette has many attributes that make its sometimes intense heat pretty tolerable. It has a rural quality, with plenty of hills and trees and a lot of open space to explore. Craig and Molly Cokeley thought it was a good place in which to find a house and raise a family.

House-hunting on a hot day in the early '70s, the Cokeleys inspected a one-story brick house with a tile roof. Craig remembers stepping inside the door and marveling at the cool interior. The mass of the tile and bricks was enough to blunt the summer sun without assistance from an air conditioner. Laid in wavy courses, the sand-molded bricks gave the house an appealing handmade look. The Cokeleys bought it, and by the mid-80s they were ready to expand the house to accommodate their needs and those of their teenage son and daughter.

Built around a barn—In contemplating their remodeled house, the Cokeleys imagined it to look like an Old English tithe barn that had been converted to a residence and remodeled by generations of inhabitants. Used by the church to store crops collected as taxes from parishoners, tithe barns were majestic structures that bore a resemblance to church buildings. They typically had a steeply pitched gable roof supported by a timber frame.

The new floor plan shows how the public spaces now occupy what can be construed as "the barn" (drawings right). In one lofty volume are the dining room, kitchen, living room, bar, entry and family room. The areas are given definition in part by a series of six simple roof trusses, made of 10-in. by 12-in. and 10-in. by 16-in. rough-sawn Douglas fir timbers, and an oak stairway that divides the room in half (photo left). In addition to all these spaces being under one roof, their finishes are consistent: The ceiling is rough-sawn fir 1x8s over 3x4

The main living areas are divided into distinct spaces by the lower chords of the trusses and by the stair (photo left). The feeling of expansiveness was inspired by Old English tithe barns.

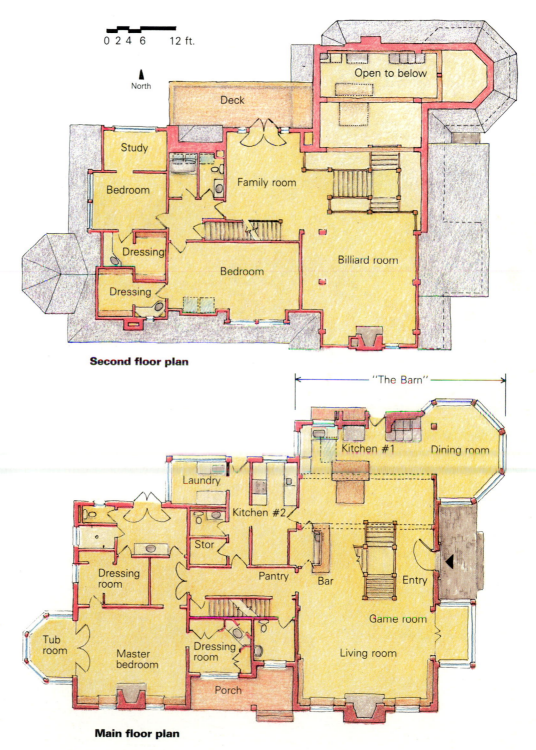

Second floor plan

Main floor plan

The eastern half of the house is a two-story gabled structure called the "barn." It encompasses the living room, game room, kitchen and dining room. Nearby is a second kitchen that's used when the owners entertain.

From *Fine Homebuilding* magazine (Spring 1989) 52:46-51

From the east, the barn is a single volume with a bay for the dining room projecting from the northeast corner. Between the chimneys, the bedroom-wing gable peaks over the ridge. Note the ridge vents; they are inverted copper gutters. The vent over the dining room has an octagonal prow to match the dormer roof.

Photo: Eric Rekdahl

With the major framing members in place, the house begins to take shape (middle photo). The third-floor ridge stops in line with the lower ridges to keep the higher mass from overpowering the form of the house. The brick walls stand where they did in the original house, while the pile of bricks in the foreground will be recycled into chimneys and the east wall. Kiln-dried clear redwood 2x12s, applied as beveled siding (photo above), clad the gable ends of the finished house.

rafters and 6x6 purlins; the walls are unpainted plaster with a slightly sandy finish, troweled to a texture that shows a few tool marks. Covering the barn floors are oak planks rescued from the original house, and rift-sawn oak wainscoting is typical throughout the barn.

The barn's ridge beam runs north/south, and it's about 24 ft. above the finished floor. Another higher ridge runs at a 90° angle to the first one. This gable appears as a later addition to the original barn, and shelters the private spaces in the rest of the house. It was important to keep this three-story portion from overpowering the rest of the house. So on its east side, the gable dies into the ridge of the barn, appearing to be but a small dormer peaking over the ridge (top photo, left). To the west, it blends with a gable over the master bedroom (bottom photo, left). This design

A dining table tucks into a timber-framed bay at the northeast corner of the barn (photo above). Next to it, a cantilevered granite fireplace allows the fire to be enjoyed from two sides. A ¼-in.-thick plate steel hood catches range vapors. Granite blocks faceted with a pitching tool surround the front door (photo center), while the entry porch is paved with granite tiles that have been finished with a torch to give them a rough, nonslip texture.

works to reduce the imposing character of a three-story gable end-wall. In almost every case, the roof forms follow the footprint dictated by the original brick walls.

A small kitchen occupies the northwest corner of the barn. Separating it from the octagonal dining room is a dark-grey granite fireplace (photo right). We used granite because it can be finished in a variety of ways. For example, the granite blocks surrounding the fireplace are finished with a pitching tool, which creates irregular facets that glisten subtly as you move about the fireplace. A granite arch over a hallway connects the fireplace with the stonework surrounding the commercial range. Behind the range, the granite is polished so it will be easy to clean.

This kitchen gets used on a daily basis for preparing meals for the family and friends. But because the Cokeleys like to entertain on a large scale, we included another space behind the bar for a combination kitchen/pantry where food can be prepared away from guests.

A floating foundation—Before we could begin gutting the original house, we got some dismaying news from the soils engineer: the soft silt of the ancient stream bed under the house was inadequate even to support the original one-story structure. That explained why, in some places, the unreinforced footings had cracked and settled as much as 2½ in. To remedy this, the soils engineer recommended a foundation bearing on 35-ft. deep concrete piers. In addition to being a very expensive foundation fix, we realized that in order to gain access for a drilling rig, we would have had to demolish several of the precious brick walls that we were trying so hard to save.

As an alternative, we devised a floating foundation based on 400 lb. per sq. ft. bearing capacity—40% of the lowest value (1,000 lb./sq. ft.) allowed by the UBC. And in addition to preserving the brick walls, our eventual solution cost about $60,000 less than the pier proposal.

All of the existing footings of the house were widened (drawing, p. 20), and new footings were poured to support the new loads from the second and third floors and the massive masonry fireplaces. The low bearing capacity of the soil meant that the 21-ton living-room fireplace would require an 8-ft. by 13-ft. concrete pad. The soils engineer's caution was shown to be warranted when, during compaction, we noticed 2-in. high waves of soil propagate from the compactor.

We inserted more than 800 rebar dowels into the existing foundation. Grouted with ep-

Section through barn

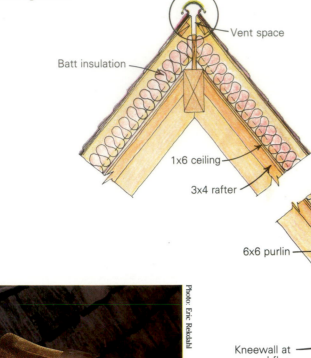

Vent space

Batt insulation

1x6 ceiling

3x4 rafter

⅛-in. by 2½-in. copper-strap cover plate and splice connection

⅛-in. by 2½-in. copper-strap mounting bracket at 3-ft. 4 in. o.c. max. welded or riveted to copper flashing

Insect screen

6-in. copper gutter

Copper flashing

Last course of shingles over copper flashing

Ridge vent detail

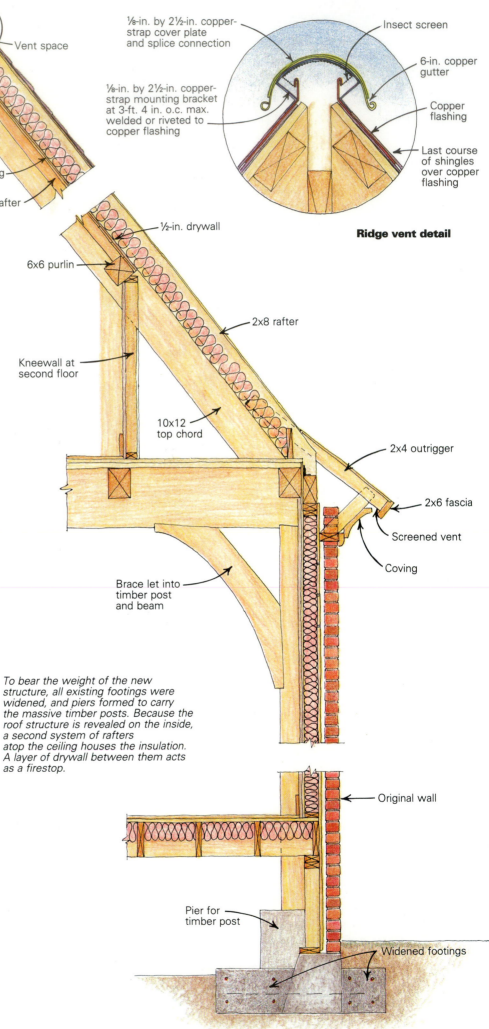

½-in. drywall

6x6 purlin

2x8 rafter

Kneewall at second floor

10x12 top chord

2x4 outrigger

2x6 fascia

Screened vent

Coving

Brace let into timber post and beam

To bear the weight of the new structure, all existing footings were widened, and piers formed to carry the massive timber posts. Because the roof structure is revealed on the inside, a second system of rafters atop the ceiling houses the insulation. A layer of drywall between them acts as a firestop.

Original wall

Pier for timber post

Widened footings

Photo: Eric Rekdahl

Copper flashings cap the ridges of the slate roof. Bronze insect screening wraps over a slot left open at the ridge, and thick copper straps tapped for machine screws await inverted copper gutters to cap the ridges.

Eave vents are screen-covered slots tucked between the fascia and a cove molding milled from clear redwood 3x12s.

oxy, they knit together the network of grade beams and widened footings that now carry the house. We poured 75 cu. yd. concrete to build this "webbed mat" system, which distributes the weight of the structure so effectively that it exerts no more pressure on the soil than does Molly Cokeley standing barefoot in her garden.

Exterior finishes—Besides the brick, Craig and Molly had very definite ideas about other materials. Since the original house was a single story and we were expanding it—therefore needing more brick—another material was necessary to cover the gable ends of the second and attic floors. Given the Cokeley's Tudor tendencies, it would have made sense to use half-timbering with stucco infill on the gables, but Molly and Craig were both adamant in their dislike of stucco on this house. A standard 1-in. clapboard siding was too weak a texture to work with the rest of the materials, so we went to a 2x12 lap siding (bottom photo, p. 18). The revealed edge of the 2x siding is beefy enough not to look out of place alongside weighty materials such as brick.

The roofing decision was easy—slate. That conclusion drawn, however, made the next problem tricky. How do we detail a ridge vent that would be in keeping with the slate? Because we wanted the structure revealed on the inside, we had to put our batt insulation atop the 1x6 ceiling decking. We used 2x8 rafters to get the bays for the insulation and left a gap at the ridge where opposing rafters meet (drawing, facing page).

Since we were going to be using copper gutters and downspouts, we developed a design that turns sections of copper gutter upside-down for our ridge vents. The design secures inverted gutters to ⅛-in. thick copper straps (top photo and detail drawing, facing page). The straps span a slot in the roof decking, which is covered with bronze insect screening, and the inverted gutters are screwed to the straps. We used the bronze screen at our soffit vents, too. The screen covers a narrow slot between a 2x6 fascia and a generous coving milled from clear redwood 3x12s (drawing, facing page).

Windows—Craig's willingness to hold out for the details that he thought most appropriate was never more apparent than in the window selection. The narrowest mullion we could find for double-pane glass was 1³/₁₆ in. Craig wanted an "old-style" window with narrow mullions—period. He liked the look of the multi-paned "T" section steel-framed windows that used to be common in industrial buildings, so we went looking for a manufacturer who still made them. We found one in southern California (Torrence Window Co., 1814 Abalone Ave., Torrence, Calif. 90501). They make steel windows that have ¾-in. wide muntins, primed with red-oxide and ready for puttied-on-site single-pane glass.

These windows would not ordinarily comply with California's stringent energy code. But since this was a remodeling, and because we were significantly improving the thermal characteristics of the original house, we could afford the luxury of the single glazing and still meet the code requirements.

Timber frame—The roof structure is a calculated conglomeration of timber framing and conventional framing. The barn's triangular trusses support a structural ridge beam that carries 2x8 rafters. In addition to providing bays for the batt insulation, the rafters share the load of the 30-ton slate roof with the exposed purlins, rafters and sheathing.

The timber roof is simple in concept: two intersecting gables with three dormers. The layout, cutting and erection, however, proved quite complex. Craig requested that we join beams using as few visible fasteners as possible. This meant that valley rafters would be let in to main truss chords, purlins would be let in to valleys and jack rafters into purlins. That meant that about 800 mortises needed to be laid out and cut.

The connections between the gable dormers and the main roofs were the toughest of all. For example, the western end of the 6x10 dining-room ridge beam is perpendicular to the upper purlin in plan. On either side of the ridge, 6x10 valley rafters tuck into the 90° angles formed by the purlin and the ridge. Visually, we wanted one bottom edge of each valley rafter to meet the bottom of the ridge beam while the other edges met the bottom of the purlin. This seemed simple, but it meant there could be no guessing or trial fitting of any of these members. We couldn't just cut them close and then scribe and trim until they fit. And because this layout affected the width of the room, some mind-boggling calculations determining the relationships between framing members had to be completed before the foundation could be poured. Precision layout was mandatory—we didn't have any spare 26-ft. 10x16s.

We struggled with the layout calculations for days, hunched over scrap plywood tablets scribbling away, double- and triple-checking the calculations. The occasional hopeful cry of, "I think I've got it!" was often followed by a string of obscenities when we discovered the next mathematical error. But persistence, born of necessity, paid off, and the equations were eventually solved.

The eight main trusses of the barn were assembled on the ground, and we brought in a crane to lift them into place. The remaining heavy timbers were lifted into place, as high as 35 ft., using a site-built derrick and a 2-ton chain hoist. This allowed us to take the time necessary for precise fitting of the massive beams, purlins and knee braces.

Saving the bricks—A major problem at the beginning of the job was how to salvage the bricks in the walls that we were dismantling. Would we be able to clean them? Could we match the original bricks if we needed more? Would we be able to match the original mortar color and texture?

Our mason examined a sample of the mortar and told us that it was an example of very hard portland-cement mortar. It was harder than the bricks, making them nearly impossible to clean. This was staggeringly bad news. The bricks were sand-molded—a type no longer made locally—and they were slightly different in size and color than anything we could find. But fortunately we came to realize that the sample analyzed by the mason wasn't indicative of the entire house. The fireplace he had scrutinized had been laid up with cement mortar for extra strength. The vast majority of the bricks were in the veneered walls, laid in relatively soft lime mortar. In all, we chiseled out more than 12,000 bricks. We hired a crew to chip away the chunks of remaining mortar with ⅜-in. thick flat steel bars. Only when we added the bricks stripped from the garage did we end up with enough, barely, for the three new chimneys and the new walls.

To help the masons match the original irregular coursing, we suggested they try laying the bricks without using their levels. This didn't work. Our masons had developed their own built-in levels. You could have aligned a pool table with the first rows of bricks they laid. Urged to loosen up, the the pendulum swung the other way and we got courses resembling ocean waves. Interestingly, it was their least-experienced crew member who was most able to duplicate the slightly out-of-level rows.

The masons used a portland cement-based mortar to lay up the new brick work—slightly greyer in tone than the original lime mortar. To get a better color match, they added lime to the new mortar. That did the trick—it's nearly impossible to tell where new work meets old.

Collaboration—From the beginning, this project was imbued with a contagious excitement. We felt we'd been given a rare opportunity to work with special materials, a design we liked, and for clients who appreciated fine craftsmanship and who allowed us to take the time necessary to do work we were truly proud of.

Adding to the camaraderie of our "through-it-all" crew (Ken Whitney, Dave Yonenaka, Tim Englert and John Kraft), was the close involvement the owners took in the project. They converted their two-car garage and guest house into their living quarters and pitched in to help on a regular basis. They were clients who were able to make significant design and building contributions without getting in the way of progress. Craig did everything from sweeping the driveway to installing the windows and building the white-oak entry door with its arched, laminated jamb. Molly took charge of sanding, staining and oiling the thousands of feet of oak trim. This house was their dream, and they weren't going to miss any of it. □

Eric Rekdahl was the architect in charge for Christopherson and Graff Architects (Berkeley, California.), designers of the Cokeley remodel. Contractor and civil engineer Joe Wilkinson was responsible for building and engineering the project.

Timber-Frame Layout

Systems for labeling the timbers and adjusting the joinery keep the frame plumb and true despite variations in dimensions

by Tedd Benson

The mystique that surrounds the craft of timber framing often clouds a full understanding of the kind of work that goes into cutting, assembling and raising a frame. It's easy to imagine yourself paring off fine shavings with a razor-edged chisel and raising timbers in communal euphoria. There's real satisfaction in pushing a tenon home into its perfectly mated mortise, or in driving the pegs to lock the joint. All these things contribute to the pleasures of framing with timbers.

But precise joinery is only a small part of

Careful planning, hard work and strict adherence to labeling, layout and mapping rules made it possible for five workers and a crane to raise this frame in one day. It has 203 individual timbers and 382 joints.

the process. Many of the frames we build contain well over 200 timbers and 350 connected joints. The frame shown in the photo above was raised in one dramatic day by a crew of five and a crane. But this day was merely the culmination of all the work that preceded it. There were five days of sanding timbers and assembling bents, and before that, many hours of work in the shop.

In order to work with speed and efficiency, there can't be any mystery whatsoever about what timber goes where. And all the timbers must fit exactly—a single misaligned joint stops a raising dead in its tracks.

We lay out, cut, and finally truck a completed frame to the site without test-fitting the joints. We're able to do this only because every frame evolves with a great deal of plan-

ning, some applied geometry, and an organized approach to layout and cutting.

With an organized system and good preparation, a beginner can get through a difficult project. Without them, even a master joiner couldn't possibly succeed.

We apply three systems to the timbers and joints. *Labeling* is a system for identifying each member so we know where it fits within the overall frame. *Layout* is a method for locating and marking each joint so that all timbers will align correctly. *Mapping* is a system of accounting for variation in timber dimension and adjusting the length of adjoining timbers accordingly, so the completed frame will be true to its planned measurements.

To demonstrate how these planning principles work, I'll use the frame shown above as

From *Fine Homebuilding* magazine (August 1983) 16:38-41

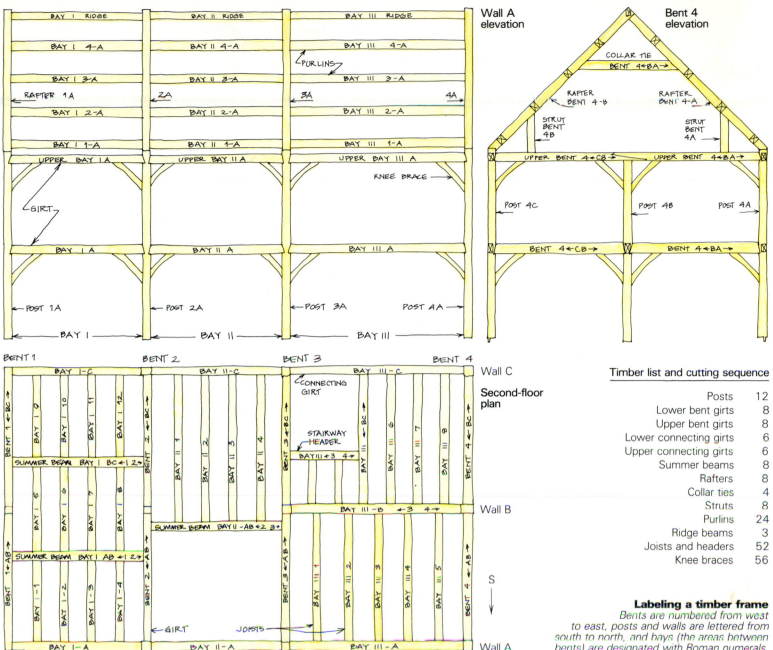

Wall A elevation

BAY I RIDGE | BAY II RIDGE | BAY III RIDGE
BAY I 4-A | BAY II 4-A | BAY III 4-A
PURLINS
BAY I 3-A | BAY II 3-A | BAY III 3-A
RAFTER 1A | 2A | 3A | 4A
BAY I 2-A | BAY II 2-A | BAY III 2-A
BAY I 1-A | BAY II 1-A | BAY III 1-A
UPPER BAY I A | UPPER BAY II A | UPPER BAY III A
KNEE BRACE
GIRT
BAY I A | BAY II A | BAY III A
POST 1A | POST 2A | POST 3A | POST AA
BAY I | BAY II | BAY III
BENT 1 | BENT 2 | BENT 3 | BENT 4

Bent 4 elevation

COLLAR TIE
BENT 4←BA→
RAFTER BENT 4-B | RAFTER BENT 4-A
STRUT BENT 4B | STRUT BENT 4A
UPPER BENT 4←CB→ | UPPER BENT 4←BA→
POST 4C | POST 4B | POST 4A
BENT 4←CB→ | BENT 4←BA→

Second-floor plan

Wall C
BAY I-C | BAY II-C | BAY III-C
CONNECTING GIRT
STAIRWAY HEADER
BAY III←3 4→
SUMMER BEAM BAY I BC←1 2→
Wall B
BAY III-B ←3 4→
SUMMER BEAM BAY II-AB←2 3→
SUMMER BEAM BAY I AB←1 2→
GIRT | JOISTS
BAY I-A | BAY II-A | BAY III-A
Wall A
S ↓

Timber list and cutting sequence

Posts	12
Lower bent girts	8
Upper bent girts	8
Lower connecting girts	6
Upper connecting girts	6
Summer beams	8
Rafters	8
Collar ties	4
Struts	8
Purlins	24
Ridge beams	3
Joists and headers	52
Knee braces	56

Labeling a timber frame

Bents are numbered from west to east, posts and walls are lettered from south to north, and bays (the areas between bents) are designated with Roman numerals.

---

an example. These systems apply to every frame we construct, but we have to modify them somewhat to meet the specific demands of each new frame.

Labeling—After we finish the blueprints for a house, we draft a complete set of shop plans for the frame. This set of working drawings typically includes elevations for each bent and wall, a plan view of each floor to show joist and beam locations, and large-scale sections or blow-ups of any unusual joinery details. At this stage, all joinery decisions have been made, and every timber has been sized in dimension to support its respective load.

Labeling begins when the plans are drawn. A consistent identification system allows us to distinguish between the many timbers in any frame that look alike but may not be dimensionally identical.

Unless your label tells you the exact location and orientation of every piece in the frame, you'll be plagued by constant remeasuring, and you run the risk of putting timbers where they don't belong. Here's how our labeling system works:

We draw plan views of the frame with south at the bottom of the page. Moving from west to east and from south to north, we number the bents, letter the posts, and assign Roman numerals to the bays (the spaces between the bents). For example, bay I is between bent 1 and bent 2; bay II is between bent 2 and bent 3; and so on. The posts in the southernmost row are A posts, the posts in the next row are B posts; those on the north side of the house are C posts and could be D or E posts on a very large frame. Posts also carry the number of the bent in which they stand. The southwest post will be 1A, for instance, and the post on the northeast corner will be 4C. The drawings above show how the various parts of the frame are labeled.

Bent girts are the horizontal timbers that join posts together to form a bent. Since the bent for a two-story frame will have more than one girt, a label like upper bent 1 ←B A→ would identify an upper girt that joins posts 1B and

1A. The arrows match the ends of the girt to the posts they will join.

Connecting girts, which we sometimes call bent connectors, are bay timbers that span between posts. They join one bent to another, and carry the braces that keep the frame rigid in the direction of the wall. They're labeled according to the bay and wall they fit in. For example, I-B would indicate a girt that falls in the first bay, in the A wall.

Summer beams, purlins and floor joists all fall within bays of the frame. Summer beams are connected to adjacent bent girts and hold the floor joists. They're labeled according to the bay they're in and by the posts and bents they fall between, for example, summer beam I AB ←1 2→ (bay I, between A and B posts and between bents 1 and 2).

Purlins are horizontal timbers that connect adjacent rafters, and are among the pieces that often appear identical but aren't, as a result of variations in rafter dimensions. A purlin would get a label like purlin III 4-A (bay III, A wall, fourth purlin up from the eave). Floor

Post layout

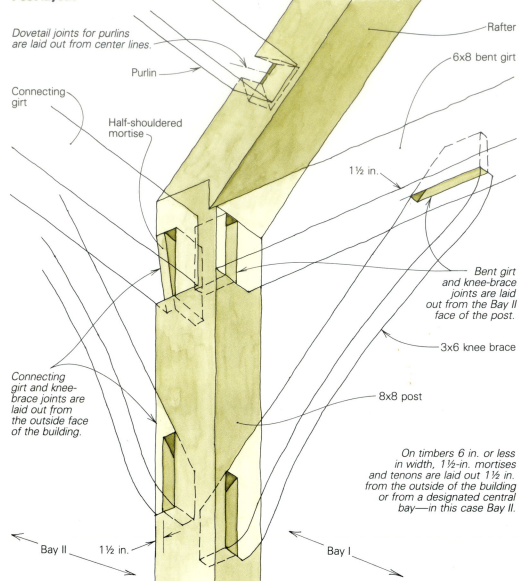

Dovetail joints for purlins are laid out from center lines.

Purlin

Connecting girt

Half-shouldered mortise

Connecting girt and knee-brace joints are laid out from the outside face of the building.

Bay II

1½ in.

Rafter

6x8 bent girt

1½ in.

Bent girt and knee-brace joints are laid out from the Bay II face of the post.

3x6 knee brace

8x8 post

On timbers 6 in. or less in width, 1½-in. mortises and tenons are laid out 1½ in. from the outside of the building or from a designated central bay—in this case Bay II.

Bay I

joists have a bay Roman numeral, and are also numbered as they fall from west to east or from south to north, as shown in the drawing.

It's important that all labels appear on the shop plans and on individual timbers. We use a lumber crayon and mark on a side of the timber that will later be covered—on the outside, for instance, or on the top. If it's an interior post and all sides of the timber will be exposed, the label can appear on any face. We sand or scrape it off later. Pieces should also be labeled on their ends, so they can be identified in a pile.

Layout—There are only about 10 different types of joints that we use in most of our designs, and all but three of these are simply mortises or tenons with added variables such as housings, shoulders, angles and tenon depths. Therefore, our layout rules are based on the relationship between the mortise and tenon. By standardizing their respective locations within each joint, layout work is simplified. Joints can be cut one at a time, with one framer taking up where another has left off without worrying about misalignments. The specifics may vary, and so may the exact dimensions used by other timber-frame crews, but these are the rules we apply to any frame:

1. All mortises and tenons that join timbers 6 in. or less in width are laid out 1½ in. from the outside of the building, or, in the case of an interior bent, 1½ in. from a designated bay. In the frame shown in this article, the pieces that would be governed by this rule are the knee braces, bent girts, collar ties, struts and connecting girts.

The 1½-in. tenon width that we use on nearly all mortise-and-tenon joints in a frame is convenient because the tongue of the framing square—our principal layout tool—is 1½ in. wide. Oak is strong enough for 1½-in. tenons; a frame of pine or fir would be better off with 2-in. wide tenons (which conveniently coincides with the width of the square's blade). In either case, we don't rely on the tenon alone to carry loads; we add a shoulder or housing to the joint for this purpose. The tenon holds the members together, but doesn't usually have to withstand shear forces.

2. When 1½-in. mortises and tenons are used to join two 8-in. wide timbers, the layout is 3¼ in. from the outside of the building, or from a central bay, bay II in this case.

3. The tenons that join the posts to the subfloor are all 1½ in. thick. Those on the perimeter are laid out 1½ in. from the outside of the building. A and C post tenons run parallel to the walls; B post tenons run parallel to the bents. Interior post tenons are centered.

4. The joints for joists, purlins, headers and

Layout rules. **Standardizing the size and location of mortises and tenons makes it possible for a timber-framing crew to work timbers individually, without having to test-fit each joint. Though the joinery in the post shown in the photograph looks complex, it is mostly mortise and tenon. The layout parameters that governed this post's joinery are explained in the drawing above.**

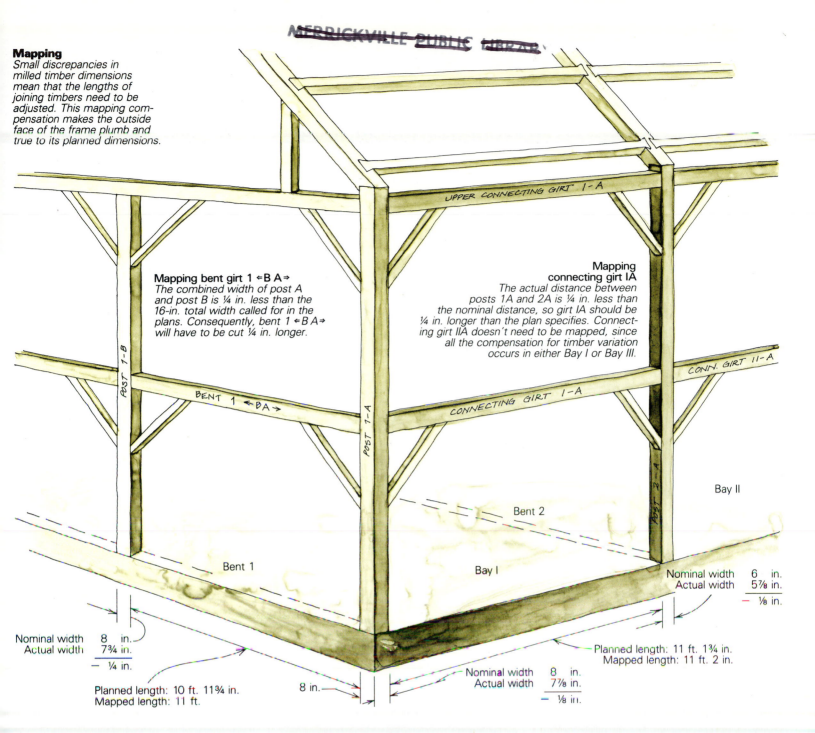

Mapping
Small discrepancies in milled timber dimensions mean that the lengths of joining timbers need to be adjusted. This mapping compensation makes the outside face of the frame plumb and true to its planned dimensions.

UPPER CONNECTING GIRT 1-A

Mapping bent girt 1 ←B A→
The combined width of post A and post B is ¼ in. less than the 16-in. total width called for in the plans. Consequently, bent 1 ←B A→ will have to be cut ¼ in. longer.

Mapping connecting girt IA
The actual distance between posts 1A and 2A is ¼ in. less than the nominal distance, so girt IA should be ¼ in. longer than the plan specifies. Connecting girt IIA doesn't need to be mapped, since all the compensation for timber variation occurs in either Bay I or Bay III.

POST 1-B

CONN. GIRT II-A

BENT 1 ←BA→

POST 1-A

CONNECTING GIRT 1-A

POST 2-A

Bay II

Bent 2

Bent 1

Bay I

Nominal width   6   in.
Actual width   5⅞ in.
— ⅛ in.

Nominal width   8   in.
Actual width   7¾ in.
— ¼ in.

Planned length: 10 ft. 11¾ in.
Mapped length: 11 ft.

8 in.

Nominal width   8   in.
Actual width   7⅞ in.
— ⅛ in.

Planned length: 11 ft. 1¾ in.
Mapped length: 11 ft. 2 in.

---

summer beams that don't fall on posts are laid out from centerlines.

Mapping—Compensating for slightly out-of-dimension timbers in the frame at the layout and cutting stages is a process we call mapping. It puts the variation in beam dimension in a predictable direction, keeping the timbers flush and plumb on the outside of the building and in any other plane that's important.

The timbers that we use to build a frame do not arrive from the sawmill cut to the precise dimensions described on the plans; they are roughsawn, and their thickness can vary by as much as ½ in. We have solved this problem by squaring the timber at the joint area with a portable power plane. We surface the rest of the timber with the plane for flatness and smoothness only. Then we compare the actual dimensions of the timber at the joint area with the dimensions called for on the blueprints. The difference between these two measurements is either added to or subtracted from

the length of the joining timber. Essentially, that's mapping.

Let's say that post 1B (bent 1, B wall) measures 7¾ in. by 8 in., rather than 8x8, as called for in the plans (drawing, above). If the bent is going to be plumb, the length of the bent girt that joins the post at its narrower width will have to be increased by ¼ in.

Some parts of a frame don't require mapping adjustments. On the frame shown here, we laid out the joinery for all the timbers in bent 2 and bent 3 from bay II, so the variance in beam dimension was thrown toward bays I and III. Girts, summer beams and purlins in this midbay can be cut to their blueprinted dimensions. Knee braces throughout the frame don't have to be mapped because the bottoms of all girts are held to a prescribed measurement. On the other hand, some timbers have to be mapped in more than one direction, making the mapping operation quite complex.

Because of this, we make charts to keep track of dimensional variations throughout

the frame as joint layout progresses. These charts are simply copies of the blueprints with blanks at each joint where actual measurements are filled in next to their nominal counterparts. We keep the mapping charts close at hand at all times, since some joining pieces are cut at different times.

Joint by joint, mapping adjustments are made according to the charts. This means we have to cut the beams in a predetermined sequence, which might change from frame to frame, depending on the interrelationship of the joints. By cutting the posts first, for example, we can note actual dimensions at the joint area and adjust the lengths of bent girts and connecting girts accordingly. After cutting the posts, we usually cut the bent girts, then the connecting girts, summer beams, rafters, collar ties, struts, purlins, ridge beams, joists and headers, and finally, knee braces.   □

Tedd Benson's timber-framing company is based in Alstead, N.H.

Sizing Roughsawn Joists and Beams
Methods and formulas for engineering your own timber frame

by Ed Levin

Structural engineering in timber design figures the allowable loads in building members, with an eye to staying safely within the elastic range of the material. The greatest challenge in designing and building a timber frame is to accommodate timber placement to the floor plan of the structure. In this process, the carpenter should always be at the service of the architect, developing a framing skeleton so that no diagonal braces have to be ducked, and no posts obtrude into the living space. Structural engineering lets you work to the designer's specifications, choosing scantlings (timber sizes) and deciding upon joist and rafter spacings.

Intuition and experience—Our medieval ancestors didn't have refined engineering tools, yet they created monumental wooden structures unmatched in modern times. An experienced carpenter seldom needs tables, and with some conventional building experience under your belt you should be able to extrapolate to dimension timber in other framing situations. For instance, in a floor where 2x8s 16 in. on center are adequate, then 3x8s 24 in. o.c., 4x8s 32 in. o.c. or 6x8s 48 in. o.c. will do just as well, with heavier flooring as spacing increases.

If you wonder whether a certain beam will be springy, block the ends up off the ground or floor and jump on the middle. With some blocking, beams and planks, you can quickly mock up a floor and try it out. Vary the timber spacing and see what happens. A little empirical knowledge goes a long way in timber design, and leaves you better prepared to deal with the complexities of the more rigorous engineering approach.

Using structural formulas—When you meet up with a problem you can't solve empirically, or you want to check on a particular frame element, it's nice to have the resources of modern structural engineering to fall back on. Joist and rafter tables in the standard carpentry texts aren't much help, because they are keyed to dimensioned lumber. There are a few books geared to the needs of the timber framer (see the bibliography at the end of the article), but even the best reference has limitations. For example, if you are checking deflection in 16-ft. long, 7-in. by 9-in. hornbeam timbers on 37-in. centers with a 95 pound per square foot (psf) live load, chances are all the tables in the world won't help

Ed Levin, of Canaan, N.H., designs and builds timber-framed houses.

you. You'll need to go directly to the formulas upon which the tables are based. These are the fundamental engineering tools in timber design.

Some pointers: allowable stress values (modulus of elasticity, extreme fiber stress, compression parallel to the grain, horizontal shear stress and so forth) for particular species and grades of wood can be found in tables in several of the books listed in the bibliography on p. 30. If working stress values for a particular species of wood are unavailable in the standard references, clear wood strength values can be obtained from the USDA *Wood Handbook*.

Most timber frames are built of green wood, which is both heavier and weaker than dry. The increased dead load due to the initial high moisture content, combined with decreased stiffness (increases of 20% to 30% are typical after green wood dries) can cause a joist or girder to dry with a pronounced sag. Take care that your floor will be strong enough when new. You may want to add temporary midspan support to beams whose green strength is questionable.

In beam design, you should check all members for shear and bending moment. An additional calculation for deflection is necessary for floor joists and in other situations as called for by code. Shear is the limiting factor in short, heavily loaded spans or if you're using narrow, deep members. Deflection governs in long, lightly loaded beams, as well as in broad, shallow ones. For intermediate situations, bending moment is usually the limiting factor.

For sizing floor joists, some codes specify live load deflection only, while others call for deflection due to both live and dead loads. Typical allowable deflections in floor joists and beams are $\frac{1}{360}$ of the length of the unsupported span if you're figuring live load only, or $\frac{1}{240}$ of the length of the span if you're figuring combined live and dead loads. The minimum standards for uniformly distributed live loads are 40 psf for first floors, 30 psf for upper floors and inhabitable attics and 20 psf for uninhabitable attics.

When you plug values into the formulas, use actual and not nominal sizes of members. Finally, lengths in formulas are usually given in inches, not feet, so keep your units straight.

The formulas here will let you size a simply supported rectangular beam that bears a uniformly distributed load or a concentrated load at the middle of a span, the two most common loading conditions on floors and roof. The formulas cover 90% of the bending and deflection problems you'll encounter in floor framing.

Deflection

Live load deflection—The dimensions of floor joists and beams are usually governed by deflection. Let's use the most common standard for a floor: a minimum first-story live load of 40 psf with a live load deflection of $\frac{1}{360}$ of the length of the unsupported span (this is the only computation in which you don't need to use combined live and dead loads). We'll run through an example, sizing red oak floor joists, 36 in. on center over a 12½-ft. span, to be covered with nominal 2-in. spruce decking.

The formula for finding the deflection resulting from a uniformly distributed load is:

$$\Delta = \frac{5wL^4}{384EI} \text{ , where}$$

Δ = The maximum deflection (in inches) at midspan;

w = the weight each lineal inch of each joist must support (in lb./in.);

L = the length (in inches) of the unsupported span;

E = the modulus of elasticity (psi);

b = the width of the joist in inches;

d = the depth of the joist in inches; and

I = the moment of inertia (in in.⁴), $bd^3/12$ (see glossary).

Begin by substituting

$\frac{L}{360}$, the maximum allowable deflection,

for Δ, and juggling the formula algebraically to solve for I, which will let us determine acceptable joist dimensions. So:

$$I = \frac{75wL^3}{16E} \text{ .}$$

We already know some values:

L = 150 in. (12½ ft.), and
E = 1,500,000 psi for red oak.

To calculate w, we first have to figure out the load each joist must carry. Each joist supports half of the uniformly distributed load on each side of it. for interior joists, this is the same as the distance between two joists (see the drawing on p. 29). In our example, this is 36 in.

$$w = \frac{40 \text{ psf (uniform load)} \times 36 \text{ in.}}{144 \text{ in.}^2/\text{ft.}^2 \text{ (so } w \text{ is in lb./in.)}}$$

Glossary of Structural Terms

Tension

When a simple beam is bent downward under load, its top is in compression and its bottom is in tension. Tension is the state of stress in which particles of material tend to be pulled apart. Ropes and cables are purely tensile elements and will not assume any compressive or bending stress. The opposite of tension is

Compression

compression, the state of stress in which particles of material tend to be pushed together. Concrete resists compression but doesn't cope well in tension. That's why it is reinforced with steel rods in areas of tensile strain. It's easy to see that knots are a greater

Compression
Tension

disadvantage in tension. This explains why they were traditionally placed in the top surface of joists and girders.

Bending stresses are greatest at the top and bottom surfaces. They decrease toward the center. Fibers in the middle of the beam are neither tensed nor compressed, and are said to

Neutral axis

lie along the neutral axis (see deflection).

Extreme fiber stress

Bending strength is limited by the maximum safe extreme fiber stress. This is the capacity of the wood to resist powerful compressive and tensile forces at the upper and lower faces of a loaded timber. For a given load, bending strength varies directly with the breadth and the square of the depth of the timber, and inversely with the length of the span

$$\left(\text{strength} \propto \frac{bd^2}{L}\right).$$

Section modulus

In bending calculations, timber size is usually expressed as the section modulus *(S)*. For rectangular beams, $S = bd^2/6$. Bending

Bending moment

force is quantified as the bending moment. For our simple beam, the moment is greatest at midspan and drops to zero over the supports.

Elastic

Wood is an elastic material, one which deforms under load, but whose deformation vanishes when the load is removed. Materials that remain deformed after loads are removed

Plastic

are described as plastic, and as with any elastic material there are limits to the loads wood can bear without behaving plastically.

Stress

A compressive or tensile force acting on an elastic material sets up stress (force per unit area, usually expressed in psi). This causes the material to be slightly shortened or stretched.

Strain

This is strain, the lengthwise deformation per unit of a material under load (expressed in inches of deformation per linear inch of material, or in./in.). The set of stress values that wood responds to elastically is called its

Elastic range
Yield load

elastic range. The point at which it begins to exhibit plasticity is its yield load. In most cases, persistent plastic behavior immediately precedes the failure of the timber.

Within its elastic range, wood deformation under load is directly proportional to that load. This proportion of load to deformation, written as the ratio of stress to strain for a particular species of wood, is called its modulus of

Modulus of elasticity

elasticity *(E)*, the constant used to calculate stiffness in beams. It expresses the linear relation between a given stress (load) and the resulting strain (deformation) in the material:

$$E\text{ (psi)} = \frac{\text{stress (psi)}}{\text{strain (in./in.)}}$$

Stiffness
Deflection

While a timber's bending strength is its ability to carry a load without breaking, stiffness is its ability to remain rigid in use. Stiffness is measured by beam deflection, the amount a loaded beam will bend below the horizontal. For a fixed load, stiffness

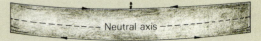
Neutral axis

varies directly with the breadth and the cube of the depth of the timber, and inversely with the cube of the length of the span

(stiffness $\propto bd^3/L^3$).

Moment of inertia

In deflection calculations, timber size is usually expressed as moment of inertia *(I)*. For rectangular beams, $I = bd^3/12$.

Vertical shear
Horizontal shear

Shear is the state of stress in which particles of material tend to slide relative to each other. Horizontal timbers under load tend to break or shear off at the edge of their supports. This vertical shear is always accompanied by horizontal shear. You can understand this phenomenon if you take a half-dozen or so

Carrying beam
Beam in span
Horizontal shear along neutral axis

pieces of wood about $\frac{1}{8}$ in. by 2 in. and lay them flat one on top of the other. Support the ends and depress the middle. You'll notice that as the center bends downward the individual strips of wood tend to slide along one another. This horizontal shear force operates the same way in a solid timber, except there adhesion between the wood fibers keeps them from sliding, which causes shear stress in the timber. The shear stress acts to split the timber along the grain, the direction in which wood is weakest. This points up another property of

Anisotropy

wood—it is anisotropic. Unlike steel, concrete, aluminum or plastic, the structural properties of timber are not identical in every direction.

Dead load

Dead load is the weight of the structure itself and all loads permanently on it. For our purposes this generally means the weight of the timber frame plus flooring or roofing and

Live load

insulation. Live loads are all loads other than dead loads—usually the weight of people and their furniture as well as wind and snow loads. You need dead load values to design a structure, but you can't determine them until after the structure is designed. So even engineers have to start with an educated guess.

Roof rafters must be strong to take snow loads, but stiffness is not a requirement unless you plan to finish the underside of the roof. So scantlings are often determined by bending strength. But floor joists and the timbers that carry them must not only be strong, but stiff as well, because you don't want a springy floor, so sizes are limited by deflection. A certain amount of deflection is inevitable in rafters, joists and beams, but you can take advantage

Camber

of bowed timbers to introduce an upward camber in the floor or roof. Then as the member settles under load it will not assume a negative or downward curvature.   —*E.L.*

b \ d	3	3½	4	5	5½	6	7	7¼	8	9	9¼	10	11¼	12
1½	3 / 2	5 / 3			21 / 8			48 / 13			99 / 21		178 / 32	
2			11 / 5			36 / 12			85 / 21			167 / 33		288 / 48
3	7 / 5	11 / 6	16 / 8	31 / 13	42 / 15	54 / 18	86 / 25	95 / 26	128 / 32	182 / 41	198 / 43	250 / 50	356 / 63	432 / 72
3½		13 / 7			49 / 18			111 / 31			231 / 50		415 / 74	
4	9 / 6		21 / 11	42 / 17		72 / 24	114 / 33		171 / 43	243 / 54		333 / 67		576 / 96
4½		16 / 9			62 / 23			143 / 39			297 / 64		534 / 95	
5			27 / 13	52 / 21		90 / 30	143 / 41		213 / 53	304 / 68		417 / 83		720 / 120
5½		20 / 11			76 / 28			175 / 48			363 / 78		653 / 116	
6			32 / 16	63 / 25		108 / 36	172 / 49		256 / 64	365 / 81		500 / 100		864 / 144
7				73 / 29		126 / 42	200 / 57		299 / 75	425 / 95		583 / 117		1008 / 168
7¼					101 / 37			230 / 64			478 / 103		860 / 153	
7½					104 / 38			238 / 66			495 / 107		890 / 158	
8						144 / 48	229 / 65		341 / 85	486 / 108		667 / 133		1152 / 192
9							257 / 74		384 / 96	547 / 122		750 / 150		1296 / 216
9¼								294 / 81			610 / 132		1098 / 195	
10						180 / 60	286 / 82		427 / 107	608 / 135		833 / 167		1440 / 240
10½								333 / 92			693 / 150		1246 / 221	
11¼											742 / 160		1335 / 237	
12									512 / 128	729 / 162		1000 / 200		1728 / 288

Moments of Inertia (I) and Section Moduli (S)

$$I = \frac{bd^3}{12}, \quad S = \frac{bd^2}{6}$$

b = breadth of timber (in.)

d = depth of timber (in.)

Moments of inertia, at the upper left of each small box, are expressed in in.^{4} Once you have figured what value is required for maximum allowable deflection, check to see that I for the timber dimensions you are considering is higher. Section moduli, at the lower right of each box, are expressed in in.^{3} After you've figured the value for maximum allowable bending, check to see that S for your timber dimensions is higher.

so w = 10 lb./in. (each inch of each joist must carry the load of 10 lb.).

Now we plug these figures into our formula:

$$I = \frac{75wL^3}{16E} = \frac{(75)(10 \text{ lb./in.})(150 \text{ in.})^3}{(16)(1,500,000 \text{ psi})}$$

$$= 105.47 \text{ in.}^4$$

By checking the table at left for moments of inertia or by substituting for b and d in the equation $I = bd^3/12$, we see several joist dimensions that would work:

3x8: $\quad I = \frac{3\text{x}8^3}{12} = 128$ in.^{4}

4x7: $\quad I = \frac{4\text{x}7^3}{12} = 114.33$ in.^{4}

6x6: $\quad I = \frac{6\text{x}6^3}{12} = 108$ in.^{4}

Combined load deflection—The other common code standard for floors is combined live (40 psf) and dead loads with deflection of $\frac{1}{240}$ of the length of the unsupported span. To find the dead load, we have to know the weight of the decking (about 4 psf) and of the joists themselves (48 lb.^{3} for red oak at 25% moisture content). A 6x6 joist, the heaviest of the three listed above, contains 432 in.^{3} of wood per linear ft. (6x6x12), or .25 ft.^{3} of wood. Multiplying this by the value of 48 lb./ft.^{3} for red oak gives us a weight of 12 lb. per linear ft. Since the joists fall on 3-ft. centers, they contribute

$$\frac{12 \text{ lb./ft.}}{3 \text{ ft.}} \text{ or } 4 \text{ lb./ft.}^2 \text{ to the dead load:}$$

4 lb./ft.^{2}	(Joist weight)
+ 4 lb./ft.^{2}	(Decking weight)
= 8 lb./ft.^{2}	(Total dead load)
+ 40 lb./ft.^{2}	(Live load)
= 48 lb./ft.^{2}	(Combined load).

Finding w as we did in the first case:

$$w = \frac{(48 \text{ psf})(36 \text{ in.})}{144 \text{ in.}^2/\text{ft.}^2} = 12 \text{ lb./in.}$$

And for $\Delta = L/240$, $I = 25wL^3/8E$. So

$$I = \frac{(25)(12 \text{ lb./in.})(150 \text{ in.})^3}{8 (1,500,000 \text{ psi})} = 84.38 \text{ in.}^4$$

all four previously selected joist sizes pass the combined load, $L/240$ test. So do a couple of new choices:

3x7: $\quad I = \frac{3\text{x}7^3}{12} = 86$ in.^{4}

5x6: $\quad I = \frac{5\text{x}6^3}{12} = 90$ in.^{4}.

To check deflection for any concentrated midspan loads, use the formula $\Delta = PL^3/48EI$, where P = the weight of the concentrated load in lb. The inverted form of this equation is:

$$I = \frac{15PL^2}{2E} \text{ when } \Delta = L/360, \text{ or}$$

$$I = \frac{5PL^2}{E} \text{ when } \Delta = L/240.$$

Maximum deflection in both concentrated midspan and uniformly distributed loads occurs at midspan. To find deflection resulting from a combination of the two, we can do the separate calculations for each and simply add the results.

In a floor with three or more members on centers of 24 in. or less, allowable stress may be increased by 15%. See values for repetitive member uses in the supplement of the *National Design Specifications for Wood Construction*.

Deflection figures are based on so-called normal loading, which assumes that a structural member will carry its full design load for an accumulated total of ten years during the life of the building. Where you expect that a beam will be fully loaded, continuously or cumulatively, for longer than that, you should reduce the allowable stress values by 10%. Timbers permanently stressed at full design load can deflect as much as 1½ times (2 times for unseasoned wood) the amount calculated for normal loading, because of long term inelastic deformation, or *creep*.

Bending

Having satisfied the deflection criteria, we should verify that the joists are strong enough in bending as well. In bending:

$$f = \frac{M}{S},$$

where

$$M = \frac{wL^2}{8} \text{ for uniform loads}$$

and

$$M = \frac{PL}{4} \text{ for concentrated loads,}$$

where

- f = maximum extreme fiber stress in psi (see glossary);
- M = maximum bending moment in inch-pounds;
- P = weight of the concentrated load in lb., and
- S = section modulus $\frac{bd^2}{6}$ (in.³).

Solving for uniform loads:

$$S = \frac{M}{f} = \frac{wL^2}{8f}.$$

Given w = 12 lb./in.,
L = 150 in., and
f = 1,500 psi for our red oak joists:

$$S = \frac{wL^2}{8f} = \frac{(12 \text{ lb./ft.})(150 \text{ in.})^2}{(8)(1,500 \text{ psi})} = 22.50 \text{ in.}^3.$$

This time we check the table on the facing page for section moduli:

- 3x7: S = 25 in.³
- 3x8: S = 32 in.³
- 4x7: S = 33 in.³
- 5x6: S = 30 in.³
- 6x6: S = 36 in.³

All six choices are adequate in bending.

As with deflection, you can find bending stress

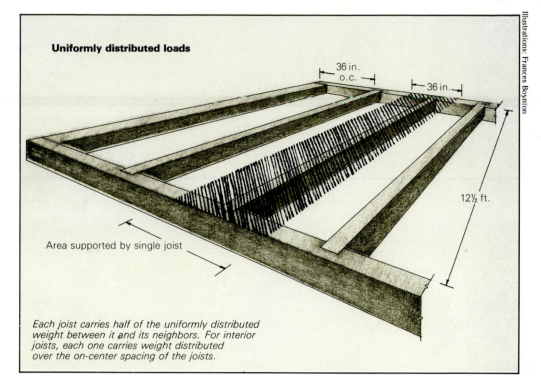

Uniformly distributed loads

36 in. o.c.

36 in.

12½ ft.

Area supported by single joist

Each joist carries half of the uniformly distributed weight between it and its neighbors. For interior joists, each one carries weight distributed over the on-center spacing of the joists.

Illustrations: Frances Boynton

Summary of most useful equations

	Uniformly distributed load	Concentrated midspan load
Deflection:	$\Delta = \dfrac{5wL^4}{384EI}$	$\Delta = \dfrac{PL^3}{48EI}$
	for $\Delta = L/360$, $\quad I = \dfrac{75wL^3}{16E}$	for $\Delta = L/360$, $\quad I = \dfrac{15PL^2}{2E}$
	for $\Delta = L/240$, $I = \dfrac{25wL^3}{8E}$	for $\Delta = L/240$, $\quad I = \dfrac{5PL^2}{E}$
Bending:	$f = \dfrac{M}{S}$	$f = \dfrac{M}{S}$
	$M = \dfrac{wL^2}{8}$	$M = \dfrac{PL}{4}$
	$S = \dfrac{M}{f} = \dfrac{wL^2}{8f}$	$S = \dfrac{M}{f} = \dfrac{PL}{4f}$
Shear:	$V = \dfrac{wL}{2}$	$V = \dfrac{P}{2}$
	$H = \dfrac{3V}{2}$	$H = \dfrac{3V}{2} = \dfrac{3P}{4}$
	$h = \dfrac{3V}{2A} = \dfrac{3V}{2bd}$	$h = \dfrac{3V}{2A} = \dfrac{3P}{4bd}$
For notched beams:	$H = \dfrac{3Vd}{2b'(d')^2}$ or $d' = \sqrt{\dfrac{3Vd}{2b'h}}$	$h = \dfrac{3Pd}{4b'(d')^2}$ or $d' = \sqrt{\dfrac{3Pd}{4b'h}}$

Δ =	Maximum deflection (at midspan) in inches	M =	Bending moment (lb.)
w =	Weight per unit length (lb./in.)	f =	Extreme fiber stress (psi)
L =	Unsupported span (in.)	S =	Section modulus (in.³)
E =	Modulus of elasticity (psi)	b' =	Net width (in.), as in dovetail waist
b =	Beam width (in.)	d' =	Net depth (above notch) in inches
d =	Beam depth (in.)	v =	Vertical shear (lb.)
I =	Moment of inertia ($bd^3/12$)	H =	Horizontal shear force (lb.)
P =	Concentrated load (lb.)	h =	Horizontal shear stress (psi)
		A =	Area of beam cross section (in.²)

due to combined uniform and centrally placed concentrated loads by addition.

Shear

Once you've chosen timber dimensions, you should check their resistance to horizontal shear stress. For the loading discussed here, shear stress is greatest directly over the supports and negligible at midspan. With loads placed symmetrically, the vertical shear force (V) is equal at both ends. The formulas for finding V are:

$V = \dfrac{wL}{2}$ in continuous loading, and

$V = \dfrac{P}{2}$ in concentrated loading.

For rectangular beams, horizontal shear force (H) is $1\frac{1}{2}$ times as great as the vertical shear force ($H = 3V/2$). Horizontal shear stress (h) is equal to the horizontal shear force divided by the area of the beam cross section (A), taken over the supports ($h = H/A$ where $A = bd$). So:

$h = \dfrac{3V}{2bd}$.

Our oak joist with the smallest cross section was the rough 3x7.

Checking it for shear stress, we find:

$V = \dfrac{wL}{2} = \dfrac{(12\ \text{lb./in.})(150\ \text{in.})}{2} = 900\ \text{lb.}$, and

$h = \dfrac{3V}{2bd} = \dfrac{(3)(900\ \text{lb.})}{(2)(3\ \text{in.})(7\ \text{in.})} = 64.29\ \text{psi.}$

An allowable h value for red oak of 100 psi puts this scantling well within safety limits. Safe h values for most species used in framing range from 65 psi to 150 psi.

Shear with notching—When a notch is taken from the bottom of a joist or beam, the cross-sectional area is diminished while the shear force remains constant, resulting in increased horizontal shear stress. The concentration of stress at the inside corner of the notch (which often lies close to the neutral axis where shear is greatest) makes splitting and eventual failure at this point a danger.

To allow for this weakness, the shear formula ($h = 3V/2bd$) is modified: The net effective depth of the timber above the notch (d') is substituted for the total depth (d). The value of the resultant shear stress is then further increased by multiplying it by a safety factor equal to the ration of the full depth to the net depth (d/d'). The revised formula looks like this:

$$h = \left(\dfrac{3V}{2\,bd'}\right)\left(\dfrac{d}{d'}\right)$$

Going back to our floor-framing example, suppose that we use a 4x7 joist and half-lap it into its carrying timber (drawing, below). Solving the formula for an acceptable d' and plugging in the acceptable h value of 100 psi, we have:

$$d' = \sqrt{\dfrac{3Vd}{2bh}} = \sqrt{\dfrac{(3)(900\ \text{lb.})(7\ \text{in.})}{(2)(4\text{in.})(100\ \text{psi})}} = 4\frac{7}{8}\ \text{in.}$$

So when using a 4x7 in this application, a net depth of at least $4\frac{7}{8}$ in. must be left above the notch. Checking the other timbers which were possible solutions to the joist problem, we find that for a 3x8, $d' = 6$ in.; for a dressed 4x8, $d' = 5\frac{5}{16}$ in.; for a 6x6, $d' = 3\frac{11}{16}$ in.; for a 3x7, $d' = 5\frac{5}{8}$ in.; and for a 5x6, $d' = 4\frac{1}{16}$ in.

It is apparent that the wider the timber, the deeper the notch that may be taken out. This sheds some light on the apparently illogical use of square-section joists and beams in traditional structures where it appears that narrow and deep pieces would have served better structurally. Not only were square timbers easier to hew from the tree, but they were also better suited to the notching necessary to fit them into the frame. It is often the case in timber framing that when a particular member seems poorly designed in structural terms, it makes perfect sense when the demands of joinery are considered.

One way of relieving the stress concentration in soffit notches, when there is no aesthetic objection, is to cut away the material below the inside corner of the notch in a gradual curve (drawing, below). This brings the strength of the joist in shear back up close to the value indicated by the net depth, unaffected by notching.

Notching the side of beams, as in dovetail lap joints, for example, also reduces the area of the cross section and increases shear stress. For these situations, substitute b' (the net effective width of the timber) for b (the total width of the timber). For a dovetail lap joint, b' is the thickness of the waist of the dovetail, and

$$h = \dfrac{3Vd}{2b'(d')^2}$$

For a dovetail lap joint with a 4-in. waist in a 6x6 joist:

$$d' = \sqrt{\dfrac{3Vd}{2b'h}} = \sqrt{\dfrac{(3)(900\ \text{lb.})(6\ \text{in.})}{(2)(4\ \text{in.})(100\ \text{psi})}} = 4\frac{1}{2}\ \text{in.}$$

The net depth above the notch must be at least $4\frac{1}{2}$ in. □

For reference and further reading

Structure in Architecture by Mario Salvadori and Robert Heller ($21.95 from Prentice Hall, Englewood Cliffs, N.J. 07632).

Structures, or Why Things Don't Fall Down by J.E. Gordon ($17.95 from Plenum Press, 233 Spring St., New York, N.Y. 10013).

Both books are excellent introductions to the basic structural concepts without mathematical overload.

Wood Structural Design Data ($12.00 from the National Forest Products Association, 1619 Massachusetts Ave., N.W. 20036).

The best structural manual for timber framers, with tables, formulas and background information.

National Design Specifications for Wood Construction ($6.50 from the National Forest Products Association).

Supplement includes comprehensive tables of design values for graded lumber.

Timber Construction Manual by the American Institute of Timber Construction ($22.95 from John Wiley & Sons).

A good basic reference, with information on working stresses and loading situations.

Wood Handbook ($10.00 from the U.S. Government Printing Office, Washington, D.C. 20402).

Another good basic reference, with information on clear wood values.

Simplified Engineering for Architects and Builders by H. F. Parker ($27.50 from John Wiley & Sons).

An introductory structural text.

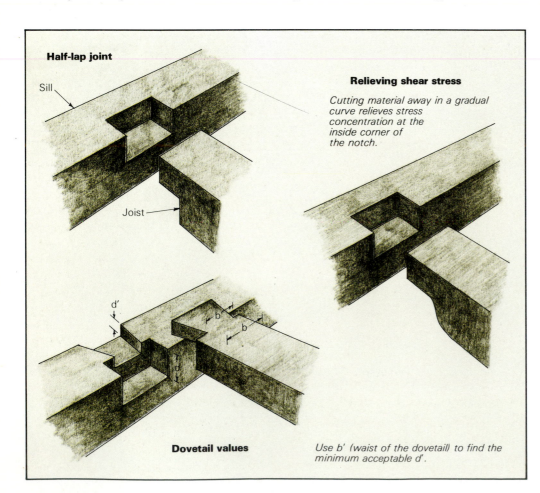

Half-lap joint

Sill

Joist

Dovetail values

d'

b

b

Relieving shear stress

Cutting material away in a gradual curve relieves stress concentration at the inside corner of the notch.

Use b' (waist of the dovetail) to find the minimum acceptable d'.

Solo Timber-Raising

A tractor, industry and common sense are all it takes

by Ross Kirk

Constructing a post-and-beam workshop was a recurring daydream of mine for two years. I had a good excuse for such musings—I needed a workshop and my house, having a dirt crawl-space instead of a basement, didn't allow for one. All of the books I read on the subject, however, maintained that you needed at least a dozen neighbors to raise a building. This was a major logistical problem. Could I achieve my goal alone? I was fairly confident I could.

Planning was the first step. Workshop functions determined the size, but what I thought I could move and carry by myself determined the design. I decided on a building 16 ft. by 24 ft.; the girts would be 6 in. by 10 in. by 16 ft. To keep the ridgepole at a height I could handle, I put a 9-ft. peak over the main part of the structure and a shed roof over the rest, resulting in a height of 19 ft. from ground to ridgepole. I chose pine and hemlock instead of oak, and though I was still handling timbers weighing about 400 lb., I could move them by sliding or by lifting one end at a time and walking them into place.

To replace the army of helpers, I used three 100-ft. lengths of new ½-in. manila rope (don't put your trust in old or frayed rope, because you'll often be working near its breaking point), a block and tackle with an advantage of four (for every 100 lb. of pull exerted, the block and tackle will pick up 400 lb.), two 16-ft. lengths of ¾-in. logging chain, two 16-in. C-clamps and a

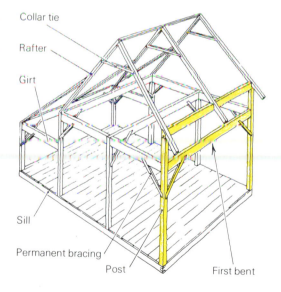

Collar tie
Rafter
Girt
Sill
Permanent bracing
Post
First bent

1-ton come-along. A 1939 John Deere model B tractor supplied the muscle and was the one tool I could not have done without. A Jeep or a four-wheel drive vehicle with an electric winch and a snatch block could replace both the tractor and the block and tackle, and would make the work easier as well. (A snatch block is a hinged pulley block that can be placed in the middle of a rope without threading from the end.)

After building a foundation of concrete block piers, I began the post-and-beam work. I squared the ends of the sill timbers and dragged each as close to the foundation as possible with the trac-

tor. Using a 4-ft. sling of rope looped around one end of the timber at a time, I lifted each into position on the foundation. After the sill and the floor girts were in place, I cut floor joists to length and custom-cut mortises for each into the sills to ensure a tight fit. I laid 2-in. tongue-and-groove flooring temporarily over the joists for a deck upon which I could cut and assemble the individual bents (sections of framing).

The first bent, of two 6-in. by 10-in. by 16-ft. girts and two 6-in. by 6-in. by 12-ft. posts, weighed about 1,300 lb., the heaviest of the lot. It was the only bent to have a double girt, the top one supporting the roof overhang. After hefting the four pieces onto the workshop floor with tractor and sweat, I placed 4x4 blocks under each to facilitate cutting the joints, assembling the bent and pounding in the treenails. Once I had cut out the various mortises and tenons of the bent, I placed the tenons of the posts directly above their respective mortises in the sill so the bents could be raised right into place. While the bent was still on the ground, I also installed the corner bracing between girts and posts.

Next, I clamped 2x10 scraps of wood to the two front corners of the sill, to guide the post tenons into their mortises. These stops have to withstand a great deal of pressure, so they must be sturdy and securely attached. Though I used 16-in. heavy-duty C-clamps, a better way might be to drill through the blocks and into the sill and

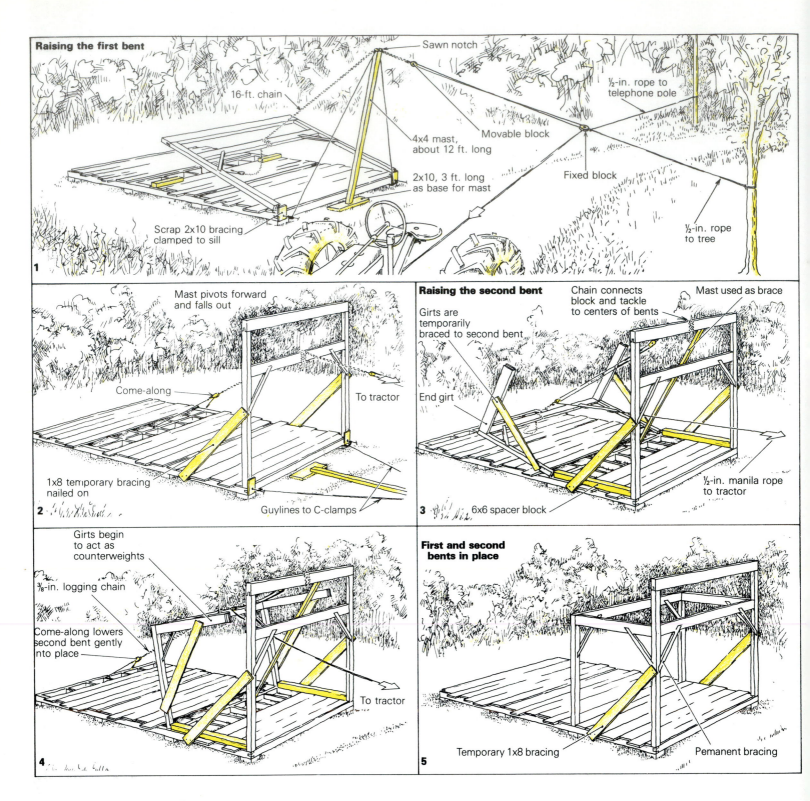

Raising the first bent

16-ft. chain

Sawn notch

Movable block

4x4 mast, about 12 ft. long

½-in. rope to telephone pole

2x10, 3 ft. long as base for mast

Fixed block

Scrap 2x10 bracing clamped to sill

½-in. rope to tree

1

Mast pivots forward and falls out

Come-along

1x8 temporary bracing nailed on

To tractor

Guylines to C-clamps

2

Raising the second bent

Chain connects block and tackle to centers of bents

Mast used as brace

Girts are temporarily braced to second bent

End girt

½-in. manila rope to tractor

6x6 spacer block

3

Girts begin to act as counterweights

⅜-in. logging chain

Come-along lowers second bent gently into place

To tractor

4

First and second bents in place

Temporary 1x8 bracing

Pemanent bracing

5

bolt them together with ¾-in. threaded rod.

Then I erected a 12-ft. high 4x4 mast with a notch in the top in front of and at the exact middle of the sill. I knotted guy ropes to the top of the mast and ran them to the two C-clamps to keep the mast from shifting. The mast needs a good, firm base—I used a 2x10, 3 ft. long. Without such a base, the mast would have been forced into the ground when the bent was lifted, and the leverage would have decreased. Next I wrapped a ⅜-in. logging chain 16 ft. long around the center of the top girt and ran it through the notch at the top of the mast and then to the movable block of the block and tackle. I ran a ½-in. rope from the fixed block to a tree exactly on the centerline, to keep the bent from falling

sideways. Then I hooked a 1-ton come-along between the logging chain around the girt and one of the floor members, with enough slack to let the bent stand upright.

Hitching the tractor up to the rope from the tackle, I took a deep breath and began to raise the first bent. The tractor took up the slack, started to pull, and everything creaked as the bent slowly began to rise. But there were problems: The terrain had made a straight pull impossible, and the fixed block was being pulled off the centerline by the tractor's pulling at a 90° angle. Setting the tractor brake, I ran a rope from the fixed block to a telephone pole directly opposite the direction of the tractor's pull. Then I gingerly continued, stopping every few feet to

check the alignment of the post tenons, making sure they would slip into their mortises. When the bent was a little past halfway up, the mast, which had been pivoting downward, dropped away. When the bent was a foot off vertical, I loosened the come-along until the posts were 1 in. shy of vertical. I took advantage of the natural stretch of the rope to nudge each one to and fro for perfect plumb, temporarily bracing them with 1x8s 10 ft. long. Getting the first bent up and snugged in place was a relief. I could finally be sure I hadn't bitten off more than I could chew.

I cut and assembled the second bent in the same manner as the first. What about the end girts, the timbers that connect the bents around

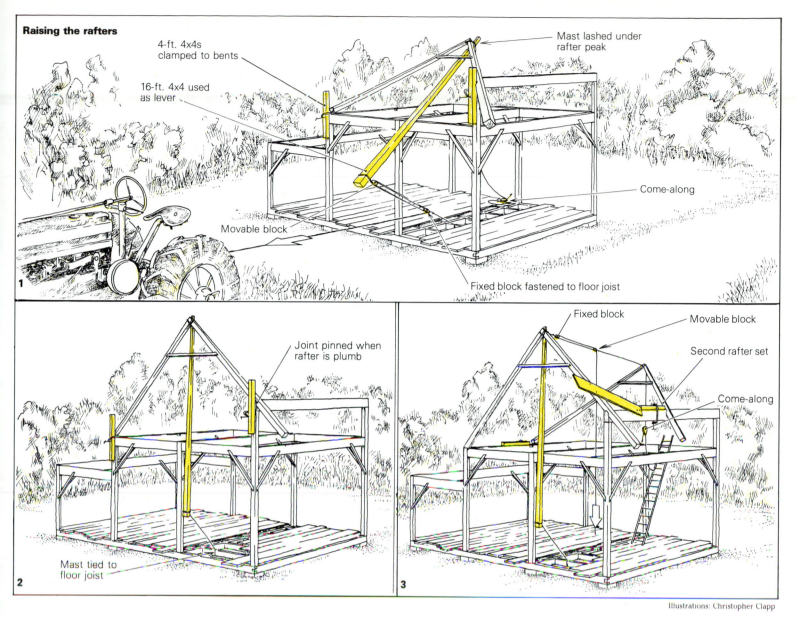

Raising the rafters

4-ft. 4x4s clamped to bents

16-ft. 4x4 used as lever

Mast lashed under rafter peak

Come-along

Movable block

Fixed block fastened to floor joist

1

Joint pinned when rafter is plumb

Mast tied to floor joist

2

Fixed block

Movable block

Second rafter set

Come-along

3

Illustrations: Christopher Clapp

the periphery of the frame? Books showed two to four people holding these up in the first bent while the next bent was hammered home. I considered many alternatives, including 8-ft. high sawhorses, before deciding to attach and temporarily brace the end girts that connect the first and second bents to the second bent. In this way when the second bent was raised, the end girts also would be lifted and would fall into their proper positions.

With the second bent ready, I cut two 6x6 timbers to fit as spacers between the bottoms of the two bents. The first bent could now be used to raise the second, but the 1x8 bracing between the first bent and the sill was inadequate to support the stress of such a raising. The mast came back into play as reinforcement. I placed the notch under the middle of the top girt in the first bent and wedged the other end of the mast against a floor joist. After a ½-in. rope failed, I used chain to fasten the block and tackle to the centers of the two bents. When the bent had been lifted two-thirds of the way into position, the end girts started to act as counterweights, pulling the bent down into place. I was ready, with my come-along secured to the bent and the

sill at the back of the building, to lower it gently. With a few taps from an 8-lb. sledgehammer, the girt tenons slid into their mortises in the first bent. I used the come-along to pull the two bents tightly together, then drilled holes in the first bent to secure the girt tenons and pounded the treenails home.

The third and fourth bents went up much the same as the second. It took me about a 10-hour day to cut, assemble and raise each bent; another day to cut and place the second-floor joists and to nail down the 1-in. tongue-and-groove flooring.

I cut all the rafters and mortises for the purlin tenons on the ground. In my earlier planning, I made sure the rafters were small enough for easy handling. I pulled the rafters up to the second floor by knotting a rope around one end and hauling. When I got them all up, I assembled an end pair. After checking to be sure their ridgepoint was square, I set the collar ties. Positioning the lower ends of the rafters, I clamped 4-ft. lengths of 4x4 timber to the bents below to guide the rafters into place and to prevent the rafter ends from kicking off the roof.

To raise the rafters, I made a lever out of 4x4

timbers 16 ft. long. I inserted one end of the lever under the rafter peak and lashed it securely into place. To the other end, which extended approximately 7 ft. over the side of the building, I tied the movable end of a block and tackle; the fixed end was tied to the first floor. A rope (or a come-along) fastened to the peak and to a second-floor joist prevented the rafter from traveling past vertical. Pulling down on the 4x4 timber (the lever) with the block and tackle raised the rafters into place. Using a plumb bob, I adjusted the rafters, then temporarily braced them. Leaving the 4x4 lever in place, I tied the bottom end securely to a floor joist and removed the block and tackle. I wanted to use this first set of rafters to raise the second: The lever tied in place would make the first rafter set stable enough to support the second. To raise the third, I moved to the other end of the building and used the technique that had worked for the first. The ridgepole of 4x4 pine was light enough for me to raise by hand, as were the rafters of the shed roof. Then, except for the purlins and the studs for sheathing, the frame was done. □

Ross Kirk, 31, is a Connecticut owner-builder.

A Timber Frame in the Hudson Valley

Fine-tuned finishes and a design inspired by a carriage house

by William Webster

During the summer of 1982, I attended a timber-framing seminar in Ohio conducted by Ed Levin, a New Hampshire designer and master builder of timber frames, and I was inspired by the structures Levin and his partners have designed and raised. But I was frustrated by how often finishes and details don't equal Levin's craftsmanship. When my brother Tom and I decided to build a spec house, we wanted Levin to design and build the frame, while we would detail and finish the house in a way that would match the beauty of the timber frame.

Although this is our first house, we are craftsmen of a different sort. Tom is an entrepreneur who also builds miniature dollhouses and is a student of the art of painted finishes, and I am a professor of aesthetics and a concert oboist by training. We thought we could build a small house that would have the elegance and intrigue of a fine dollhouse. Timber framing appealed to us because the structural frame can be used to

define space. The focus of our house would be a powerful, expansive interior. A timber frame could give us the kind of great room we imagined, and would be a framework for intricate details and fine finishes.

Inspiration from a carriage house—Tom and I grew up in a small town in Iowa before we moved to big eastern cities for graduate school and work, so it seemed natural to head for the country when we decided to build. We looked in upstate New York for property that would

This timber frame encloses living, dining and cooking areas in one 24-ft. by 32-ft. great room. The four gable ends and the center are over 21 ft. high. A motorized, domed skylight on the 4-ft. sq. lantern can be opened by a switch. Adjustable spotlights light the frame from the two tie beams and lantern. The Rumford fireplace has trim identical to the exterior cornice; the hearth is tiled with hand-molded terra-cotta.

have some topographical excitement and that would be an easy weekend commute from New York City. We finally found land in Columbia County that fit the bill—a wedge-shaped two-acre site on a hilltop. The hill is covered with oaks, birch and pine, and was thick with trees where the house was to stand. We cleared some 200 trees on the western slope, which drops dramatically toward a wide, uninterrupted view of the Hudson Valley. The village of Harlemville lies southwest of the site, and woods remain to the north and south. To the east, the hill is covered with outcroppings of bedrock.

About a half-mile away is a 19th-century cross-gable carriage house that intrigued us with its timber-frame design. In 1985 we showed Ed Levin the property, and he began designing the frame for our house, using ideas from Tom and me and drawing on the form and structure of the carriage house nearby. The trick was to design a house that would be small enough to be

As a beginning timber framer in the early 1970s, I worked on a five-story Post-Modern tower, a split-level contemporary with cathedral ceilings and a number of buildings in more traditional styles. I assumed that my early career was typical and that my colleagues and I would continue to build an interesting mix of ancient and modern structures. The years since then have told a different story—today's timber frames are largely a reprise of the American 18th century.

As an associate of Ken Rower, who has long argued for adapting timber framing to modern building forms, and as a founding director of the Timber Framers Guild of North America, I am eager to see timber framing break out of its Colonial straightjacket. The pairing of timber frame and stress skin is analogous to the familiar I-beam and curtain-wall combination, and as such is well suited to modest-scale buildings of all uses and styles. Many of the humdrum buildings done today with exposed steel or gluelam beams could be quite spectacular with joined heavy timber frames. In our shop, we welcome commissions for capes and saltboxes, but we are always on the lookout for other shapes to build, such as rectangular

compositions under a flat roof, intricate hip-and-valley designs and curved framing—our house specialty.

In the spring of 1985, I was delighted when Bill and Tom Webster asked me to build a timber-frame house that would be out of the ordinary. A couple of years earlier, Bill had taken a workshop with us in Ohio, provoking our curiosity as to why a professor of aesthetics would want to learn how to cut a timber frame. It turned out that he and his brother had caught the building bug and hoped to put their ideas to work as spec builders. We were to design a weekend house in rural New York, provide architectural and structural drawings, cut and erect the timber frame and subcontract the installation of stress-skin panels on the upper level. The Websters would take care of everything else. They gave us a free hand in the design within the limitations of the program, and encouraged us to do original and creative work.

By coincidence, the Websters' lot was next to architect Raymond DeRis' house and office, which was the only timber-frame building we had then built in New York State, so I knew the neighborhood well. We took

inspiration from the 19th-century carriage house that DeRis had relocated nearby and renovated for use as a library. The carriage house, a 29-ft. by 36-ft. rectangle, is capped by intersecting gable roofs with a cupola over the crossing. The clapboard-and-shingle exterior is dominated by the original heavily molded trim, pediment and entablature.

In our practice, the design process requires steady traffic between shop and office because several of us double as joiners and designers. Each project has two or three designers of record, and the plans are available to everyone, resulting in a collaborative design. For the Webster house, Nori Bokum took floor plans through preliminary drawings, while Ken Rower concentrated on elevations and detailing exterior trim. I worked out the timber-frame design on our CADD system and entered the architectural drawings into the computer, overlaying floors, walls and roof on the framing plans and elevations.

The Webster house gradually took shape on the computer screen. The building was 24 ft. by 32 ft. in plan, with crossing gables at a 12-in-12 pitch. The design of the main level was based on the medieval notion of an open hall

with the timber frame as its principal ornament. Outside along eaves and rakes, we applied a molded cornice reminiscent of the old carriage house, but omitted its heavy entablature. Windows and doors would be a mix of custom millwork, salvage and off-the-shelf components. Even the smallest cupola seemed to unbalance the elevations, so we designed a short, square lantern topped with an operable dome skylight.

The timber frame was of both red and white oak, with blind mortise-and-tenon connections and white oak pegs, most of which were blind as well. The 24-ft. square crossing was carried on four 7x11 valley rafters, which rose from 8x8 valley posts to join at the 4-ft. square lantern frame at the peak. The valleys received 4x6 jacks on 40-in. centers. The open plan wouldn't accommodate interior posts or partitions, so we stiffened the roof structure by ringing the walls with horizontal braces, forming a large octagon at the plate level. We also added arched braces, which joined valley posts and rafters in a smooth curve. Elaborating on this curved motif, timber arches spring from corner and valley posts and follow the inner edges of the gable-end rafters and collars, and wind braces echo the curve of the arches.

These curved timbers probably consumed more human and fossil-fuel energy than all the rest of the frame combined. We had intended to bandsaw the arches out of 6-in. thick stock, but were discouraged by past experience with sawn curves. New England oak doesn't grow large enough to provide thick stock that's free of heart center, and curves cut through the heart in green timber fare poorly in drying. In any case, we weren't able to find the required blanks for sawing, heart or no heart.

Instead, we began to stockpile clear, straight-grained 6x6 oak and to build a large steambox and bending table, wondering if we had ourselves a prescription for a nightmare. But phone calls to boatbuilders led us quickly to Ed McClave of Noank, Conn., an engineer, boatbuilder and expert on the physics of steambending, springback and overbend. Armed with the theory of the mechanics and with assurance from McClave that we weren't crazy, we went to work. A few weeks and several hundred pounds of propane later, we had our pile of curved timber ready for joinery and raising. □

The frame stands alone. This frame has no interior posts. All four gable ends were raised, then temporary staging was assembled to hold the lantern. After the lantern was hoisted by a crane to the peak, the crew fit the valley rafters to the structure, then installed intermediate rafters and jacks.

cozy yet big enough to justify a timber frame (which can cost one-third more than conventional framing). Levin and his colleagues came up with a timber-frame design that was more innovative and enchanting than any other we had seen (sidebar, facing page).

Fitting the house to the hill—The sloped site gave us the chance to have at-grade entrances to the house on two levels and to hide the full height of the house on the main-entry side. The house comes into sight only as you drive up the curved, marble-chip driveway. At first it appears to be a modest story-and-a-half with a formal entry, but as you round the last bend, the back of the house comes into view, two-and-a-half stories tall (photo right).

To make the most of the view from the upper floor, we decided to invert the usual scheme of living space on the first floor and bedrooms on the second. In this house, the bedrooms and laundry room are on the ground floor, with most windows on the south and west and the only doors on the west, or downhill, side (drawing, right). Upstairs, the main entry is at grade, and the kitchen, dining and living rooms look west to the octagonal deck and vista beyond.

Composing the frame—Walls at the lower level are constructed of cast-in-place concrete and wood-stud framing. The stud walls are two layers thick, with a 2x4 wall butted to a 2x6 wall. This gave us finished walls that provide a foundation for the tons of oak to be supported. Levin and his crew raised the timber frame on the structure below, and the frame was covered with stress-skin panels, which had been pre-assembled from exterior chipboard sheathing, rigid urethane insulation and drywall.

The frame itself is a complex structure of straight and curved timbers. To make the arched timbers, Levin built a steambox and a bending form, and after steaming the timbers, he coaxed them into their curves with a come-along. As far as we know, this is a first for American timber framing in the 20th century. The raising was tremendously exciting, in part because there are no internal posts. There were no permanent supports for the four gable-end frames until the valley rafters were locked into the lantern. The 1,500-lb. lantern, which had been constructed on the ground, was hoisted onto staging with a crane and held there while the valley rafters were set (photo facing page).

Finishing the frame—Immediately after the frame was erected, we began the task of finishing the oak. At the time the frame was raised, the oak had been cut for about six months, and while the wood was clean and planed, it needed a final dressing. We scraped and sanded the wood, then varnished it. In all, we gave three rounds of sanding and varnishing to the oak from the horizontal braces (at 7 ft. above the floor) up to the peak, and four coats to the frame below 7 ft., where it is within reach of hands and furniture. The color and texture of the oak are quite remarkable: it resembles fine, hand-rubbed furniture. We gave the drywall three brushed-on coats of flat linen-white paint,

View from the western slope. A pressure-treated deck on several levels spreads out from the back of the house. Peter Taylor helped design and engineer the 19-ft. dia. octagon with a continuous bench/rail. The deck is supported by a trunk that is built of four 4x6 posts. Eight braces hold up the deck as branches might hold up a treehouse. The bluestone terrace under the deck connects to the front of the house by a winding bluestone walk.

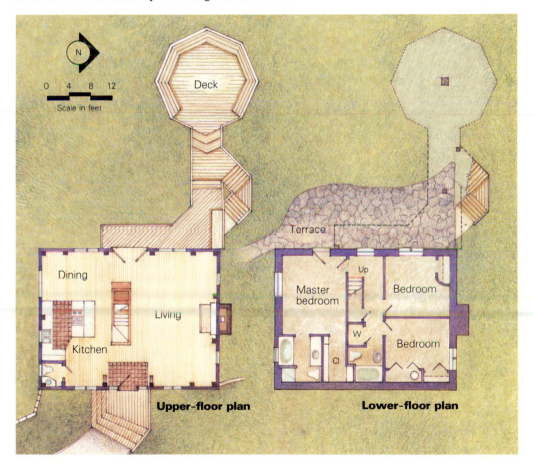

hand-sanding between coats so that the surface looks like smooth plaster.

This attention to finishing the oak and the drywall was crucial to creating the look that we wanted. It's been said that an oak frame is never more beautiful than after it is set and standing against the sky. This doesn't have to be the case if the neighboring surfaces and details are finely finished. The central space of this house is defined and enlivened not only by the frame, but also by the background to the frame—the ceiling, walls and floor. You sense upward movement here because there is no horizontal ridge beam to interrupt your eye. The valley rafters and lantern are powerful, yet they are balanced by the delicacy of the smaller rafters and jacks, making the massive oak appear light and airy (photo p. 35). Behind the oak, the white background seems to float, and recalls the memory of the bare frame set against the sky.

Finishing the details—We continued the arch shape of the frame on the three curved windows: the semicircular 1840s English win-

A semicircular window over the entry determined the proportions and detailing of the door, transom and sidelites. Two short walls that flank the door and terra-cotta floor tiles define the entrance. A cooking/preparation island separates the kitchen from the living and dining areas. White plastic-laminate cabinets with oak edging echo the colors of timber frame and walls to minimize the presence of the kitchen. The timber frame and all of the oak trim were sanded and varnished three times. Painted trim and walls got three brushed-on coats of oil-base paint, with hand-sanding between coats.

Cloud detail. The author's three-color glazing on the master-bedroom walls turns the room into a Hudson River School painting.

dow above the front door (photo above), the new custom 8-ft. dia. window in the south gable (photo p. 34), and the Victorian window with a curved head in the west wall. The front door, sidelites and transom were custom made to match the antique window above. We wanted all windows to have true divided lites in order to define and articulate the view. Instead of sill-and-apron window trim, we did not want the three-piece trim to be interrupted, so the upstairs windows are "picture-frame" trimmed. In the walls downstairs, the window jambs and casings sit near the exterior, with drywall returns at jambs and heads and deep sills of oak or marble. All window and door trim was three-piece, custom made by Ron Roland (393 N. Pearl St., Albany, N. Y. 12207), who also ground his own router bits to make the one-piece trim on the curved windows match the three-piece straight trim.

All surfaces that needed finishing got close attention. The seven-piece custom gable trim and the window and door trim, inside and out, received three coats of oil-base enamel paint, with hand-sanding between coats. We used 4-in. red cedar siding on the exterior and gave it three coats of rich, reddish-brown oil paint after nails were set, filled and sanded. The colors in the T&G oak flooring ranged from white to orange to almost black, and the figure was wild and wiry, so we bleached the oak. After bleaching and three coats of varnish, the floor is a subtle complement to the darker oak frame.

Special finishes for the walls—We labored the longest over the walls in the bedrooms, where Tom put his training in painted finishes to work. One such finish is wall glazing, a classic technique presently being revived as an elegant

way of covering walls. Unlike opaque paint, which doesn't let light pass through, glazed surfaces provide the illusion of depth, texture and movement by the layering of transparent paints. But glazing is an involved process that can take you and your tools around a room six or more times, from primer coat to varnish.

We prepared the drywall by filling imperfections and thoroughly sanding the surface. Next, we applied two coats of oil-base primer. When it dried, we rolled on and brushed on the underlying color coat. Then we laid down the color (or a combination of colors) and worked it wet. This layer can be oil or latex-based and is both applied and taken off with cheesecloth, natural sponges or chamois. Finally, we ragged on the glaze coat—a combination of oil-base paint, mineral spirits and glazing compound, a transparent material made by McCloskey Glaze Coat (7600 State Rd., Philadelphia, Pa. 19136). After 24 hours, we applied a flat or eggshell varnish with cheesecloth to give the wall surface more depth and to provide protection.

We used a single color in one bedroom, a double color in another and a three-color glaze in the master bedroom. Here, we applied beige-brown and caramel-brown paint at the same time with cheesecloth, then laid on turquoise for the second coat. This gave the walls the soft and rich patina of age (photo left).

Tom and I set out to build a spec house, but cranking out a house wasn't the point—we wanted to build the best timber-frame house we could. We've been asked why we don't keep such a labor of love, but to us, the process of building means more than the finished product. For us it was putting mind to matter and hand to brush that brought the structure to life. □

Tools for Timber Framing

A housewright's implements
for measuring, marking and cutting,
and how he keeps them sharp and true

by Edward M. Levin

The recent interest in timber framing has led to the revival of woodworking techniques long in decline or disuse. These methods call for implements not found in most carpenters' tool kits since before the turn of the century, along with new uses of more familiar tools. Here is an introduction to the use and care of some of the fundamental tools of the housewright's trade.

Measuring—The framing square is the essential tool. Apart from its chores as a straightedge, and in squaring up assembled framework, we use it to measure and mark across timber, as in

the photo above, to test flatness and, with screw-on fixtures, to repeat roof and stair angles. Two framing squares, one set at either end of a beam, make excellent winding sticks to test for and quantify twist (drawing, below).

A sliding bevel complements the framing

square and fixtures for laying out joints, testing angles and setting up machinery. Use a bevel with a slotted screw-tightening mechanism. If your sliding bevel has thumbscrews or wing nuts, it's best to replace them with slotted screws or hex nuts, and tighten with a screwdriver or a wrench to fix the angle securely. A bevel that slips is worthless.

Combination squares have largely replaced the traditional try square for checking mortises

(as in the photo above), notched and lapped joints, the shoulders of tenons, and for squaring across end grain. The 12-in. size is standard, but the 6-in. size is handy to square drill bits to a surface and to work in tight spots. The blades of combination squares can serve as straightedges to test surfaces for flatness. To check inside different-sized housings and gains, we often supplement them with a variety of special straight-

edges made of ⅛-in. by 1-in. brass or aluminum with edges filed flat.

We use templates to lay out frequently repeated joints like notches, lap joints and dovetails, as well as decorative chamfer stops. The ideal template material is thin (about ⅛ in.) but stiff and can be cut with a knife, but resists damage by knife or scribe while in use—I haven't found it yet. Brass, aluminum or steel work well for permanent templates, but they must be cut out tediously with hacksaw and file. Wood and hardboard must be sawn out and erode away in use. For the most part we use throwaway tem-

plates of dense grey cardboard (newsboard or chipboard), like the one in the photo above.

For measuring lengths in timber work, I have found a 1-in. by 25-ft. power return tape to be best. The 1-in. width makes it easier for a person working alone to extend the tape without its

---

1⁵⁄₁₆ in.

1. Set squares at both ends of a timber (say, an 8-in. wide beam). Their blades will sit at different angles if there is any twist.

2. To find the amount of twist, position yourself to site down one edge of the timber, aligning the top end point of the far square with the top edge of the closer one.

3. Moving your eyes but not your head, site across the closer square and take a reading at the point its top edge seems to intersect with the vertical scale of the far square (1⁵⁄₁₆ in. in this example). This is the difference over the full 24-in. length of the rear square. But you want to know the deviation (twist) over the 8-in. width of the beam itself.

4. Divide the length of the square blade by the width of the beam to find the ratio of one to the other: 24/8 = 3.

5. Since this beam is ⅓ as wide as the square blade is long, its twist will be ⅓ the deviation you noted on the square, or 1⁵⁄₁₆ in./3 = ⁷⁄₁₆ in.

---

folding over. Try to use the same tape throughout a frame, since graduation may vary significantly from tape to tape.

We use an unchalked carpenter's line to check beams and assemblies for straightness and alignment and to measure the crown in bowed timbers. A chalked line comes in handy when we have to lay out a beam from its centerline because its edges are irregular.

Marking—Gauges are best for laying out the sides of mortises and tenons, the backs and bottoms of notches, the depths of housings and to mark any straight line parallel to the edge of a timber. Standard marking gauges have a useful reach of about 4 in. Beyond this point, switch to a panel gauge.

Gauge stems carry three spurs to scribe the centerline and both sides of mortises, as in the

photo. I make these spurs from hardened sheetmetal or drywall screws chucked in an electric drill and pointed on a grinding wheel while both wheel and drill are spinning. The screw thread allows you to adjust the heights of the spurs to keep all three marking evenly.

Once the centerline is determined, use an awl or an automatic center punch to mark drillcenters. The dimple will engage the worm of the auger used to bore out waste.

A knife is best for marking across the grain, as in the first photo on p. 39, and a scribe for marking with it. Pencils won't stay sharp on rough lumber, and they leave fat, ambiguous lines that make for sloppy fits. (They are, however, useful for marking out decorative chamfers and stops, and in other applications where a residual scribed line is undesirable.) Cut and scribed lines can be split cleanly by setting the edge of your chisel right in the line when paring or chopping a joint. There are other advantages: Cut lines aren't erased by light surfacing and can be recovered or "darkened" without benefit of straightedge since the knife or scribe will track in the path of the existing line. An incorrect mark can still be changed—the sideways pressure of the tool cutting a new line will close up the grain in the adjacent old one. Finally, grain will not chip up beside a cut line when you're crosscutting with a circular saw. This not only makes for neater work, but also signals when you are cutting off the line, since in that case the saw will begin to raise flecks of wood.

Marking knives, awls and striking tools incorporating both knife blade and scribe are available from mail-order tool houses. For cut lines, I use an ordinary utility knife, and for scribing, a homemade awl made from a hardened nail pointed like the gauge spurs and hafted in an adjustable file handle or a pin vise. Both knife blades and awl points are easily reground or replaced when they wear away or break.

To identify timbers and joints for later assembly there are several options: The traditional tool is the timber scribe or race knife, which consists of a handled blade, often made out of an old file, bent back on itself in a hook or V shape. It is pulled toward the user, and scoops out a groove (the race) in the wood. You can use a chisel for the same purpose, or turn to number and letter stamps or lumber crayons.

Knives and planes—If your marking knife can't do double duty, a pocket or utility knife is as essential for miscellaneous tasks in timber framing as in all carpentry. A drawshave (also called a drawknife) will remove bark and, along with a spokeshave, will clean up wane (rounded or bark corners), and cut decorative chamfers and stops on beams.

The carriage or coachmaker's rabbet plane (photo below, right) is the unsung hero among timber-framing tools. We use this versatile plane (Stanley #10, Record #010) to knock off bumps around knots and checks, to level crowned timber surfaces before marking out, to dress housings or gains, finish cheeks and sometimes shoulders of tenons, and to surface scarf joints.

For hand-planing timber, a short, wide smooth plane like the Stanley #4½ or Record #04½ (photo below, left) is best, but standard smooth

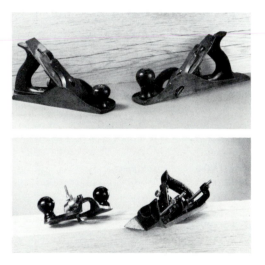

or jack planes are adequate. Grind the iron in a shallow curve so the corners won't dig in.

The photo above shows other useful planes: A fillister or duplex rabbet plane (Stanley #78, Record #778) with 45° wooden fences attached (right) makes an excellent chamfer plane. And (left) a hand router (Stanley #71, Record #071) will clean up stopped or blind housings that the bench rabbet can't get into. An electric router will also do this, but its voracious appetite for wood is not always satisfied with waste. If the gain is wider than the tool, attach a wooden base or leave intermediate ridges in the work for the router to ride on. You can chisel these off later.

Among tools for power planing, I find the Makita model #1805B (photo above) unsurpassed. It cuts a 6⅛-in. swath and, when sharp, leaves a glassy surface on which tool marks are barely discernible.

Chisels—Several different patterns of chisel are handy in timber framing. The standard tool is the framing chisel, a category that ranges from tanged firmer chisels like the one in the photo on the facing page, bottom right—a tang is a spikeshaped extension of the blade, which extends into the handle—through heavier socketed varieties, all the way to stout mortise chisels and millwright's chisels. This last is often a two-man tool (one to hold, one to strike) capable of chopping a mortise straight out of the solid wood with little or no pre-drilling. It has pretty much vanished from the scene. Advances in drill-bit and drill technology make it more convenient and more efficient for the carpenter to bore out most of the waste in a mortise.

Tanged chisels used for chopping the ends of mortises should be somewhat narrower than the mortise width, lest the tool become wedged in the joint. Thicker socketed framing chisels can take the prying force necessary to free them, and so can be used full width. The sharper the corners of the top of the chisel (the beveled side), the better it will cut the sides of the mortise when levered forward.

One caution: Many carpenters take a straightbacked chisel for granted. Since most old and many new framing chisels are not flat on the back (unbeveled) side, check carefully when purchasing a tool. The English chisels available through mail-order tool catalogs are usually reliably flat. And you can repair most others— more about this later.

A large (1-in. to 1½-in. wide) bevel-edged chisel is useful for cleaning up inside acute angles (as in dovetails) along with a small one (⅜ in. to ½ in. wide) for even more restricted areas. The corner chisel, as its name implies, cuts two adjacent perpendicular surfaces at once. Using this chisel requires an unusual combination of concentration and dexterity. Since corner chisels are a nuisance to sharpen, I don't recommend them. A sharp framing chisel is perfectly adequate.

The slick—3 in. to 4 in. wide and 30 in. long— is the king of chisels. With its handle offset to clear the work, the slick is used to surface large areas, often for roughing out the area in advance of a plane. Slicks are paring chisels—they are always pushed, never struck.

Saws—Contractor's circular saws get a real workout in timber framing. The ideal power saw for this kind of work will cut at least halfway through the narrow dimension of your largest stock, without being unduly heavy. Four candidates are the Rockwell 510 Speedmatic 10¼-in. saw (which cuts 3⅝ in. deep at 90°, but weighs 35 lb.), the Makita 5201N 10¼-in. (3¾ in., almost 20 lb.), the Makita 5103N 13-in. (5 in., 22 lb.) and the Skil 860 10¼-in. (3⅞ in., 17½ lb.).

An 8¼-in. worm-drive saw makes up in tenacity what it lacks in depth of cut. And don't despair of your 7¼-in. saw. There are many operations in timber framing where a small, light saw is best (roughing out housings, cutting tenon shoulders and so forth). However, you will have to finish cutoffs and deep shoulder cuts by hand.

For sawblades, I recommend the chisel-tooth combination pattern, filed as a ripsaw. If your saws are in heavy and continuous use, you might consider carbide. After many years of using steel blades, we switched over several years ago when I realized that saw sharpening had become an almost daily chore. Our saws range from an 8¼-in., 18-tooth, 14-gauge blade which makes a .125-in. kerf, to a 12-in. 24-tooth, 12-gauge blade with a .159-in. kerf. The tooth pattern on all our blades is left/right/raker, which is free cutting on both rip and crosscuts, yet doesn't tear or leave a ragged cut.

A basic handsaw kit includes a 7 or 8-point crosscut, a 4 to 6-point crosscut and a 3½ or 4-point ripsaw. Finding coarse-toothed saws can be a problem. A pruning saw makes an acceptable heavy-duty crosscut. Docking saws can be filed to rip or to crosscut. Most of my saws with fewer than 7 teeth per inch started life with a finer tooth pattern and were retoothed and refiled by the local saw doctor. Cutting edges should be straight or slightly crowned in order to work down to a line when sawing joints.

A well-sharpened two-man crosscut saw makes fast and surprisingly accurate work of cutoffs and tenon shoulders.

Drills—These days, most of the work of cutting peg holes and boring out waste in mortises and notches is done with hand-held electric drills. Use a powerful (6 amp or more), slow-spinning

(300 to 600 rpm) reversible, ½-in. or larger drill with long handles. Guard against binding, lest the drill spin instead of the bit. You can guide the drill by eye, with a small square on the surface or a batten attached to the side of the work, or by attaching a circular bubble level to the tool. For the first and last of these methods, it's important to have leveled up the timber beforehand.

The 19th-century boring machine (photo above) is a sensible hand-powered way to drill timber. Out of production for many years, such machines are scarce, but they are a joy to use. The coffee-grinder handles give the workman tremendous leverage. When the desired depth is reached (indicated by a scale on the side of the machine or by a built-in adjustable depth stop), a set of gears is engaged to retract the bit and most of the chips. A 2-in. hole can be drilled 4 in. into oak in less than a minute.

A drill press is useful for repeated operations on smaller pieces such as diagonal bracing and light floor joists or purlins.

The Scotch-pattern auger is the appropriate bit for most timber-framing applications. It is identical in most respects to the more familiar Jennings pattern—a double-twisted body, a nose with flat cutting edges and a screw lead—but instead of downward pointing spurs, the Scotch auger has upward-facing side wings at the outside of the cutting edges (the difference is apparent in the drawing at left). This leaves a rougher hole, but makes for a freer-cutting bit with less drag. A Jennings auger is an acceptable substitute if the Scotch is unavailable.

Other bit patterns include the ship's auger (single twist, single cutter and side wing with worm) for peg holes, a long barefoot auger to finish deep holes, brad-point twist drills for use in a drill press, and the Irwin bit (single twist, solid center) for general work. Drills without screw leads (multispur, Forstner, power bore, spade, and so forth) have trouble clearing chips in all but the shallowest holes and are not recommended for timber framing.

Mallets—Wooden mallets are kinder to trunnels, tool handles and timber surfaces than steel hammers, but don't stand up well to heavy use with steel-hooped chisels. We like to use mallets with rawhide-faced iron heads (photo below). Carver's mallets have a cylindrical or conical

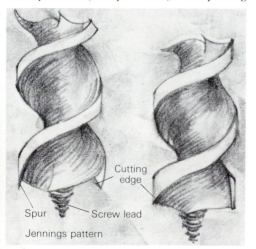

Cutting edge

Spur   Screw lead

Jennings pattern

head that is parallel to the handle. Carpenter's mallets have a cylindrical or rectangular head that is perpendicular to the handle. The carpenter's mallet is more common in timber work, but personal preference rules. Some carpenters prefer to use dead-blow mallets of shot-filled plastic for driving pins or knocking light framework together, and in other situations calling for a heavy blow without bounce. The commander is the grandfather of wooden mallets. It weighs

20 to 30 lb. and is used to drive beams or wall sections together and shift them into place, as shown in the photo above.

Tool rehabilitation—There is no guarantee these days that new tools from the manufacturer will arrive in good working order. They are often poorly tempered and carelessly ground (or belt sanded instead). They may have been machined while their castings were still green. There are also a lot of old tools out there in attics, antique shops, junk stores and flea markets. They may be rusty or out of adjustment, but many of them, along with lots of less than perfect new tools, can be made perfectly serviceable with a little tinkering.

Metal straightedges can be trued up with a long flat or mill file. A small wooden guide block

clamped or held to the file (photo above) will help maintain square. Alter your filing pattern for even wear on the file, and clean the file regularly with a file card and a brush. This is especially important when you are filing brass or aluminum, which clog up ordinary files very

rapidly. (If you do a great deal of soft-metal filing, get special-purpose files.)

To test tools for flatness and square, keep a master straightedge and square. You can also test squares by marking across a straight board and reversing the body of the square, as in the

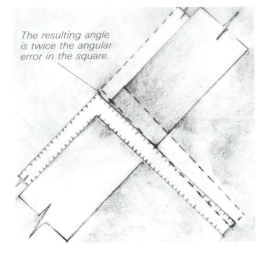

The resulting angle is twice the angular error in the square.

drawing. If the blade of the tool and the line still coincide, the square is true. If they don't, the angle they form is twice the error in the square.

Out-of-square combination squares can be repaired with a small, thin file (a 4-in. flat or mill file will do). File the base of the slot in the body of

the square (photo above). The drawing below shows how to true up framing squares. Scratch a line between the corners at the juncture of the body and the tongue. Place the square on an anvil or the other solid support and, using a ham-

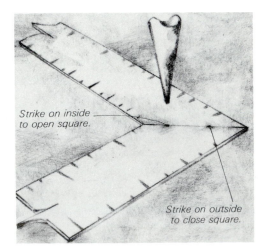

Strike on inside to open square.

Strike on outside to close square.

mer and center punch, strike on the scribed line. A blow toward the inside corner of the square will open the angle, and one near the outside will close it.

Small deviations from flat in the backs of chisels or bottoms of planes can be eliminated in several ways. Joint the tool on sandpaper or an abrasive belt attached with spring clamps or with rubber cement to a flat surface like the bed

of a jointer (photo above). Or you can lap it with abrasive compound (tripoli, carborundum powder or valve-grinding compound) on a flat piece of plate glass. Polish the tool with fine-grit paper on the jointer top, polishing compound on the glass, or on a large sharpening stone.

More pronounced curvature in chisels and planes can be taken out on the flat side of a grinding wheel, but this is a touchy business, and it's probably best to consign these tools to the surface grinder of a competent machinist. The same applies to rabbet planes whose sides are not square to their bottoms.

Here is a procedure to follow for resuscitating an iron plane:

1. Disassemble the plane. Examine and treat the parts separately (drawing below).

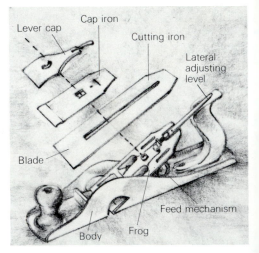

Lever cap Cap iron Cutting iron Lateral adjusting level Blade Feed mechanism Body Frog

2. Remove the cap iron. Clean up rust and flatten the back of the cutting iron on an India stone, removing scratches with an Arkansas stone. Reassemble and check for daylight between cap and iron. There should be no play between the two when the screw is tightened. Twist or insufficient spring tension in the cap can be cured by placing it in a vise and bending it slightly. If the

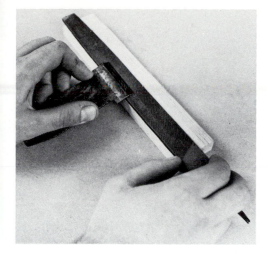

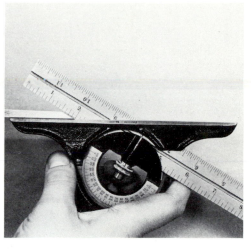

Grinding and sharpening—To sharpen drill bits, file the top side of the flats (photo below left) and the inside of the spurs or side wings (photo below right) with a bit file. Be sure to remove material evenly from both sides.

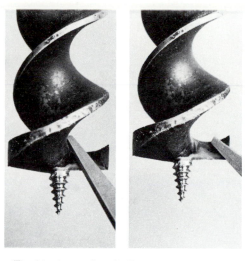

cap still does not touch the blade along its full width, then it must be jointed. Block a file or stone up off the bench, as in the photo above, and flatten the contact surface of the cap with the heel resting on the bench. This should ensure that cap and iron meet at the leading edge of the cap, preventing shavings from becoming wedged between the two. Grind and hone the cutter (see grinding and sharpening, at right).

3. Clean up the frog. If the feed mechanism doesn't work freely, spin the knob off and examine it and the stud it rides on. Damaged male threads can often be repaired with a needle file or a thread-repairing tool or file. The knob or stud can also be replaced, either by cannibalizing a spare-parts plane or by ordering from the manufacturer (Stanley maintains a comprehensive repair and spare-parts catalog). Recutting the threads is difficult as they are often odd-sized or left-handed. The lateral adjusting lever can usually be freed up by lubricating and working it vigorously back and forth.

4. Remove rust from the body using penetrating oil and a stainless-steel sponge. For more serious cases, use a light application of the jointing techniques described above. Ease sharp corners with a file or emery cloth. Replace the frog (set at the widest opening) and install the iron. You may need to file the forward edge of the throat if the opening is too narrow for timber work. (The same may be necessary with the apertures for chip clearance in the sides of a rabbet plane.)

To remove rust or pitting on drill bits, carefully stone or file the bottoms of flats and lightly polish the outside of the spurs or side wings with a stone or buffing wheel. This is the only time these surfaces should be touched. If a bit drags or won't feed in test holes, try the following:

1. Check chip thickness. If one side of the bit is taking a thicker chip, file back the leading cutter until both cut to an even depth. Match the height of the spurs on Jennings augers. On a Scotch auger, the leading edges of side wings and edges should coincide so that both cut simultaneously. Remember to file only the tops of cutters and the insides of wings or spurs.

2. Check the screw lead. Damaged or shallow threads can be filed with a needle file.

3. Check the cutter angle, and file it down if it appears too steep. For timber work, 30° to 35° is about right.

4. File down the spurs on Jennings augers to reduce drag.

The big danger in grinding edge tools is burning the tool and drawing its temper. To avoid this, use a sharp wheel. Dress it with a carborundum, a star wheel or a diamond dressing tool when it becomes uneven, glazed or clogged. White aluminum oxide wheels wear quickly, but stay sharper and are an improvement over the older-style grey wheel. Avoid excessive pressure, and check the tool regularly to see that it doesn't overheat. One way to do this is to dip the plane iron or chisel into water and grind only until the droplets just begin to steam off the edge before dipping again.

If you do burn a tool (you can tell by the discoloration at its edge) or have one that is too soft (the edge rolls over and nicks easily) or too hard (the edge chips or corners break off), you can usually have it retempered by a competent blacksmith or metalworker.

We grind large tools on a belt grinder with an 11½-in. contact wheel (photo below). Plane irons

and smaller tools are ground on a 6-in. hand grinder since the large wheel doesn't leave a sufficient hollow in the narrower bevels. A 7-in. or 8-in. grinder is a reasonable compromise between the two.

First check and correct the edge for square. If the sides of the tool are not parallel, split the difference. We grind most timber-framing tools at

an angle of 30°. Check the angle with a sliding bevel or bevel protractor as in the photo above. Another test for a 30° angle: The length of the bevel is just twice the thickness of the tool. Experience may dictate a larger or smaller angle on certain tools. Experiment. Grind until you raise a wire edge, checking for straightness and square, and then hone at the same angle, with the bevel laid flat on the stone, until a shiny narrow line appears at the edge. Whet the tool only until all the scratches from grinding are clear of the edge. This should leave enough steel for several additional honings before the bevel is flat and has to be reground.

Hone plane irons on the standard 6-in. or 8-in. stones. With careful grinding you can go directly to a soft Arkansas stone (photo below). If this works too slowly, take a couple of strokes on an India stone first. For a razor edge, finish with a hard Arkansas stone. Whet the back of the tool last to remove the burr. Light mineral oil makes an excellent and inexpensive honing oil.

Since it can be very difficult to hand-hold framing chisels and other large edge tools at a steady angle while moving them over a sharpening stone, try moving the stone rather than the tool. Lay the chisel on its back and hone with small India and Arkansas files. This method works for all edge tools and is especially handy when retouching edges away from the workshop, since you don't have to tote around several large and fragile stones.   □

Ed Levin, of Canaan, N.H., designs and builds timber-framed houses.

The Fairbanks House

Modern carpenters trace the roots of American architecture as
they reconstruct the nation's oldest wood-frame building

by Ed Levin

From *Fine Homebuilding* magazine (February 1983) 13:22-27

The Jonathan Fairbanks house in Dedham, Mass., built in 1637, is the oldest wood-frame structure in North America. The lean-to addition, left, was added to the rear of the house before 1668. In 1980, Ed Levin and his crew cut and raised a replica frame of the Fairbanks house on the Boston Common (above).

It was in the early 1630s that a yeoman farmer named Jonathan Fairebanke left the village of Sowerby in the West Riding of Yorkshire and crossed the western ocean, landing in the new town of Boston in the Massachusetts Bay Colony. In the spring of 1637 he was granted twelve acres in the new settlement of Dedham, just south of Boston; and in that same year unknown carpenters, themselves newly arrived in the wilderness of New England, built him a house that still stands today (photo facing page). The Fairbanks house, having outlasted all of its contemporaries, is the oldest surviving wood-frame building in North America.

Three hundred and forty-three years later, in July of 1980, I was one of a crew of modern housewrights who erected a full-scale replica of the timber frame of the Fairbanks house on the Boston Common as the centerpiece of a fair honoring the 350th anniversary of the city (see p. 49).

The Fairbanks house is an important example of the beginnings of American domestic architecture for two reasons. First, it has come through nearly three-and-a-half centuries relatively unscathed by the waves of alterations, remodelings and "restorations" that have destroyed or obscured the original construction of most surviving 17th-century houses. The Fairbanks house presents its original face to the researcher and eliminates a lot of sleuthing and guesswork.

Second, the design and construction of the house make it a good example of 17th-century building on both sides of the Atlantic. Its construction came right on the heels of a period of drastic changes in house building in England, and the Fairbanks house features many of the innovations of its time. However, the carpenters who worked on the house were recent emigrants from a backwater of County Suffolk, so it retains archaic elements as well. The evolution of English building technique is most evident in the frame and the plan. The exterior, on the other hand, represents a real departure from European tradition, and is one of the clearest examples of an emerging American architecture.

The English tradition—In the early 1500s, the house of the ordinary English farmer was a central hall open to the roof flanked by sleeping and service wings set at right angles on one or both ends. Glazing was non-existent. Windows were either open to the elements or closed with wooden shutters. Cooking was done in an outbuilding; the notion of including the kitchen in the house did not come into fashion until the 1630s. Ovens were unknown in rural farmhouses—bread, if any, came from the baker. The hall was heated by an open fire kindled in the center of the dirt floor. Smoke escaped through vents high in the end walls or roof.

The upsurge in economic activity under the Tudors (1485-1603) brought a new prosperity to many English farmers and tradesmen. This culminated, during and after the reign of Elizabeth I (1558-1603), in a housing boom accompanied by dramatic changes and improvements in the buildings themselves—a period sometimes known as the Housing Revolution. Much of what we today consider inexpressibly ancient can be traced back to this time.

The most radical change was the replacement of the open hearth by a central masonry chimney. Multiple fireplaces made it possible to heat separate spaces, so the open hall was broken up into rooms by vertical partitions. Similarly, since second-story rooms could be heated by their own fireplaces, a second floor was introduced. The chimney stack, often including a bread oven, was placed toward the rear of the house, leaving room at the front for a staircase to reach the new second floor. The cross wings at the ends of the central hall disappeared. Kitchens, glass windows and wood first floors were other contributions of the Housing Revolution. This two-story house with central chimney and two-room plan is the basic structure that the colonists brought with them to New England. It was the starting point of American domestic architecture.

Site and plan—The Fairbanks house sits on a slight rise just to the east of the Charles River. The house faces due south, as did most homes of the period. Out of 125 Massachu-

setts houses whose orientation is known, 98 (78%) were south-facing, and all but a handful of the rest were located in towns where small lot size restricted siting options. Windows were concentrated in the front wall, and the north wall was left blank. Clearly the 20th century has no patent on passive-solar design.

The original building measures about 33 ft. by 16 ft.; both these dimensions and the length-to-width ratio (about 2 to 1) are typical of the period (see the floor plan on the next page). The front door opens on a narrow entry (3½ ft. by 8 ft.). A cramped stairway takes up 2½ ft. of the chimney bay, the rest of which is occupied by the enormous chimney mass, itself 8 ft. by 9 ft.

To the left (west side) is the hall. The main living room and original kitchen, it contains the largest fireplace and, with its smoke-blackened joists and ponderous summer beams, is the most imposing room in the house (photo next page, bottom right). Underlying the west end of the hall is an early example of that American innovation, the underground cellar.

The parlor at the east end of the house was a slightly narrower room than the hall, 11 ft. as opposed to 13 ft. It served as the master bedroom and probably as a sitting room as well. The parlor was enlarged during early alterations to the house, and the original summer beam replaced.

Upstairs (photo next page, bottom left), the hall and parlor chambers sit above their first-floor counterparts. These rooms were used for sleeping and storage. The hall chamber is unfinished and is also the only room in the house without its own fireplace.

The Fairbanks house was built at a time when the brick bread oven was still a novelty, and its original chimney contained none. Similarly, evidence also indicates the lack of a stairway when the building was new. A ladder is still the only means of reaching the unfinished attic.

One other archaic feature is ceiling height. In the hall, the distance from the top of the first floor to the bottom of the second floor is 6 ft. 4 in. Head clearance under the joists mea-

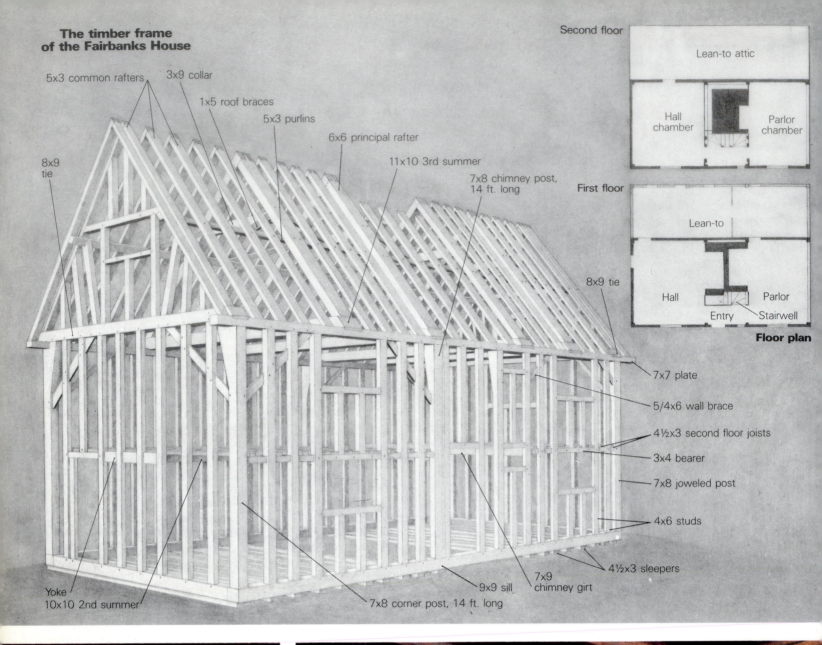

The timber frame of the Fairbanks House

5x3 common rafters

3x9 collar

1x5 roof braces

5x3 purlins

6x6 principal rafter

11x10 3rd summer

8x9 tie

7x8 chimney post, 14 ft. long

8x9 tie

7x7 plate

5/4x6 wall brace

4½x3 second floor joists

3x4 bearer

7x8 joweled post

4x6 studs

4½x3 sleepers

7x9 chimney girt

9x9 sill

7x8 corner post, 14 ft. long

Yoke

10x10 2nd summer

Second floor

Lean-to attic

Hall chamber

Parlor chamber

First floor

Lean-to

Hall

Parlor

Entry

Stairwell

Floor plan

sures 6 ft. 1 in., and under the summer beam it is 5½ ft. Sill-to-header distance in the rear door barely exceeds 5 ft.

Exterior—The original Fairbanks house had a very different appearance from its English counterparts, not because of the Housing Revolution, but because of the vastly different conditions on the new continent. Wattle and daub was the most popular walling material for timber-framed houses in England. First stout splits of oak, pointed at the ends, were sprung into shallow slots in the studs. Then smaller splits or withies were woven in vertically around the horizontal staves to complete the wattle. The daub, a mixture of clay and straw, was applied inside and out, filling the spaces between the studs (photo bottom right). In 16th-century England, the outside of the daub received a thin layer of lime plaster and perhaps a coat of white or color wash to complete the exterior finish. By the time of the Fairbanks house, this half-timber walling was going out of style. Brick laid with clay mortar had largely taken over as the preferred infill, and studding and infilled panels were no longer exposed to the weather. Instead, the entire house was lathed over and covered with a layer of plaster called roughcast.

The Fairbanks house is one of two surviving American houses that have the archaic wattle-and-daub infill. Its exterior surface, however, sported the new wooden clapboard finish, which was rapidly becoming the universal siding material in New England. The original clapboards on the house were riven, or split, and shaved from swamp cedar. Oak was the other wood commonly used for clapboards on early New England houses. In the Fairbanks house, daub was applied from the inside only, with the clapboards—nailed directly to the studs without sheathing—serving as a backstop for the clay fill. The lack of half-timber or roughcast exteriors in New England was due to the scarcity of lime for plaster in the early days of the Colonies, and the severe weather, which eroded the daub out of the walls on a number of early houses.

Most English roofs of the period were either ceramic or stone tile, or thatch. But tile roofs are the product of a more settled and finished society than pioneer New England, and the long winters increased the danger of fire always present with thatched roofs. The abundance of timber in the Colonies again suggested wood, and both oak weatherboard and the more common shingle roofs can be traced back to the first houses.

Shingles were made in much the same way as clapboards, with the preferred materials being cedar and pine. Unlike tiles and thatch, which were applied over widely spaced poles or battens, shingles were nailed to a solid layer of roof boards. Shingled roofs did not require the steep slopes necessary for tile and thatch (tile because of its great weight, thatch in order to shed water), but the Fairbanks house retains the steep pitch of 17-in-12, or 55°, associated with the older materials.

Another characteristic of early houses that is shared by the Fairbanks house is the absence of a framed overhang at the eaves. While these were common on gable ends, the only protection afforded to the side walls was provided by the extension of the roof sheathing a short distance beyond the top plate.

The few surviving original windows in the house show glazing technology at an early stage. Small diamond-shaped panes of hand-blown glass were set in lead cames (grooved rods) to make the individual lights. These were then inserted into the framed openings between the mullions and jambs. Grooves in the sill and header received the leaded-glass lights, which were first raised into the deep slot at the top and then lowered to engage the shallower one at the base. The fragile windows were supported by steps rabbeted into the large ovolo mullions and applied to the jambs, and were wired to the small intervening diamond-shaped stay bars.

Interior—In England, the framing, sheathing, flooring, interior finish and trim, windows and doors were likely to be made of oak. The colonists, while retaining the traditional oak frame, switched to pine for most other applications. In the Fairbanks house the floors, trim, roof boarding and wall sheathing are all of pine. The partitions separating the hall and hall chamber from the chimney bay are made of shiplapped vertical boards in the typical single-wall colonial style—one thickness of plank spanning from floor to ceiling without intermediate support. The exterior walls of the hall are covered with unusual clapboard-like sheathing of shiplapped horizontal boards nailed to the studs, as shown in the drawing, top right. The parlor and parlor chamber are plastered.

By 1668, when Jonathan Fairbanks died, a full-length shed lean-to had been added to the back of the house. This follows the standard practice of expansion in early American houses. Typically, a third ground-floor fireplace opening into the lean-to was added to the original chimney mass and the kitchen was moved into this new wing. Utensils, food and drink were also stored there.

The addition of a lean-to became almost universal as the 17th century progressed, and by the end of the century it had ceased to be an addition, and had become an integral part of house construction. Thus the saltbox was born. In the early 18th century, a second story was added to this integral lean-to, and it disappeared under the main roofline. And, in the final step in the development of this house plan, dual chimneys replaced the single massive central stack. These were relocated either at the gable ends of the house or against the back walls of the hall and parlor. The former chimney bay became a central hallway, and

Sheathing in the Fairbanks house

Front entry

Stairwell

Hall

Framing for four-lite window in attic

Section

Plan

The builders of the Fairbanks house filled between studs with wattle and daub, above. The oaken, horizontal wattles on the left are sprung into slots in the stud. The drawings show sheathing and window details.

The main room, (facing page, right) was the original kitchen. The musket hangs on a summer beam, into which the second-story floor joists are mortised. Molded, horizontal sheathing on the outside walls is shiplapped and nailed directly to the studs. A narrow stair (facing page, left) hugs the chimney.

Illustrations, E. Marino III; photo this page courtesy of the Society for the Preservation of New England Antiquities

the winding stairs were turned and straightened, rising from front to back in a single run. This central-hallway plan—well established by 1770—is the prototype for many houses built in our own time. Those who grew up in a 20th-century "colonial" house will recognize the model for their childhood homes.

18th-century embellishments—Dominated by their massive oak frames, 17th-century buildings were simple and unadorned. Clothing of the frame was minimal and entirely subservient to the structure. By 1750, an enormous change had taken place. New applied decorative elements were everywhere. The frame had shrunk, both literally and figuratively. Its importance was downplayed, and its beams and posts vanished under a welter of fine finish work. The effect was refined, sophisticated, classical—American architecture had belatedly entered the Renaissance.

If the 17th century was the century of the carpenter, the 18th was the century of the joiner (the ancient equivalent of the modern cabinetmaker and finish carpenter), and this shift had a profound effect on the timber skeletons of colonial houses. The frame was the heart and soul of early houses, and as such received the bulk of the decorative treatment. Arrises—or sharp edges—of major beams were given flat or molded chamfers ending in elaborate carved stops. In the Fairbanks house, almost every exposed member—everything but the studs and wall braces—received some kind of chamfer and stop, ranging from a quick swipe with the drawknife on joists and common rafters to careful work with plane, saw and chisel on girts, summers, tie beams and door jambs to produce the singular treatment that was the signature of the builders.

Other embellishments of early timber work included carved decoration on jowled or flared posts, serpentine braces, pinnacles crowning rooftops, pendants below posts in second-story overhangs and molded mullions in early window framing.

As the decorative emphasis shifted from frame to skin, these carved adornments disappeared, and the frame itself began to recede behind paneling and plaster. Finally, floor joists vanished behind plaster ceilings. Summers, girts and posts were cased or reduced in size so that they too disappeared, and with them went all visible evidence of the timber frame, detectable at this point only in unfinished attics and basements. The 20th-century penchant for exposed beam ceilings in 18th and 19th-century-style houses is a fad with little historical basis—except as a harking back to earlier and simpler days. The marked decline in the quality of timber framing, along with the ascendancy of joinery over carpentry, was hastened by the early 19th-century development of balloon framing, which rapidly replaced traditional timber framing for house construction.

Research—To accumulate the vast amount of information needed to recreate the frame of the Fairbanks house, we supplemented the available documentation with hours of on-site inspection and measurement. The old house was reluctant to give up its secrets, and many pieces of evidence were missing. The sills, first floor, and lower ends of studs and posts were lost to decay; the parlor summer beam and east wall were removed during early remodeling. Others were buried under sheathing, plaster or daub. You can't just tear into the walls of historic buildings to satisfy your curiosity about original window locations, so where wire probes and intuition failed us, we resorted to X rays. Several important questions were settled by the ghostly images of framing taken through the wood and plaster.

Most of this archaeological work in the Fairbanks house was done during the winter of 1980. The building had not been lived in for 80 years and had never been modernized. When we stepped through the front door, we left the 20th century behind, and the days of stooping under low ceilings in the dim light and bone-chilling cold of the unheated house were arduous ones. The conditions were offset by the pleasure of the work. There was a steady stream of discoveries, and occasional moments of high drama, such as the time we stumbled across a small secret room behind a loose board in the hall chamber. (In our elation we almost missed the footprints of our many predecessors in the brick dust around the chimney.) Most rewarding was the rare chance to encounter history face to face, without the intermediary of books.

Many old buildings have a special quality, a trace of the accumulated lives of their inhabitants. In the Fairbanks house—birth-and-death place for nine generations and silent witness to the comings and goings of four more—this aura of personal history was very strong. Walking through the house I often felt that I was brushing past the people whose paintings and photographs adorned the walls.

On my final day of note-taking, I arrived early and worked straight through lunch. Time passed quickly, and it wasn't until the orange glow began spreading across the floor that I realized the day was drawing to a close. The midwinter sun was sinking into the empty woods bordering the Charles River when my flashlight batteries expired. Determined to finish the task at hand, I started for the spare set in the car when a hush fell over the house. The buzz of the rush-hour traffic died away, and the building was enveloped in that awesome silence in which you can hear a single snowflake fall. My footsteps echoed strangely, and I stopped just short of the entry. Perhaps it was only a lull in the traffic. But I still wonder whether I could have opened the door onto the forests and fields of the 1630s. In any case, I waited silently in the gloomy hall until the noises of the world returned. Then I walked out into the 20th century and got my batteries. □

Ed Levin is a housewright in Canaan, N.H. For more on early American buildings, see The Framed Houses of Massachusetts Bay *(Abbott Lowell Cummings, Harvard University Press, 1977).*

Raising the Replica

Work on the replica of the Fairbanks timber frame got off to a shaky start. One of the drivers of the 10-wheel crane trucks delivering timber to my Canaan, N.H., shop missed a turn and got hopelessly mired in the mud several miles down a little-used country road. One drive-shaft and many hours later, men and truck emerged, mud-splattered but triumphant, buoyed by the thought that we had probably just fulfilled our disaster quota for the entire project. Happily, this proved to be the case. Three months later, our five-man crew laid down their chisels, having shaped nearly 9,000 bd. ft. of oak into 300 separate members. The array of timbers was impressive—11x10 summer beams that weighed half a ton, 8x9 girts and ties, 7x7 plates, and almost 100 4x6 studs mortised into 9x9 sills. In all, we cut over 700 joints and 550 oak pins for the 1,000-sq. ft. house. The whole project was funded by the Northeastern Lumbermen's Association.

The Fairbanks frame replica, like the original, was built of green oak. Modern folktales notwithstanding, timbers were almost never seasoned; they were cut, joined and raised in the same year they were felled. Drying the logs or beams wasn't realistic since it takes many years for large oak timbers to reach equilibrium with atmospheric moisture, and the seasoned wood is so hard it's practically unworkable.

Because our budget was limited, we did much of our sawing and boring with modern tools. When we could, though, we used 17th-century methods. A fair number of our timbers were hewn, pitsawn, laid out and bored the same way as the original Fairbanks frame.

For boring out the hundreds of 1½-in. mortises in the original house, the carpenters used a 1¼-in. shell auger, or nose auger (photo facing page, bottom). This tool is basically a half cylinder with a flat bottom and a T-shaped

Most of the timbers in the replica were roughly shaped with power tools, but 17th-century implements were used whenever possible for truing the timbers and cutting the joints. Facing page, bottom: A shell auger bores waste from a mortise. Top, two men pitsaw a beam on trestles. The crew donned period costume for the raising (photo above).

handle. Half of the bottom is beveled to form the cutter; the other half is cut back to serve as a depth gauge and chip escapement. Since it's difficult to start boring on a flat surface with a shell auger, we chopped shallow conical holes with a gouge to get it going. Like many of the other 17th-century tools we used, the shell auger turned out to be a pleasant surprise. It was by no means effortless, but it bored smoothly, and the geometry of the cutter made it essentially self-feeding.

Confronted with a pile of timber, a 17th-century carpenter couldn't pull out his power-return rule and framing square to lay out beams. The Fairbanks house, like its contemporaries, was probably laid out with a long measuring stick called a story pole. All of the lengths and locations needed to lay out the frame were marked on it. The story pole itself was laid out with 1-ft. rules, 2-ft. rules, a 10-ft. rod and dividers. It is more versatile than it sounds, and after the Fairbanks replica was done, I began to use story poles for all repeated layouts in my own timber framing. The advantage of a story pole is that all the necessary layout data is written on one device that can be laid directly on the beams. This allows the timber framer to position joints away from faults in the lumber because all of the various points are clearly marked on the stick. The story pole also minimizes careless errors in repeated measurements, and eliminates the need to memorize increments or constantly refer to the plans for them.

There were sawmills in New England in the 1630s, but none near enough to Dedham to be of any use to the builders of the Fairbanks house. Major timbers—sills, posts, summers, girts, plates, ties and principal rafters—were hewn from logs with a felling ax and broadax. To cut stock for the scantlings (smaller pieces such as studs, joists, braces, purlins and common rafters), a large log was first hewn square and then pitsawn.

Pitsawing implies setting a log over a large excavation and then neatly sawing it into various lengths with a two-man whipsaw. Pits, however have their disadvantages. They are difficult to dig in rocky soil, they provide homes for creepy and crawly things, they are wet and muddy, the scenery is terrible and, perhaps worst of all, a pit is not very portable. It's unclear whether the Fairbanks house

carpenters sawed over a pit or used trestles as we did (photo facing page, top). The coarse ripping teeth of the 8-ft. long saw take a big bite, 2 in. per stroke in a 6-in. pine timber, about one-third that in oak, but it's still a lot of strokes from one end of the log to the other. Twice per rip the saw must be dismantled, removed from the kerf, and the timber relocated to avoid sawing through the supports. It's no wonder that sawyers in England were noted more for their fondness for taverns than for their native intelligence.

Contrary to myth, our sawyers preferred the bottom position (pit man) to the top (tiller man). It takes more strength and staying power to pull the saw up than to pull it down through the cut. Sawdust was also more of a problem for the tiller man because it accumulated on the log and obscured the line of cut. The pit man needed to worry about sawdust only when the wind blew his way.

In the first two years of its life, the Fairbanks replica frame has had four homes. After a trial raising in Canaan, N.H., the frame was disassembled and shipped to Boston where it was raised in July of 1980 on the Common amidst the trappings of a 17th-century market fair. It took six of us three days to raise the frame, with occasional help when extra hands were needed for heavy timbers. The job could have been done in a long day, but the celebration turned the event into theater, and we took our time, did some teaching and enjoyed ourselves. The current Jonathan Fairbanks, who is the curator of American Decorative Arts at the Boston Museum of Fine Arts, helped with the raising. His daughter Hilary, a 12th-generation descendant of the original Jonathan, worked with us on the wattle-and-daub infill.

The end of the project was as eventful as the beginning. Rob Tarule, now curator of Mechanick Arts at Plimoth Plantation, had been its originator and director. At the last minute, he and I realized that we had forgotten to make a plumb-bob level, the 17th-century predecessor of the modern spirit level. We didn't want to pull out an anachronistic tool in front of the throngs watching us on the Common. On the other hand, we did want a plumb and level building. So we plumbed the frame by aligning it with the distant, vertical sides of modern Boston's skyscrapers. —E.L.

Rhode Island Stone-Ender

A 17th-century style house planned and built under the practiced eye of a sculptor

by Roger Schroeder

The early Welsh settlers in Rhode Island combined their Old World skills of joinery and stone-masonry to build what we know as the stone-ender, a post-and-beam house with a massive chimney-wall enclosing one end. Built mainly during the 17th century, few survive today in this country.

When Armand LaMontagne, of North Scituate, R.I., started his house in the spring of 1973, 300 years had gone by since the last stone-ender had been built. A wood sculptor by profession, LaMontagne had already custom-built a number of houses, among them a Rhode Island gambrel and a Connecticut Valley saltbox with a double overhang. Building a traditional stone-ender gave him the opportunity to work with two of his favorite materials—wood and stone. Near his home, he found two old examples to study and to draw his plans from: the Clemens Iron House in Johnstone and the Eleazer Arnold House in Lincoln. LaMontagne's experience was further enhanced by his having dismantled a stone-ender that was slated to be razed to make way for a shopping center.

Planning and materials—Once he had a good idea of the amount and dimensions of lumber that the post-and-beam frame would require, LaMontagne ordered his wood from a local sawmill. He used unseasoned, roughsawn white oak, just as the early Colonists did. Strong, yet easy to work when green, the white oak tightens the frame as it seasons. To cut the framing joints, LaMontagne used a chainsaw, an industrial drill with an assortment of bits, and an extensive selection of chisels—all tools he uses regularly for wood carving.

LaMontagne gathered some of the granite for his chimney-wall from old barn foundations. Most of the stone, however, came from the Oneco quarry in northeastern Connecticut. Rather than construct the chimney solely from stone, LaMontagne also planned to use cinder block and ceramic flue liners. The block would reduce the weight of the wall—the massive chimneys in old stone-enders tend to lean. The flue liners would make the chimney safer, more effective and easier to clean. Both these modern adaptations would be hidden behind the fine masonry work that gives the traditional stone-ender its unique appearance.

One final planning detail bears mentioning: LaMontagne went ahead with the construction without blueprints or working drawings. Determined to do most of the work himself and accus-

LaMontagne's stone-ender reflects the fine craftsmanship that went into similar houses built over 300 years ago by Welsh settlers in Rhode Island. Clapboard siding, hand-split shingles and diamond windows add to its authenticity.

tomed to working by eye, he saw the house as a giant sculpture. LaMontagne rarely resorts to complex measurements or drawings when completing a wood sculpture; why should building a house be any different? When pressed for an explanation, he argues that early American post-and-beam builders created finely scaled houses by relying more on their sense of dimension than on engineered plans. (He did, of course, use a tape measure to size the structural elements.)

Concrete—The early settlers used stone to build their foundations. LaMontagne excavated for a full basement and poured a concrete foundation into standard forms. Local building codes specify a concrete foundation, and in this case the builder felt that the merits of cement over stone warranted the change. The chimney-wall would exert tremendous downward pressure on its footing, and extra reinforcement would eliminate the chance of settling or weight shift. To hold the wall, he dug down 3 ft. below the basement slab level, erected forms, and then positioned three layers of ¾-in. rebar (crisscrossed on a grid) to make the slab into a rigid beam. The concrete used for this footing was an extra strength (3,500-lb.) mix.

To ensure structural stability, stone-enders are built so that the wood frame and the stone chimney can stand independently of each other. Traditionally the post-and-beam construction is

done first; it then serves as staging for the stone-masonry that follows to complete the house. Once the foundation was poured, LaMontagne began raising his timbers.

Woodwork—When he is sculpting a large block of solid wood, LaMontagne has developed the habit of working rapidly. This experience proved valuable when it came to shaping the timbers and cutting the joists. Using a chainsaw to cut his timber to size, he laid sills on the foundation and then let in girders across its 30-ft. width. These girders were braced underneath with posts resting on the basement floor. To complete the framing for the first floor, LaMontagne mortised 4x6 joists between sills and girders, spacing them on 24-in. centers. For the subfloor, he used ¾-in. ponderosa pine boards in random widths; these were simply butt-joined and nailed across the floor joists.

The completed subfloor provided a working surface for the rest of the house framework. Lacking blueprints, LaMontagne used the floor as his working drawing. He snapped chalklines to mark locations for posts and girts, writing in labels and instructions where necessary. Once the rough work was complete for the rest of the house, the finish floor deck of wide pine boards could be laid.

The posts for the house extended from the sill to the top plate on the second floor. LaMontagne had to set up long ramps and sturdy sawhorses to work on these timbers, using a lumberman's peavey to turn and position the stock. He made each post wider at the top than at the base. Often called a shouldered or gunstock post, the extra width at the top of the post can hold a larger, stronger joint. Rather than rest the posts on the pine subfloor, LaMontagne cut away these small sections so that each post could be tenoned directly into the oak sill.

Summer beams are a distinguishing feature on early American houses. So named because the sum weight of the floor falls largely on this structural member, the summer beam is laid between girts and supports the floor joists (photo, facing page). LaMontagne cut his summer beams from 12x12 oak, using housed dovetails at the girt junctures. While working the beam, he also cut

LaMontagne planes a joist beneath the nearly finished timber frame of his house. The summer beam above his head connects two girts and supports the joists for the second floor. The gunstock post (at top right) supports the third-floor girt.

From *Fine Homebuilding* magazine (December 1981) 6:42-47

Photo: Jim Baird

LaMontagne drills through a mortise-and-tenon joint so it can be pegged with trunnels.

Photo: Myron Taplin

pockets to receive the 3x4 joists (spaced 24 in. on center).

In many 17th-century houses, the exposed timbers were planed smooth or embellished with molded edges. By the 18th century it was common practice to box timbers to conceal any sign of hand hewing. Since the stone-ender style dates from the earlier period, LaMontagne hand-planed each timber and chamfered or rounded the exposed edges of all posts and beams. He also carved lamb's-tongues at the ends of the beams, where the chamfers are stopped.

Fitting work—LaMontagne completed all the sizing and joint-cutting work himself. He then hired a crane and enlisted some friends to lift the finished posts and beams into position. The posts were fitted into position first and secured to the sill with temporary diagonal braces. Then the crane hoisted a girt into position between posts while the crew fitted its tenons into the post mortises. A come-along forced the joints closed while LaMontagne drilled holes to receive the trunnels to secure the joint (photo, above left). Repeating this hoist, fit, and peg operation joined the girts to the posts and formed the perimeter framing for the second floor.

The next step was to install the top plate beams so that the rafters could go on. Here again the crane was used to hoist the beams; LaMontagne and his crew maneuvered them to fit into the slots that had been cut in the top of the posts.

The steep roof pitch (60°) of the stone-ender is probably its second most noticeable feature. LaMontagne built the roof trusses for his house from 4x6 white oak timbers. Each is 24 ft. long, and collar ties (4x4 stock) were cut to 12-ft. lengths. LaMontagne used the traditional pinned slip joint at the peak, a mortise-and-tenon for the collar ties, and bird's-mouth joints where rafters join the top plate. The fastest way to erect trusses is to fasten the first truss to the top plate, brace it plumb, and secure adjacent trusses with blocking. Purlins can be let in once all the trusses are in place. The crane did the lifting; LaMontagne and his co-workers received the trusses and anchored them to the frame and to each other. Using random widths of 1½-in. stock, the workers furred out the roof with purlins. Around the chimney hole, solid board sheathing was used for extra stability and to provide a safe staging area for the roof-based masonry work to come.

Stone ending—"Seventeenth-century masonry," says LaMontagne, "is the finest in this country." European settlers brought with them the

Masonry work on the house begins after most of the wood framing and siding are complete. At left, the base of the stone end rises from LaMontagne's vast selection of rocks. Plastic sheeting protects the inside of the house during construction and marks the interior dimensions of the chimney. Aluminum flashing, nailed to the joists that frame the stone end, will be bent tight against the stone as the wall rises. Inside the house (facing page), the concrete block core of the wall awaits its stone face. Using blocks rather than solid stone reduces the weight of the wall, cuts down on the amount of stone required, and makes the work go more quickly. The recession at the back of the firebox is designed to keep the draw of the fire against the back stones.

Illustration: Barbara Smollover

skill and tradition of castle-building. For these New World masons, mortar was used to fill gaps, not to hold stones together—just as well, since 17th-century mortar had very little inherent strength or adhesive power.

As was the case throughout the building project, LaMontagne drew on his sculpting savvy to build the chimney, stone by stone. Wisely, he first erected a smaller fireplace and chimney on the side of the house opposite the stone end. With this practice behind him, LaMontagne felt confident enough to tackle the major masonry that would enclose the other side of his house. Having more than enough stones for the job is important. Otherwise too much time is spent splitting and dressing rocks to size. Even with a good selection of sizes and shapes, LaMontagne still had to do a substantial amount of dressing, using a 4-lb. dressing hammer. To split larger stones, he used a 20-lb. pointed sledgehammer. Traditionally, holes were drilled into the rock, and wedges were hammered between specially made half-cylinders called feathers to split the piece. LaMontagne used this method, and also found that a large stone could be split by striking it near the middle, on a line where stress would be more or less equal on both sides.

The broad, reinforced footing provided a sound base for the stone, while the house itself gave the builder and his helpers plenty of platform space. The carefully laid stone exterior of the chimney-wall hides a core of cement block

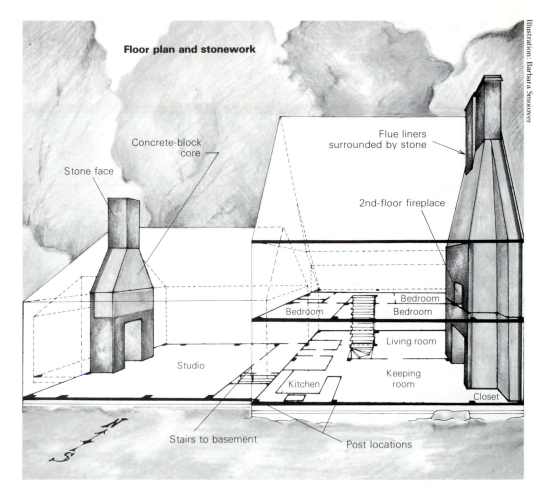

Floor plan and stonework

Concrete-block core

Stone face

Flue liners surrounded by stone

2nd-floor fireplace

Bedroom
Bedroom
Bedroom

Living room

Studio

Keeping room

Kitchen

Closet

Stairs to basement

Post locations

Photo: Myron Taplin

Finishing touches reflect the builder's careful attention to historical detail. The back door, above, was made from two bookmatched oak planks, handcut nails and wrought iron fixtures. Overhangs and copper flashing around the chimney, top right, protect the surrounding shingles from storm water runoff. Handmade windows like this one, center, with diamond panes and wrought iron hinges, were found on stone-enders of 300 years ago. The woven clapboard corner, at right, is another traditional feature.

The keeping room has wide plank floors, post-and-beam joinery and a cavernous fireplace, a fitting setting for the Colonial furnishings.

and flue liners. Over the main hearth in the keeping room (photo above), LaMontagne used a 10x18 lintel of white oak, 12 ft. long and cambered like the traditional stone-ender lintel. Once the chimney-wall was completed, copper flashing was woven into the remaining roof shingles as they were nailed in place. This is the only real connection between wood and stone, although the fascia board at this end of the house appears to enclose the masonry mass solidly beneath the roof.

Shingles, siding and floors—Early in the construction, LaMontagne had noticed a grove of sassafras trees not far from the site of the house. Thick, tall, and lacking lower limbs, each tree could provide a pile of clear-grained shingles. After felling the trees and cutting the trunks into 2-ft. lengths, LaMontagne split out the shingles in the traditional way—using a froe and a mallet. Porous and rot-resistant like cedar, the sassafras shingles are beginning to weather to a silver-grey. LaMontagne estimates that they will last 75 to 100 years. Nailing shingles over purlins is better practice than shingling over sheathing, since sheathing tends to trap moisture, while purlins provide air circulation beneath the shingles. The roof peak around the chimney hole was left unshingled, so flashing could be installed when the chimney was complete.

The exterior sheathing for the stone-ender consists of ¾-in. by 6-in. white pine clapboards, nailed directly to the post-and-beam frame and 3x4 oak studs with handcut 16d nails. Instead of butting the clapboards against vertical corner boards, LaMontagne chose to detail the corners in more traditional fashion. The courses overlap at the corners, so that every other board extends to the outer edge of the sheathing on the adjacent side. To weave the corners in this way, LaMontagne had to run each clapboard course around the entire house. This sheathing method, which today has been replaced by faster techniques, recreated the clean horizontal lines found on the original stone-enders.

Wide pine boards (16 in. to 24 in.), dressed to a full 1¼ in. thickness, were laid directly on the second-floor joists and secured with 2½-in. rose-head wrought-iron nails. LaMontagne built his floors like those he found in traditional stone-enders. He cut slots in the edges of his planks and splined them together, substituting ¼-in. plywood strips for the oak splines used by the Welsh settlers. Splining provides a dust barrier and allows for shrinkage in board width without having voids appear between boards. LaMontagne used plywood splines because they are stronger and more resilient than oak splines. The pine flooring is the finished ceiling for the first floor. LaMontagne installed the same wide-board floor over the sub-floor on the first level. He later found that while the double floor de-

veloped a few squeaks, the second-story floor stayed quiet—another argument in favor of single-layer floors.

To give his floors an aged appearance, LaMontagne used a technique he had developed for wood sculpture. First, he created surface burns in the flooring with an acetylene torch. This required a delicate touch and a knowing eye, since even a slight overexposure to the flame can damage the wood. Then he covered the surface loosely with beach sand and used it with a floor buffer to remove the darkest carbon spots. The final step was flooding the surface with three separate applications of Clorox bleach, stopping when the wood's coloring had reached the aged look he was aiming for. Two coats of satin polyurethane varnish completed the job.

Diamond-pane windows and diamond-studded exterior doors are historically authentic features. LaMontagne also had wrought-iron strap hinges, door knockers, latches and other hardware made by a local blacksmith to look like early American fittings. A year after construction began, LaMontagne had completed what he calls his largest sculpture. To those who visit the house, it is a pleasing reassurance that the craftsmanship of this country's first settlers still continues. The stone-ender lives on. □

Roger Schroeder, of Amityville, N.Y., is a teacher and freelance writer.

A Carved Timber Frame

Conventional framing encloses a
first floor of oak timbers embellished
with carved details from the 18th century

by William R. Cadley

Carpentry can take you in many directions. The work that I've done in the last 10 years has ranged from condos and contemporaries to restoration projects and restaurants. I started to get interested in traditional timber-frame construction about six or seven years ago. New England is full of old houses, and if you've ever had to take one apart or replace beams that were hand-hewn and cut to fit with mortise-and-tenon and dovetailed joinery, your appreciation of fine craftsmanship really grows.

In addition to working on several restoration projects, I started to visit old historic houses and read about early Colonial architecture. Frederick Kelly's book, *Early Domestic Architecture of Connecticut* (republished in 1963 by Dover Publications, 31 East Second St., Mineola, N. Y. 11501), was especially inspiring because I was actually able to visit some of the houses that are described in the book. My interest grew, and it soon became obvious that the house I'd been planning to build for my family would have to be based on the traditional timber frame.

The best of both worlds—I decided on a Cape Cod style design. Of all the old houses I'd visited or worked on, my favorites were Capes built during the early 18th-century Colonial period. The delineation of space in a Cape is simple and appealing. Bedrooms are upstairs, while eating and entertaining happen downstairs. The stacked space is easy to heat, and I wanted to be able to incorporate both passive-solar and energy-saving features in the design.

Although I admire the old Capes, I didn't want the second floor of our new house to resemble in any way the second floor of a period home. There just isn't any headroom or storage space to speak of in these early houses. In our upstairs, we needed enough space for two bathrooms, three bedrooms and plenty of closets.

Insulation was another consideration. I didn't want to enclose my frame with stress-skin panels (see *FHB* #24, pp. 54-59) because of their expense, and because I don't feel comfortable about living in a super-tight house. I wanted to insulate primarily with fiberglass batts, so this

meant that I'd have to build a frame of dimensioned lumber outside of my timber frame.

I decided that the best approach would be to build a traditional timber frame downstairs and to use conventional platform framing upstairs. As unusual as it sounds, this combination was ideal for me. The big timbers and fine joinery would enhance the first floor, the more public part of the house. Upstairs, there would be plenty of space. And once the first floor's massive post-and-beam frame had been raised, the second story would go up with no surprises, which meant that I could close the house in quickly. Even the long shed dormer I wanted to build into the south roof could get done easily. Using 2x stick framing upstairs also solved the problem of insulating the roof. R-30 fiberglass batts could be installed between the 2x10 rafters.

The idea of embellishing the first-floor timber frame struck me a month or so after I started to cut the first joints. I knew quite a few people who were building timber frames, but nobody was putting on finishing touches to give their

From *Fine Homebuilding* magazine (August 1985) 28:58-62

work an individual flavor. The logical way to carry exposed post-and-beam joinery one step further is to decorate the wood with carved details. Of the old timber-frame houses I'd visited, the most impressive ones were those that had carved embellishments. These more ornate frames, most of them near the coast, were probably built by shipwrights.

The frame—The basic house is 36 ft. long and 26 ft. wide. All the framing members are cut from native red oak. I bought the timbers roughly sized and planed them square and smooth using a Makita 6⅛-in. portable power plane. Despite the green, unchecked surface of the oak as it came from the mill, I knew that once inside a heated house my framing members would check and shrink considerably as they continued to dry out. Inside a house, green oak will dry at the rate of about 1 in. per year, so you have to expect some checking, or cracks in the surface of the wood. These checks have no effect on the overall strength of the frame.

I designed the frame with four bents, each one spanning the width of the house and consisting of three gunstock posts that support 8x9 beams, or girts (photo bottom right). Each girt is actually made from two or more 8x9 beams, joined together with double-bladed scarf joints (for more on timber-frame terminology, see *FHB #16*, pp. 38-41).

Adjacent bents are joined by summer beams, which in turn hold the 4-in. by 5-in. ceiling joists. The summer beams that join the two central bents are actually chimney girts—8-in. by 8-in. beams that frame the masonry chimney. This hierarchy of framing (photo top right) makes a traditional timber-frame ceiling a lot more interesting to look at than one framed with 2x10s.

The floor joists are dovetailed into the girts and summer beams, and all summer-beam-to-girt joints are housed dovetails (photo facing page). Though they take longer to cut than simple mortises and tenons, dovetails really lock the framing members together, keeping the joinery solid as the wood continues to dry out.

The gunstocks—Like its namesake, a gunstock post tapers from one end to another. In timber framing, the broader end of the gunstock always faces up to provide a larger bearing surface for the beams that join over it. The tops of my gunstock posts are 8x12, and they taper down to 8x9. Rather than go with a straight taper, I decided to use a series of carved lamb's tongues and chamfers to reduce the size of the post. The models for these carvings were the

Not content with massive timbers alone, the author decided to ornament his oak frame with carved details resembling those in several historical houses that he'd visited. Top right, all posts taper from top to bottom in a series of carved lamb's tongues and chamfers. Summer beams have coved edges, and floor joists are given a full quirk bead on each lower edge. Right, the frame contains four bents, or post-and-beam sections, that span the 26-ft. width of the house. Facing page, housed dovetails lock the major beams and joists together as the wood dries out.

Embellished gunstock posts. The top-heavy gunstock post provides extra bearing surface for the beams that join over it. In the photo above, a double-bladed scarf joint is used to join two girts together over the post. The carving on the gunstock begins 1¼ in. down from the top shoulder of the post with a 2¾-in. long lamb's tongue, an S-shaped chamfer. Then there's a 7½-in. long tapered chamfer that runs into a 6½-in. long lamb's tongue. The curve of this lamb's tongue is carried across the entire width of the post, ending at a ½-in. stop above a ⅝-in. reveal. Below the reveal, a straight, 2-in. wide chamfer extends to the bottom of the post.

gunstock posts found in the old Acadian house in Guilford, Conn. The carved edges on these posts are the most elaborate of the early 18th-century period, and I'd never heard of anyone trying to reproduce them. Even in Colonial times, this degree of ornamentation was rare because only the wealthy could afford it.

I wouldn't have been able to complete the 12 gunstock posts without the help of my brother-in-law, John Stainer, who works as a shipwright at the Mystic Seaport Maritime Museum. Apart from his familiarity with timber-framing tools and fine wood joinery, the 350-lb. weight of each of my 8-ft. long posts was too much for me to handle alone.

Here's the basic anatomy of the carved gunstock (photo above): 1¼ in. down from the top shoulder of the post, the embellishment begins with a lamb's tongue broach 2¾ in. long. A lamb's tongue is an S-shaped chamfer that takes the place of a straight taper as a transitional element. At the bottom edge of this first lamb's tongue, a 7½-in. tapered chamfer begins. Then there's a 6½-in. long lamb's tongue whose curve is carried across the entire width of the post. This dies into a ½-in. stop above a ⅝-in. reveal. At this point, the gunstock's taper to an 8x9

Carving the post. The gunstock post's straight chamfer is made by cutting into the edge with a handsaw every 6 in. to within about ⅛ in. of the layout lines; then the waste is removed with a drawknife, top left. Middle, the curved taper near the top of the post is roughed out with a series of closely spaced saw kerfs across the width of the timber. Shaping and smoothing are done with chisels followed by hand-sanding. At left, the gunstock nears its final shape as the stop, reveal and lamb's tongue are cut. The lamb's tongue has to be carved by working the chisel from both ends of the curve.

cross section is complete, and from the edge of the reveal to the base there's a straight, 2-in. wide chamfer.

This carved detail on the gunstock is almost as intricate as it sounds, so it was important for us to devise an accurate way to lay out its various parts. The first thing that we did was to make up separate templates for each lamb's tongue and chamfer. Using these and a combination square, we were able to put down layout lines that described the borders of the upper carved sections of the post. A separate large template gave us layout lines for the long chamfer that starts at the base of the post and for the broad lamb's tongue that extends across the full width of the post.

To carve the chamfers, we first used a crosscut saw to cut into the edges of the posts every four inches or so, stopping just shy of the layout lines. Then we used a drawknife to remove most of the waste wood (photo top left). We finished the chamfers off with chisels and finally planed them smooth.

We used a skillsaw to start the broad lamb's tongue, adjusting the depth of cut so that it came to within ⅛ in. of the layout lines on the sides of the post. After a series of parallel cuts was made across the width of the post, the resulting waste was broken out to expose a rough curve that we cleaned up with chisels. Then we used chisels and spokeshaves to chamfer the sides of the curve and carve out the ½-in. stop and the ⅝-in. reveal (middle and bottom photos at left).

The smaller lamb's tongue just below the top of the post had to be chiseled out entirely by hand. Because of its S-shape, we had to carve this type of lamb's tongue from both ends, which can be a problem if the grain happens to run up in one direction. A sharp chisel, a steady

Ceiling joists. The author used the custom-made router bit shown above to cut full quirk beads along the bottom edges of all floor joists. Two separate passes are required for each corner. The bit's pilot bearing is guided first by the bottom edge of the joist and then by the side of the joist.

hand and careful attention to the coarse grain of the oak are important.

Once the lamb's tongues and the tapered chamfers were done, the carving was finished. I sanded the flat areas of each post with a belt sander, followed by an orbital sander. I sanded the curved sections by hand. Then we oiled the entire post with a 50/50 mix of linseed oil and paint thinner. When this had dried out for two weeks or so, we shellacked the posts in an effort to slow the checking process.

Summer beams and ceiling joists—The carved summer beams in the Deacon John Graves house, in Madison, Conn., are the nicest I've seen, and I decided to carve my own to resemble them. I changed the design just slightly to accommodate the difference in timber size. My chimney girts and stairwell girts also received the same treatment. The embellishment consists of a 2-in. cove molding carved into the bottom edges of the timber and inset between 5/16-in. stop reveals that run the full length of the coves. The coves and their reveals terminate at a 5/16-in. stop 8 in. from the end of the timber, where a small (4-in.) lamb's tongue takes you out of the carving and back to the 4 in. of hard corner that's left in the beam (photo top right).

The layout for the beams is as follows: After the housed dovetails were cut at both ends of the beam, I measured in 4 in. from the shoulder, then drew the layout lines for the lamb's tongues against a template. The 5/16-in. stop between lamb's tongue and cove was drawn next, with the layout lines perpendicular to the corner. Then I drew lines 2 in. from each bottom edge, running them the length of the beam until they intersected with the layout for the stop.

The first cuts were the stop reveals that border the coves. I set up a ¾-in. straight bit in my

router to make a 5/16-in. deep cut, and routed out to both 2-in. lines along each corner. Next, I scribed a 5/16-in. layout line off the rabbet edge to give me a guideline for the cove, and to establish the 5/16-in. rabbet stop at the ends of each cove (photo middle right). Then I cut a series of perpendicular kerfs that stopped just shy of my cove layout lines and started to remove the beam edge with a draw knife and a 2-in. slick.

With the boundaries for the 2-in. cove chamfer established, I used a 2-in. gouge to rough-shape the cove and then a 2-in. convex-sole plane to get the cove even smoother. The final shaping was done with a 2-in. cove scraper (photo bottom right). Finally, I sanded the curved surface by wrapping the curved face of the plane with sandpaper after retracting the plane iron.

The lamb's tongues on the beams were cut the same way as the ones on the posts. The subtlety of these curves led me to design all the knee braces for the frame with a slight curve too. There's something very interesting about breaking the straight lines of a support brace, and it seems in keeping with the decorative elements on the rest of the timbers.

With the major timbers carved as they were, I couldn't just leave the ceiling joists untouched. I decided to put a full quirk bead along both lower edges of each joist. Because of the size and weight of the joists and the slight crowns and surface variations in the wood, I didn't want to cut the quirk bead with shaper knives on my table saw. Instead, I had a special quirk-bead bit custom made for my router. I sent a piece of stock showing the quirk-bead profile to a local dealer (Brian's Tool Sales, 19 Kreyssig Rd., Broadbrook, Conn. 06016), and a few weeks later I had the bit. As shown in the photo above left, it's got two carbide cutters mounted on a ¼-in. shank, and a ⅜-in. dia. ball-bearing pilot. The cutters describe a semicircular bead along with a 3/16-in. deep quirk.

Each full quirk bead took two separate passes to complete. One pass runs the pilot bearing against the bottom edge of the joist. To complete the cut, you turn the router 90° and the pilot bearing runs against the side of the joist. In true early 18th-century tradition, the beading really shows off the tulip-poplar board ceiling used throughout the downstairs.

Around and above—Once my ornamental frame was up, there wasn't any time to stand back and admire it. I had to start enclosing the first-floor walls with 2x4 studs and framing the second floor. The dimensioned lumber outside

Beam ornamentation. Top right, the lamb's tongue near the shoulder of each beam is 4 in. long and dies into a 5/16-in. stop reveal. There are also stop reveals flanking the 2-in. cove that runs between lamb's tongues along the bottom edges of each beam. Middle, the first cutting is done with a router, using a ¾-in. straight bit to make the 5/16-in. deep stops that border the cove. Then the lamb's tongue stops are cut with a handsaw, and layout lines are made for cove and lamb's tongue. Right, a gouge, a curved plane and a scraper, all with a 2-in. radius, were used to carve the cove.

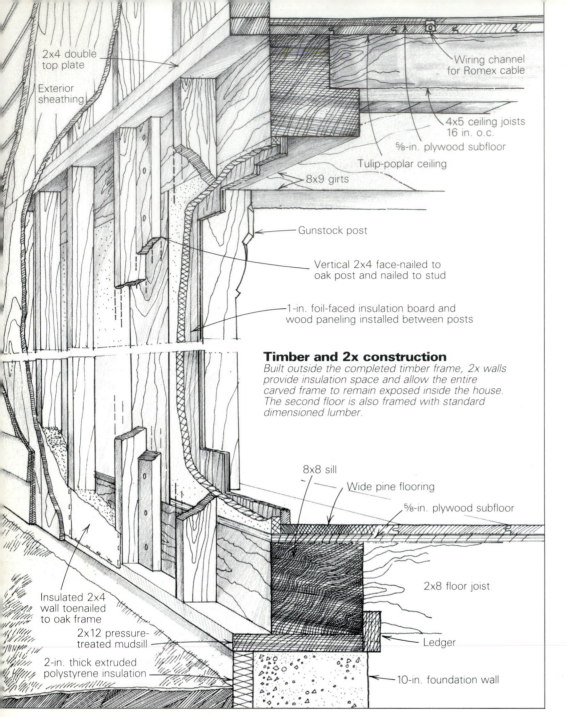

2x4 double
top plate

Exterior
sheathing

Wiring channel
for Romex cable

4x5 ceiling joists
16 in. o.c.

⅝-in. plywood subfloor

Tulip-poplar ceiling

8x9 girts

Gunstock post

Vertical 2x4 face-nailed to
oak post and nailed to stud

1-in. foil-faced insulation board and
wood paneling installed between posts

Timber and 2x construction
*Built outside the completed timber frame, 2x walls
provide insulation space and allow the entire
carved frame to remain exposed inside the house.
The second floor is also framed with standard
dimensioned lumber.*

8x8 sill

Wide pine flooring

⅝-in. plywood subfloor

2x8 floor joist

Ledger

10-in. foundation wall

Insulated 2x4
wall toenailed
to oak frame

2x12 pressure-
treated mudsill

2-in. thick extruded
polystyrene insulation

As the interior nears completion, partition walls that butt against timbers are built with 2x3 studs
to maximize timber exposure. Foil-faced insulation board covers the 2x4 wall that was built outside
the oak frame to hold batt insulation and exterior siding, as shown in the drawing above.

and above the timber frame would later be
sheathed and insulated conventionally.

Studding out the first floor went quickly because the extended 2x12 mudsill provided a
3½-in. ledge for the 2x4s, which are 3½ in.
wide. As shown in the drawing at left, these
studs are exactly as high as the oak frame, from
the sill to the top of the girt. All studs are toenailed to the outside of the frame. Instead of
toenailing studs against posts, these studs were
face-nailed to a vertical 2x4 nailer that was in
turn face-nailed into the post.

The stud wall is topped off with a 2x4 double
top plate to which the dormer studs or rafters
are nailed. Against the inside edges of the studs
I nailed up 1-in. thick foil-faced foam insulation
board (photo bottom left). Combined with 3½ in.
of fiberglass batts in the stud cavities, this yields
an R-value of 23. The wide-plank pine paneling I
plan to install will be nailed in place directly
over the insulation board.

Interior finish—I decided to frame up all the
partition walls downstairs with 2x3 studs rather
than with 2x4s. None of these walls is structural,
so I didn't have to worry about losing strength
with 2x3s. And because most of the partition
walls butt against posts and beams, I wanted the
walls to be thin so that more of the oak timbers
would show.

In order to run wiring to several first-floor
ceiling fixtures, I had to rout channels in the
tulip-poplar ceiling boards and in the ⅝-in. plywood subfloor that covered the tulip poplar
(drawing, left). All I did was to chuck a ¾-in.
straight bit in my router, set the depth to ¼ in.
and follow the layout lines I had penciled onto
the wood, being careful to avoid nails. I routed
an identical channel into the underside of the
subfloor. After the Romex cable was placed in
the channel, I covered it with ⅝-in. dia. metal
conduit that I ripped in half by clamping the
conduit in a vise and cutting it with a reciprocat-
ing saw. The metal protects the wiring, so that
future remodelers working upstairs needn't worry about nailing through the cable.

My main goal after closing in the house was
to get the upstairs finished and the downstairs
livable so that we would be able to move in.
Plumbing, electrical, insulation and drywall work
upstairs went as smoothly as we had hoped.
Downstairs we installed the kitchen and laundry
appliances and completed the bathroom. Just
before we moved in, the mason completed the
Rumford fireplace and the chimney, which also
carries the flue for a multi-fuel furnace located
in the basement.

The major work still to be done downstairs is
the paneling. Slowly, I'm accumulating the wide
pine, butternut and chestnut boards that I'll use
for the walls and cabinetwork. This will have to
be done as time allows, since I'm now working
on other houses similar to my own. But I don't
want to rush finishing up my own place. If the
work is done right, you should feel like you're
going back into the 1700s when you step through
the front door. □

*William Cadley's company, Pagoda Timber
Frames, is based in Chester, Conn.*

Drawing: Victor Lazzaro

Mountain Passive

An Appalachian house of vernacular form and solar aspect

by Robert McGahey

Unlike most of you, I never dreamed of building a house. It's just that where my family chose to live, housing was in extremely short supply. But once I was committed to it, the project became my whole life for two years: one year for salvaging material, for logging and for designing around the best of what I could get, and one year for building. Like other fortunate owner-builders, those were among the best years of my life.

We had joined a 1,100-acre land trust that had been set up in western North Carolina in the 1940s as an alternative means of living in a community; much of the land was still available for house sites. I walked many acres, checked prevailing winds, measured slopes, observed vegetation for cues to soil fertility, watched

where the sun rose and set at different times of the year and measured spring flows.

It was getting to be time to put in a road before winter when I finally narrowed my choice down to two sites. At this point my dog died. I had to find the proper place to bury him, and it was obvious that it should be where we would build our home. His grave is on the ridge of the site I chose, and the house fits below it into the southwest slope.

Living in a land trust makes it important to build as simply and cheaply as possible. We have "holding agreements," which amount to lifetime leases, and we can sell our houses only to incoming members of the trust. If there is no purchaser during the first two years after a member leaves, the community will buy the

dwelling, but the maximum reimbursement is $19,000. Since we limit our rate of growth to two or three new members a year, the market for selling is slim. Thus our houses are places to live, not investments. For this reason, we gave ourselves a ballpark budget of $30,000 for building the house.

Design for the mountains—Certain things were clear to me from the start. I wanted an earth-tempered solar house, largely passive. But I was tired of "functional sheds," the awkward and often downright ugly solar buildings I had seen. We liked several features of the houses we saw in the mountains around us: steep rooflines (often with dormers), board-and-batten siding and tin roofing. I decided to

Timber rafters are round poplar, shaved off to carry the decking; poplar also panels the stud infill walls. Floors are T&G oak. The river-rock chimney adds heat and mass to the upstairs bedrooms. Large dormers allow space for sleep and study and bring light indoors.

Up on the second level, a framer tapers the end of a round poplar cross tie in preparation for joining it to timber rafters.

combine the solar features with the mountain-home features in a post-and-beam design. I wanted to use post-and-beam framing and to stain it with used engine oil, so that it would stand out against the paneling.

In addition to the basic building primers and passive-solar manuals, the book I used most was *A Pattern Language* by Christopher Alexander and his associates (Oxford University Press, 1977). Alexander's book is designed to help the designer by identifying patterns involved in building. Since the patterns are laid out like a cross-referenced grammar book, I was able to start the design process wherever I wanted. We worked out how our family would use each space, then modified the patterns and fit them into the design.

We began laying out spaces by placing the bathroom at the northeast corner of the house at the bottom of the stair. I placed the kitchen between the bathroom and the greenhouse (so the two can share plumbing). The kitchen opens to the dining and living areas to make one large, south-facing space. A music room is tucked behind the living area and fireplace. Bedrooms are upstairs, with the children's room to the east and the master bedroom to the west. *Pattern Language* inspired us to fit beds and desk into the large dormers, to use closets and bookshelves as room dividers, and to add a loft to the children's room as extra playing space.

Combing the hills for salvage—I began salvaging materials to save money, but once I got into it, I had a lot of fun as well. As I salvaged materials for over a year, I would draw and redraw the house design to fit the materials I'd found, which made the design process similar to fitting the pieces of a puzzle together. In recent years, prices for used materials have risen steadily, making pulling nails less attractive. There are still plenty of bargains for the

persistent scavenger, though. I found most of the best deals in *IWanna*, a mountain newspaper that advertises used materials. Many of my windows and all of my fixed glazing came from the reject pile of a glass company in Asheville. These insulated-glass windows, which I bought at $.50/sq. ft., were either returns, odd lots or discontinued styles. It was fairly easy to get plate glass that had been removed from old storefronts and have it cut to my specifications for glazing the solar batch heater. The day after I considered changing the roof pitch on the drawings from 12-in-12 to 10-in-12 to make installation easier, I came across a bunch of triangular windows that fit almost perfectly in the east and west gable ends, only ½° off a 10-in-12 roof pitch.

Another find was yellow pine siding from a tarpaper shack, which we left tarred on one side, then milled and finished on the other. We used this for the kitchen and bath cabinets, stair risers and stair railings. On another occasion, I visited a local moonshiner on a tip that he might have some cherry I could use for window trim. Once I got there, the old guy just wanted to swap stories and drink rye whiskey. I finally got a look by flashlight at the boards, which were in a dark corner of his barn. We agreed on a price, and I made it home after midnight. When I took a look at my purchase in the morning, I found a small pile of cherry floorboards covered with chicken manure. It took a lot of milling to produce some "wormy cherry." I also had only a little better than one-quarter the amount of window trim that I needed, but I was able to get the remainder from a family expressing gratitude to my wife, who is a doctor, for special care that she had administered to them.

I got a lot of framing material (used for blocking), copper pipe and most of my plumbing fixtures by keeping an eye out for special deals. One of the best was a pedestal bath-

room sink replete with water fountain and a gracefully curved splashback, which must have come from an old elementary school.

Laying up walls—Several local builders—Eric Thurston, John Senechal and Tom Trout—worked with me to build the house, and friends helped us with the timber raising. For the Trombe half-wall between greenhouse and living space and for the parts of the first floor that are below or partly below grade, we used concrete block—12-in. block at the north wall, 8-in. block at the east and west walls and 6-in. block at the Trombe wall. For strength, we reinforced the block with rebar and concrete every 4 ft. or so and for additional heat-storage capacity, we filled remaining cores with mica tailings that we got free from a local mica plant. In order to add even more solar storage capacity, we hung a shelf on the Trombe wall for 90 plastic milk jugs, which have not held up well because of the breakdown in sunlight.

Instead of laying the block up with mortar, we applied Surewall to both sides of each block wall. Surewall (W. R. Bonsal Co., Lilesville, N. C. 28091) is a surface-bonding material made of portland cement and glass fibers. Troweled to about ⅛ in. thick, this tinted cement bonded the walls, giving them shear strength and assisting with waterproofing (photo p. 65). Two coats of tar and a layer of 6-mil. plastic complete the waterproofing. The Surewall finish looks good inside, like stucco, but it is quite rough to the touch, so I troweled over some of the interior surfaces with a thin layer of drywall compound.

To add to the R-value of the wall, we fit sheets of 2-in. styrofoam for below-grade use over 2x2 pressure-treated nailers. Then we plastered over metal lath wherever the masonry wall was to be above grade. We bermed earth around the outside of the block walls up to 6½ ft. high on the north

Photos by Robert McGahey except where noted.

The core of the house. A river-rock fireplace heats both the house and water. Water loops through the black pipe grate at the hearth and rises to an electric quick-recovery water tank upstairs, which is supported by the stone masonry.

side and 3½ ft. high on the east and west. This provides plenty of insulation in both winter and summer.

Timber framing—The five North Carolina mountain counties together boast more than 250 small sawmills. Oather Pritchard, whose mill is just four miles away from our site, custom-cut lumber for me for two years. The timber I carried to him came from a swath of oak that I cleared for a road and from a stand of poplar at the house site. We used a pole trailer retired from phone company use to haul most of the logs. On the south wall, on sections of the east and west walls that are above grade, and for the entire upper floor, we used a post-and-beam structure. The oak was used for 4x6 posts, 6x10 central beams, a free-standing post by the kitchen (bark left on one side because Oather wanted to avoid a nail) and as 1x subflooring for the upstairs. I had most of the poplar cut into half-rounds for the exposed rafters and rafter tie beams (see photo left). I also used the poplar for paneling, which we shiplapped at the site, and for shelving. Poplar has a pleasing blond color that doesn't darken appreciably unless it is exposed to direct sunlight. Among the softest of the hardwoods, it is pretty easy to work with. I did have a problem with warp in the shelving; now, I would suggest using hefty weights on it during drying.

We framed the upper floor with 4x8 yellow pine joists. Where the joist ends fit into support-

South-facing windows glow at dusk. Solar panels for preheating water fit into the roof over the entrance. Upstairs to the left is the master bedroom; the studio is in the center and the children's room is to the right. At ground level, a terrace abuts the living room at the left. Water jugs for additional heat storage line the Trombe wall in the greenhouse at the right.

ing notches in the block wall, we wrapped the joists with metal pans, then drilled holes and inserted bolts through the sides and lag bolts into the ends of the joists. After setting the joists in place, we mortared around the wrapped joist ends and bolts to lock everything in place.

Because our timber was only minimally seasoned, we bolted all of our post-and-beam joints to keep the timber from twisting during drying. Where joists meet over the central east-west beams and where they abut the posts on the south wall, we used simple lap joints fastened with ⅜-in. carriage bolts. The 4x6 posts

along the south wall are continuous over two stories with the joists mortised into the posts. Beams and joists bear on the central chimney. I understand that in California, and perhaps elsewhere, it is against the building code to frame wood into a chimney because of the hazard of fire. It's allowed here, but as a precaution we flashed the ends of each of the timbers butting into the chimney and used a vermiculite mortar mix (which transfers heat more slowly than mortar with sand) to fill in gaps around the flues to insulate the beams from the heat. The beams have never gotten hot.

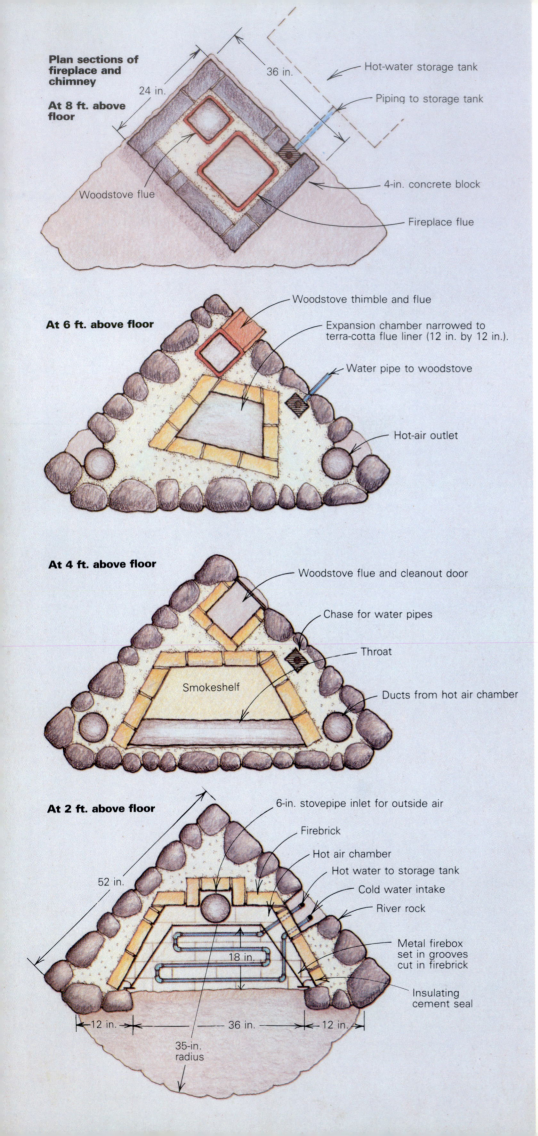

Plan sections of fireplace and chimney

At 8 ft. above floor

24 in.

36 in.

Hot-water storage tank

Piping to storage tank

Woodstove flue

4-in. concrete block

Fireplace flue

At 6 ft. above floor

Woodstove thimble and flue

Expansion chamber narrowed to terra-cotta flue liner (12 in. by 12 in.).

Water pipe to woodstove

Hot-air outlet

At 4 ft. above floor

Woodstove flue and cleanout door

Chase for water pipes

Throat

Smokeshelf

Ducts from hot air chamber

At 2 ft. above floor

6-in. stovepipe inlet for outside air

Firebrick

Hot air chamber

Hot water to storage tank

Cold water intake

River rock

Metal firebox set in grooves cut in firebrick

Insulating cement seal

52 in.

18 in.

12 in.   36 in.   12 in.

35-in. radius

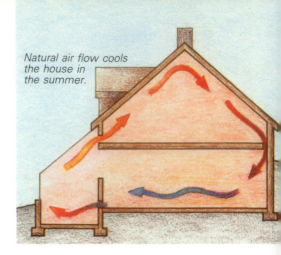

Natural air flow cools the house in the summer.

Raising the roof—The half-round poplar rafters are hinged at the peak with lap joints, fastened with ½-in. carriage bolts, and bolted to half-round poplar tie beams. The joinery here was the most exacting because of fitting curved shapes to square, but also the most rewarding. We used an electric chainsaw, which was indispensable for mortising, and I hired a good axman, on leave from building log cabins, to taper the tenons (photo right, page 62). We assembled each pair of rafters and its tie beam on the floor of the upper level, then got a crew together to raise them. I expected this process to be a slow one, but it took only about four days with three of us working on it. Scribing round logs was awkward, but when we went to attach subflooring for the play loft across the tie beams over the kids' room, they were dead level. We also framed up three large dormers, giving us space to sleep and work in. Some time after finishing the house (and after these photos were taken), I stained window and dormer trim with transmission oil, which enhanced the figure of the wood.

A thick floor—I decided not to lay oak flooring over the oak subfloor upstairs because of potential sag between joists and the risk of noise transmission. So we ended up framing a 24-in. grid of 2x4 studs, which we attached to the floor joists. We cut squares of feltboard to lay in the spaces to damp the noise and slow down heat transfer to the upstairs, then attached plywood to the grid and installed the hardwood flooring. One advantage of this was to give us a space to run the pipes to and from the hot water tank, which for optimum convection, was installed upstairs, directly above the heating core.

Unfortunately, we didn't protect the subfloor from the weather before roofing, so the surface exposed to the first level became stained with watermarks. At first I was bothered by its appearance, but several visitors who know that I salvaged material for the house have looked up at the ceiling and admired the "nice barn siding" (top photo, previous page).

Tin roof—The roof was fairly expensive, but we built it to last. We laid 2x6 T&G decking on the flat, top side of the poplar rafters, extending the decking almost 2 ft. at the gable ends as a generous overhang. Then we nailed 1x4

The north wall is constructed of dry-laid concrete block stiffened with white surface-bonding cement. Bituminous waterproofing coats the wall below grade; insulation will be added before berming. The subroof is built up in several layers, with 2x6 secondary rafters raised up on 1x4 strapping over tar paper, which is laid over 2x6 T&G decking and timber rafters. Insulation will be fit between the secondary rafters.

strapping to the decking over tarpaper and nailed on 2x6 secondary rafters at 16 in. o. c. (photo above). We vented the roof at both soffit and ridge to allow air to flow freely between the tin roofing and the insulation. It's a fairly fancy roof, but the strapping and rafters were mostly salvage material.

The biggest headache was the installation of the galvanized steel roofing—or "tin" as many roofers call it—and flashing around the dormers. It is important to stick with galvanized flashing on a galvanized roof because otherwise you will get a galvanic reaction between incompatible metals, as we did in places where we mistakenly used aluminum for flashing. Fortunately, all the dormer valleys are flashed with galvanized steel.

A masonry heat core—We considered using a woodstove instead of a fireplace, but the longer I thought about it, the more I thought how important it was to have a masonry heat core as the heart of the house (top photo, p. 63) with supplemental heat from a woodstove. I asked Steve Magers for help in designing the fireplace and chimney after reading *Fireplaces: The Owner-Builder's Guide* (Scribner, 1978, now out of print), which he wrote with Ken Kern. I told him we wanted to build in a hot-water heating system and a Rumford fireplace and top it with a spring-loaded damper. It was not too difficult for an experienced chimney-builder like Eric Thurston to execute the transition from a triangular corner fireplace to the chimney rectangle, aided by Steve Magers' cross-sectional drawings (facing page, left).

Building the fireplace and chimney was very satisfying. We gathered the stones from the banks of the South Toe River, mostly from a little over a mile away. The whole family got in on it, including my youngest son Jesse, age 2 then, who picked up colorful little stones as if they were jewels. Building with river rock is like assembling a puzzle with round pieces. You don't want to introduce hard edges by breaking the rock to get a tight fit.

Piping hot water—To get hot water, we set up a system of convective loops, using tips and details from Art Sussman and Richard Frazier's *Handmade Hot Water Systems* (Garcia River Press, P.O. Box 527, Port Arena, Calif. 95468, 1978), an invaluable source. Incoming water is preheated by a 40-gal. solar batch heater over the main entrance and stored in a secondhand 52-gal. tank. This water is circulated through both the black pipe grate that holds logs in the fireplace (drawings facing page) and through copper coils in the throat of the woodstove. Heated water rises naturally through copper piping to a used electric quick-recovery hot-water tank installed on the second floor next to the upstairs fireplace and resting on the fireplace masonry below. In the summer we use electricity to heat water but during winter, we get most of the hot water we need from this system. When it's sub-zero and the woodstove is cranked up, the water gets scalding hot, so we periodically run water in the tub to "dump" it from the loop before it boils.

Natural cooling—The pit greenhouse on the south wall provides an air-circulation system modeled in part after some pioneer solar homes nearby that were designed and built by Wendal Thomas in the 1940s and 1950s. These are passive-solar houses with greenhouses, basements and perimeter floor vents that allow for natural convection. In our house, hot air loops from the greenhouse to the upstairs via vents in the kneewall. The two vents are about 4 ft. by 6 in. and are screened to keep out insects. Cool air flows down the north wall

through the 4-in. slots left by omitting floor boards in the closets, which don't have doors. The moving air not only keeps the house cool in the summer but keeps condensation from forming on the buried north wall.

The cycle drives in reverse on a cold winter night, protecting the plants from freezing. We turned several concrete blocks sideways at the slab level of the Trombe wall, leaving gaps for venting the greenhouse. We also left space at the sill of the greenhouse doors. To keep most of the heat downstairs during the winter, the vents at the greenhouse peak and the door at the top of the stairs are kept closed from late in the day to the next morning. Upstairs winter temperatures stay about the same or four degrees cooler than downstairs—comfortable for both levels. There is some heat buildup in summer, though the highest temperature we've recorded is 78°F.

The house works quite well. It's like a living organism, requiring that we adapt to its rhythms. During our first Christmas, when my parents were visiting, I fed the woodstove like a steam-engine boiler to raise the temperature from 68°F to 72°F, trying to get my mother to take off her fur coat. But I've learned that the house prefers certain temperature ranges, which we find quite livable: mid to upper 60s in the winter and 70°F to 75°F in the summer.

Though it looks like a mountain house, it performs like a solar house. Our average wood use in this mountain valley (with around 4,200 degree days) is a little over one cord. About 60% of the energy required for hot water and heating the house comes from the sun. The total cost of the house, including a 225-ft. well, was $33,000. □

Robert McGahey commutes from Burnsville, N. C. to Atlanta, Ga., where he is an instructor and doctoral candidate at Emory University.

Drawings: Vince Babak. Rendered from originals by Steve Magers.

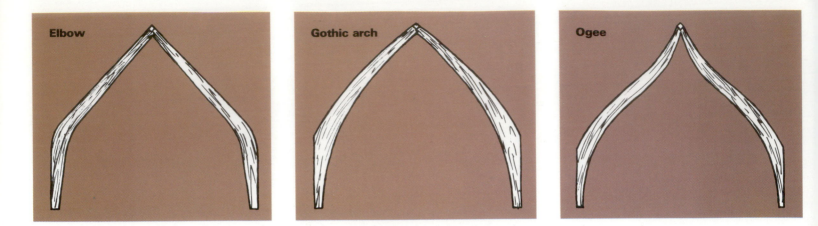

Elbow

Gothic arch

Ogee

Cruck House

An early timber-frame technique relies on curved tree trunks for principal structural members

by Jack Sobon

From *Fine Homebuilding* magazine (October 1987) 42:40-44

When my friend Susan Girard asked me to design and build a small house for her on land that she had purchased in Windsor, Mass., I immediately decided upon a cruck-frame design. Though usually the needs of my client determine the layout and size of the house, the design of the timber frame is left to me. I had always wanted to build a cruck frame, and here was my opportunity.

A brief history—The cruck frame is different from the box frame, or braced frame. Instead of vertical posts, pairs of inclined crucks, also called "curved tree principals," rise from the base of the sidewalls to meet at and support the roof at the ridge (photo facing page). The cruck pairs form rigid triangles at each bay interval, stiffening the structure in the transverse direction.

The origins of this unusual structural system date back to medieval England. B. Bunker, author of *Cruck Buildings* (a self-published book I found in an English bookshop) maintains that crucks were brought to England by Anglian settlers who arrived after the Romans departed (sometime after 400 A.D.). Other historians hold that cruck-frame construction arrived with the Normans in the 11th century. Whatever its origin, over 3,000 cruck buildings are still left to study.

In a cruck frame, the cruck pairs are most often matched halves cut from crooked trees and dressed to a rectangular cross section. The curved cruck blades follow the line of the walls and roof closely, protruding less into the interior space than a straight timber would. The most common shapes, the elbow, Gothic arch and the ogee, are shown in the drawings on the facing page. In some old buildings you find all three shapes.

Where the crucks join at the ridge, they might be half-lapped and notched to form a cradle for the ridge beam. In some old cruck-frame buildings, one or more cruck pairs weren't long enough to reach the peak. To solve this problem, the tops of the short crucks were joined with a collar beam that supported a king post which rose to support the ridge beam. Building widths are commonly 14 ft. to 18 ft., with as many as seven bays. The largest existing cruck building is the Leigh Court Barn, Hereford and Worcester, England, with an interior cruck span of 33½ ft.

Making the crucks—For the Girard house, I had planned to find and cut the crucks at the wooded six-acre site. This proved to be more difficult than I had anticipated. Because of the 2,000-ft. elevation, most of the forest was red spruce and balsam fir, with a few mixed hardwoods. Spruces naturally grow straight. A more southerly forest with its oaks and other hardwoods would more likely harbor some potential cruck blades.

A thorough search of Susan Girard's property turned up three trees that were large enough

and curved in only one plane. Two of them were black cherry, the third was quaking aspen. Each would render two cruck blades of matched curvature. The aspen was an elbow shape; one cherry was an ogee, the other was curved like an ox yoke. The maximum length available was 18 ft. This, along with structural considerations, limited the width of the building to about 16 ft. (drawing, below).

Old cruck blades are mostly 6 in. to 8 in. thick and as much as 24 in. wide at the butt. Our crucks were small in comparison: 5 in. thick and about 12 in. wide at the base, tapering to about 7 in. at the ridge. In the old days, a matching pair of crucks could be sawn out of a curved tree, or split out and then hewn square. My partner Dave Carlon and I chose a more modern method, using a portable chainsaw mill from Sperber Tool Works (Box 1224, West Caldwell, N. J. 07007). While a regular sawyer would have a difficult time positioning a boomerang-shaped

The humble exterior of this 650-sq. ft. house belies a finely joined structural system. As shown in the photo on the facing page, matched pairs of naturally curved timbers support the ridge beam and are contained within the symmetrical frame of the house.

Building layout

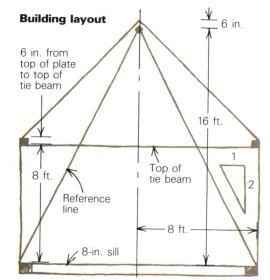

6 in. from top of plate to top of tie beam

8 ft.

Reference line

8-in. sill

6 in.

16 ft.

Top of tie beam

8 ft.

log on his carriage, this sort of cut is no problem for the Sperber mill.

After felling the tree and levering the log up onto short cross-log supports, we began laying out for the first cut, which would halve the log. We used Will Malloff's approach (*Chainsaw Lumbermaking,* published by The Taunton Press). The log was positioned with the curve lying level in a horizontal plane. Then 2x4 or 2x6 blocks were nailed on each end with their top edges both level and equidistant from the proposed cutting plane. Checking these with a level ensured a cruck free from winding problems. Two strings were stretched across the 2xs as a reference. Then ¼-in. lag bolts were screwed into the log until their heads were just below the strings. At a spacing of 3 ft. or 4 ft., these lag-bolt heads would support the guide plank that is used with the mill. Of course, the bolts were not so long as to pierce the cutting plane and catch the saw teeth. After one last check, the strings were removed and the guide plank was set on the log. Our guide plank was a 2x14, 14 ft. long. It had to be moved halfway through the cut. After the first, or halving cut, the bolts and planks were removed, since the fresh-cut surface provided a guide for the mill to complete the slabbing cut.

Since these 5-in. slabs were still too heavy and awkward to carry out of the woods, we hewed off the wane with an ax, following the natural curve of the piece. This surface was later planed or spokeshaved to form a continuous, attractive curve. We checked the curves the way you might check the straightness of a board, by sighting down the edge. Abrupt changes were quite noticeable, and we took them out with a hand plane. But even with the reduced weight, Dave and I barely managed to shoulder the cruck blades and carry them out of the woods to the work site near where the house would stand.

The black cherry was a delight to work with, and its color and aroma added to our pleasure. The aspen, however, gave us no end of trouble. First of all, the tree was leaning severely, and though Dave and I are experienced tree fellers, the aspen tore a section of its stump right out of the ground as it came down, splitting partway up the butt. This necessitated cutting off part of the butt, wasting some of the tree. The lean of the tree and its elbow shape had caused it to develop lots of reaction wood. As we finished sawing through the heart, stresses in the log were released, and the slab ends sprang apart with great force, almost catching me on the chin.

Handling the aspen cruck blades was equally unnerving. Not only were they elbow-shaped, but they were also warped. These pieces would not sit flat on our shoulders, or on sawhorses. On several occasions an aspen cruck started to roll off its sawhorses with no help whatever. After hitting the ground it seemed to flop about like a fish out of water. All I could do was get

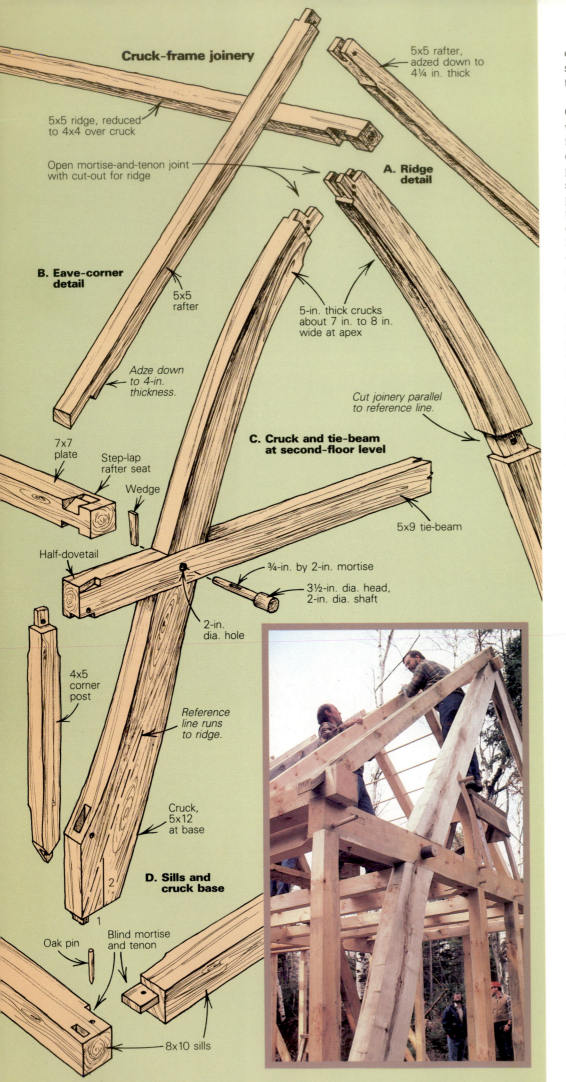

Cruck-frame joinery

5x5 ridge, reduced to 4x4 over cruck

Open mortise-and-tenon joint with cut-out for ridge

5x5 rafter, adzed down to 4¼ in. thick

A. Ridge detail

B. Eave-corner detail

5x5 rafter

5-in. thick crucks about 7 in. to 8 in. wide at apex

Adze down to 4-in. thickness.

Cut joinery parallel to reference line.

7x7 plate

Step-lap rafter seat

Wedge

C. Cruck and tie-beam at second-floor level

Half-dovetail

¾-in. by 2-in. mortise

3½-in. dia. head, 2-in. dia. shaft

2-in. dia. hole

5x9 tie-beam

4x5 corner post

Reference line runs to ridge.

Cruck, 5x12 at base

D. Sills and cruck base

Oak pin

Blind mortise and tenon

8x10 sills

out of its way until it came to rest. These pieces seemed to be full of energy until we framed them into the house.

Cruck joinery—After hand planing both sides, we laid out the joinery on each cruck blade from a single chalkline snapped on it. This reference line represented an imaginary line from the peak of the roof diagonally down to the top outside edge of the sill beam (drawing, previous page). The building was 16 ft. wide by 16 ft. to the ridge, so the angle formed between the line on the cruck and the horizontal read as 16/8 or 2/1 on the framing square. All angles were laid out with a framing square from the line, and all measurements were made on the line. Thus all the joinery could be cut without scribe fitting.

Ridge, plates and sills are all continuous in this house. To gain some extra strength, I extended the ridge and plates an additional 3½ in. past the ends of the building (photo below left). These protrusions are buried in the finished thickness of the exterior wall.

Crossing each cruck pair at second-floor height is a single horizontal 5x9 tie-beam that extends to the edges of the frame and supports a pair of horizontal 7x7 plates. Vertical posts, mortised into the tie-beam, also provide support along the sidewalls (drawing B, left).

Where the second-floor level tie beams crossed the crucks, we used a lap-type joint that Charles Hayward *(Woodwork Joints,* Sterling Publishing Co., 1979) calls a "strengthened halving" (drawing C, left). It provided additional bearing for the tie beam and allowed us to cut the walls of the lap at exactly a 2/1 angle, regardless of the actual angle of the curve at that point on the cruck blade. The only variable was the distance of the lap from the chalkline.

Traditionally, this halving joint was secured by boring multiple peg holes at opposing angles to prevent withdrawal of the joint. We made use of a more elaborate but stronger fastening design—large wooden forelock pegs, turned on a treadle lathe at nearby Hancock Shaker Village. Each had a 3½-in. dia. head, a 2-in. dia. shaft and a mortise for a ¾-in. thick wedge to draw the joint tight and allow for some adjustment after seasoning. We used an assortment of woods for the bolts and wedges including oak, hickory, maple, elm, beech, cherry, walnut and shadbush. The heads of the pegs on the exterior cruck pairs would be buried in the thickness of the wall in the finished house.

An open mortise-and-tenon joint (sometimes called a tongue-and-fork joint) was used to join the crucks at their apex, with a 4x4 notch cut out for the continuous 5x5 ridge beam (drawing A, left). The ridge not only ties the cruck pairs together but also supports the open mortise-and-tenon rafter pairs. The rafter-to-plate connection is a step-lap seat (drawing B, left). When pegged, this is an extremely strong joint.

The Girard house rafters span from the ridge to the plate, though in many traditional cruck frames, intermediate purlins framed into the top side of the crucks would support them at midspan. Bracing from the purlins to the cruck blades would stiffen the frame longitudinally. Because our frame had no purlins or purlin braces, we added let-in braces at two opposite corners to provide longitudinal bracing.

In the eastern end wall, two short raking struts connect the tie beams and crucks. These black cherry pieces, once short curved branches in a fallen tree, were hand-hewn and planed, provided with lap-dovetail tenons, and inserted into the assembled bents in just two hours.

As is customary in our frames, all the joinery in this house was cut by hand, without the aid of power tools. Most of the timber is roughsawn pine and hemlock bought from a local sawmill and hand planed ($.20/ft., and $.25/ft. for the longer timbers). This kept our overall costs down, though there is considerable labor in hand work. The timber for the frame, excluding crucks, cost less than $600.

The frame was raised by hand in November of 1984, during a traditional raising party with close to 100 attendees. Because we had pre-assembled the cruck bents on the deck the day before, the raising took under an hour and a half, but the celebration carried on into the night. Though cutting the joints was enjoyable, raising the frame (top photo, next page) was the most gratifying part of the job, especially since all the joints fit properly.

Finishing the cruck house—The frame was designed to be completely exposed on the interior, so the insulating skin is built up right on the frame. First, 2x8 T&G mixed spruce and pine planking was nailed to the outside face of the frame. This sheathing is the interior finish and nailing base for the exterior insulation and sheathing. Next came a 6-mil polyethylene va-

Cruck-frame hovel at Plimoth Plantation

In the spring of 1987, Plimoth Plantation, the living museum of 17th-century life in Plymouth, Mass., needed to replace one of its rotting post-hole type buildings. After researching temporary and transient house types in England and Holland (the Pilgrims stayed in Holland before they sailed to America), curator Jeremy Bangs decided on a cruck-frame hovel design for the replacement.

The hovel is a crude shelter, often below ground level, for the poorer classes. Hovels were still in use in Europe into this century as huts for charcoal burners and other artisans. Cruck framing, once used mainly by the upper class, had become popular for the lower classes in later years.

The Plimoth Plantation cruck was a two-and-a-half week effort by staff carpenter Ted Curtin and myself. It is a two-bay, three-cruck pair frame, 12 ft. by 20 ft., of mostly white oak. The curved trunks for the crucks were hand selected from the forest, sawn out with the Sperber mill, and framed up using only hand tools. Some timbers were adzed, while many were left with the "vertical" saw marks of the sawmill, representing pitsaw marks appropriate to the 17th century.

Hewing, surprisingly, was less of a tradition than sawing for the English builders of the period. Crooked, knotty timber typical of English forests lent itself better to sawing, which yielded more usable wood from a given log. Sometimes logs were squared up first in the forest by hewing to remove bulk, then pitsawn into smaller members. The Plimoth hovel's timbers imitate this by having saw marks on surfaces adjacent to adzed surfaces.

The Plimoth cruck-frame hovel is fairly traditional in its details. As the photos show, the cruck feet sit on large flat stones directly on the earth. The plates, at waist height, are supported by tie beams on the end walls and by cruck spurs in the center cruck pair. The spurs are dovetail-

Ted Curtin

lapped and skew-pegged into the cruck blades. Purlins were lapped across the backs of the crucks to support rafter poles at their midspan.

One end pair of crucks, the least curved, required cleats to build them out to the roof plane in order to support the purlins. The apex detail of the crucks is a short yoke piece joining the crucks and supporting the ridge. Curved collars also connect each cruck pair just above head height.

Because of the number of lap joints and the hardness of the white oak, we used axes to rough out joints. This saved time, wear and tear on our arms, and of course was the traditional way. We also used the "scribe rule" system of timber-frame layout and cutting, typical of English buildings during the period but virtually unused today. Many of the joints were scribed.

Riven white oak planks were laid against the frame below grade, and the earth was backfilled. The thatched roof, when complete, will run to the ground. Inside, the floor is earthen and heated by a hearth with a wooden smoke hood supported on curved projecting supports. At the other end will be a sleeping chamber and an animal pen, as well as a dormered entrance in the roof. —J. S.

This two-bay cruck frame at Plimoth Plantation was cut and erected in about three weeks. The bottom ends of the frame sit below grade on large flat stones; dovetail-lapped and pegged spurs on the middle cruck pair at waist height support the plates.

From above and below (left), a wall plate receives enthusiastic support as it is positioned atop the tie-beams. The matched cruck pairs that will support the ridge beam were raised first. Below left, the black cherry blade of an end-wall cruck shows up strongly against the light pine boards used on the walls and ceiling. A wedge, driven into a 2-in. dia. peg, holds the lap-joint connection between cruck blade and tie-beam.

por barrier, then 2-in. rigid urethane insulation. The exterior walls were finished with 1x8 ship-lap pine siding. The roof vapor barrier and insulation board were installed in the same way and then covered by a layer of ½-in. plywood. Cedar shingles were nailed down over this base.

Rough window openings were cut out after the 2x8 planks were installed. A full 2x2 nailer applied around the exterior side of the opening stiffens it and provides nailing for the window trim. The diminutive size and simple, low-maintenance exterior of the house belie its cruck-frame origins (photo p. 67).

The floor sandwich was built up somewhat differently. First, full 2x4s were nailed face down along the center of each 6x7 floor joist and around the sills. This left 1 in. or more of bearing surface on each side of the 2x4. Between these nailers was set ½-in. CDX plywood, followed by 1½-in. urethane insulation and a continuous sheet of polyethylene vapor barrier. Fastened to the nailers was the finish floor—more 2x8 T&G planking. R-values for the house ranged from 14 for the floor to 19 on the roof. These values are not very high, but the house's small size and unbroken insulated skin make the interior easy to heat. A small woodstove does the job with electric baseboard backup.

All of the underfloor plumbing was confined in one joist bay. Here the pipes run in a box filled with 12 in. of fiberglass-batt insulation. The incoming waterpipe is wrapped with heat tape as extra insurance against freeze-up.

Traditional cruck frames were raised off the ground on stone piers called "stylobates" and had an earthen floor. Ledge near the surface at the Girard site made a full basement foundation impractical. Instead, we used 18-in. sq. concrete piers poured right on the bedrock and finished above grade with stonework. Between the piers, we plan to construct a dry-laid stone wall.

From the outside, you'd never guess that this small (650-sq. ft.) house was built around an ancient structural system. Only when you get inside (photo bottom left) do the crucks present themselves as the dominant element in the design. The final cost of the house was about $43 per sq. ft. (not including site work), well below the average for the region. □

Jack Sobon is co-author of Timber Frame Construction *(Garden Way Publishing, Pownal, Vt. 05261). For more information on cruck construction, read* Discovering Timber-Framed Buildings *by Richard Harris (Shire Publications, Ltd., Cromwell House, Church St. Princes Risborough, Aylesbury, Bucks, England HP17 9AJ) and* Timber Building in Britain *by R. W. Brunskill (Victor Gollancz Ltd., 14 Henrietta St., London, England WC2E 8QJ).*

Raising Heavy Timber

Tools and tips for maneuvering big beams

by Trey Loy

When there were many gigantic redwood and fir trees in the Pacific Northwest, huge logs were milled into massive timbers to build sawmills, bridges, wharves, warehouses and buildings for heavy industry. Lumber 12 in. square was common, though larger beams were also sawn. (The largest piece I've seen is 18 in. square and 42 ft. long, but the old-timers say they milled bigger ones than that.) The joinery of these structures was simple, relying on steel pins, bolts and plates for strength.

Today, many of the big-timber buildings are dilapidated beyond repair. Often the owner just wants to get rid of the old wreck, so salvage rights can be obtained before the wrecking crane is called. Salvaging any material is sound economy, and in recycled lumber there are some terrific finds like clear, tight-grained redwood, and well-seasoned fir that is suitable even for fine cabinetry. Used lumber, cleaned of paint and grime by rough-planing, sandblasting, and wire-brushing, reveals a new and rugged complexion that's quite pleasing to the eye, with nail holes and blemishes adding character.

We recently built a house using timbers purchased before it was designed. The timber had framed a navy warehouse in Eugene, Ore.; we bought 2,400 linear feet of Douglas fir 12x12s in 10-ft., 20-ft. and 30-ft. lengths, and 9x18s 32 ft. long. Many pieces had several coats of paint, and others were covered with dirt, grime and grease. The lumber was roughsawn and box-cut; its width sometimes varied more than an inch from one end to the other, and many beams were twisted along their entire lengths. Wide checks had further distorted dimensions. Broken nails and the torched ends of pins protruded from the surface—nasty stuff to work with. We pulled most of them with a nail puller and a crowbar. After the house was framed, we cleaned the exposed surfaces with a portable sandblaster, keeping the nozzle moving to avoid gouging grooves in the earlywood.

Moving and raising timber—Maneuvering heavy posts and beams is no great task if you've got a crane or boom truck. But the four of us on this job didn't have access to any such large equipment. So we used a few old-fashioned but effective tools: a peavey, a sweet william, a pulley, a ramp (inclined plane) and a gin pole.

A peavey is a stout hardwood pole, usually of ash or maple, about 6 ft. long and hollowed at one end to receive a pointed steel pin (photo, right). A tapered steel collar keeps the pin from splitting the end of the handle. The upper part of the collar is fitted with two eyes through which a bolt passes to secure a large steel hook, shaped like a fishhook, which swings parallel to the pole. If you want to move a beam laterally, swing the peavey so the hook digs into the side of the timber and place the pointed end on top. Lifting and pulling on the handle pivots the timber. It is easy to flop the timber over and over until you get it where you want it. If you hook the peavey into the end of a timber, you can make a dead lift.

A sweet william, sometimes called a timber packer, is similar to ice tongs, except that the hooks are suspended so they swing and swivel from a steel collar fastened to the center of a 6-ft. wooden handle. The tongs grab opposite sides of a timber, and the scissoring action holds the timber firm. Two workers can lift the end of a beam for carrying or help drag a load up a ramp. These tools left some deep gouges in our timbers, but the new wounds were hardly noticeable among the old scars.

Ramps are great back-savers for moving logs or timber to a higher level. To load a truck use two stout planks at least 3 in. thick and wide enough to walk on and place one at each end of the truck bed. Roll the timber over and over with peaveys, walking the beam up the ramp. If the luck of the day left you with only one peavey, tie a rope to the other side of the truck bed, run it around the center of the timber two or more turns, then back to a person standing on the bed. The turns of rope act like a continuous lever. As one person pushes with the peavey, the other pulls on the rope (drawing, top of next page).

Rollers under a timber make light work of moving a beam end first. Firewood-size logs work fine on rough ground; on the smooth surface of a ramp or subfloor we use lengths of 2-in. pipe. You alter the direction of travel by

Using a peavey in the end grain, you can either push or lift a heavy timber. For lateral movement the hook digs into the side of the beam, and leverage is applied through the hardwood handle.

Photos: Park Loy

Using a rope as a lever

When you've got only one peavey, a few turns of rope around the center of a timber will create the leverage you need to work it up an inclined plane.

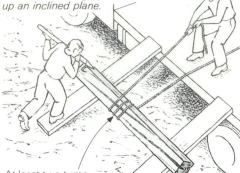

At least two turns

Lever and fulcrum

You can maneuver huge timbers with the proper application of leverage.

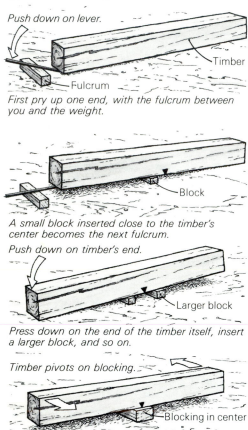

Push down on lever.

Timber

Fulcrum

First pry up one end, with the fulcrum between you and the weight.

Block

A small block inserted close to the timber's center becomes the next fulcrum.

Push down on timber's end.

Larger block

Press down on the end of the timber itself, insert a larger block, and so on.

Timber pivots on blocking.

Blocking in center

Once the timber is high enough you can rotate it on a fulcrum block set under its center.

The gin pole has been raised, and the trucker's hitch on one guy line is being tied off. The tackle that will raise the timber is dropping straight down from the yardarm. A ⁵⁄₁₆-in. braided steel cable supports the pole from the rear.

tapping the roller askew; the timber follows the rollers' path.

The posts for this house were light enough to be carried by three men using a peavey and a sweet william. Once on the subfloor, we man-handled each post into an upright position, plumbed it as well as possible, and braced it with 2x4s nailed temporarily to the stem wall and to stakes driven into the ground at right angles to the building's face. We moved heavier pieces onto the subfloor by rolling them up a strongly braced 2x8 ramp, using a wedge of wood behind each roller as a brake to prevent the timber from rolling back down.

Though we tried to put the lumber we'd need first on the top of the pile, invariably the timber we needed was at the bottom. At those times a lever and fulcrum came in handy. Using a lever, it's best to have the load on the other side of the fulcrum so you are pushing down with your weight to raise the load. With the load between you and the fulcrum, you have to lift up, and that's the kind of lift that can bust something loose inside. For levers we used steel bars, the peavey, and lengths of lumber. By prying up the end of a beam so it is slightly raised and slipping a block of wood underneath as far toward the middle as possible, you turn the beam itself into a lever. I'm always amazed at the small effort needed to seesaw a half-ton of wood back and forth. By alternately placing fulcrums of increasing height on either side of the balance point, you can raise the beam higher and higher, as shown in the drawing at left. With the fulcrum at the balance point, the timber can be swiveled in a new direction.

The gin pole—To raise the top plates, ridge beams and rafters into place, we used a gin pole. This is an upright pole with three guy lines for support; a block and tackle hung from the top does the lifting. A gin pole works only for vertical lifts and must be repositioned for every piece, but it can be moved around the site easily by two workers, though four are required to raise loads. You can set up the gin pole anywhere there is a solid place for its butt.

Our pole was a fir sapling 22 ft. long, straight, true and measuring 4½ in. in diameter at the butt and 3½ in. at the top. We passed a ⁵⁄₈-in. steel pin 18 in. long through a hole drilled 1 ft. from the narrow end to serve as a yardarm for the rigging; a loop of chain hung over the top of the pole and resting on the yardarm supported the upper block of the block and tackle. When we moved or set up the pole, we ran out the lower block and tied it to the bottom of the pole. The guy lines are spliced with eyes that slide over the pole and rest on the yardarm. We used ⁵⁄₁₆-in. braided steel cable 120 ft. long for the main guy line directly supporting the pole (cable won't stretch) and two lengths of ½-in. rope 100 ft. long for the side guy lines that position and brace the pole.

To set up a gin pole, first find the balance point of the timber to be raised, and then determine where this point will be after the piece is in place. Directly under this imaginary point, mark an X on the floor or ground. Four or five feet back from the X, make a chock to hold the

butt of the pole by nailing two pieces of lumber on the floor in a V-shape, or by digging a shallow hole in the ground. Then lay the gin pole over the X, with its butt end resting in the chock. Raise it to about 75°, with the tackle plumb above the X. This will keep the load from rubbing against the pole during the lift.

The main guy line should run in a straight line behind the pole. Stretch the side guy lines out to either side of the pole, slightly behind the chock. The farther from the pole you anchor the lines, the smaller the angle of pull, which means less force is needed to raise and secure the pole. We usually fasten the main line at least 100 ft. from the pole and the support lines at least 50 ft. away. Loop the lines around something stable, like a tree or solid framing, or drive stakes in the ground at an angle away from the pole. We use 2-in. steel pipe 4 ft. long, driven 2 ft. into the ground with a maul.

The main guy line is run to its stake and given a couple of turns around the pipe or anchor. The side guy lines are secured with a knot capable of retrieving slack called a trucker's hitch (drawing, facing page, top). The pipe and the loop of the hitch act like two pulleys, and though there is some friction, this method makes it easier to haul the pole up. In fact, the friction works to keep the load from slipping back when the lines are held together.

On our job, one of us manned each of the three lines and a fourth worked the pole, lifting the end of it over his head and walking toward the butt. After the pole reached about 45°, we raised it the rest of the way with the lines alone, as the fourth man made sure it didn't slip out of the chock.

When the gin pole is nearly in position, untie the lower block and holding the falls (the rope you pull on) firmly with one hand, attach a weight to the lower block hook (we used a chunk of timber) for a plumb bob to center the block and tackle over the X. Once the tackle is plumb, draw the guy lines taut, secure them, and double-check everything. Tie off the lower block again to keep tension on the pole. Now roll the timber in place, positioning it with its mid-section over the X.

Lifting—It took quite a bit of time to prepare for each lift, and because of the size of the timbers, some days we got only one rafter into place. (The gin pole can work well and quickly to raise lighter weights like standard ridgepoles). We tried to maintain an even pace, with two of us preparing the rigging and two working on the next piece. Dealing with these tremendous weights requires teamwork. First we chained the timber to the lower block hook. Those of us who had to lift used our legs, and a short countdown was called out so we could heave in unison. As two of us hauled in on the falls, the other two guided the timber into place with tail lines tied to the ends of the timber. It's easy to swivel the beam in an arc and rock it like a seesaw to maneuver it around stuff that is already in place. □

Trey Loy is a carpenter. He lives and works in Little River, Calif.

Tying the trucker's hitch

Truckers often have to tighten loads down on flatbeds. This hitch, a modified slipknot, lets them do it quickly without a lot of trouble. It comes in handy any time you have to snug up a line that's fastened at one end

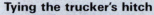

Standing part (guy line)

Free end

1 Make a loop with a double twist in the section of the rope leading to the gin pole—the rope's standing part. Make another loop below the first loop.

2 Insert the second loop within the first loop, creating yet a third. Snug things up a bit.

3 Take the free end of the rope around the post and back through the third loop, formed by the other two

To pole

Free end

4 Pulling on the free end will first tighten the hitch, then move it toward the post, pulling the guy line taut. Be sure both to start the hitch far enough away from the post and to leave enough slack in the line as you begin to tie it. When you're done, tie things off with two half-hitches in the free end around the doubled rope between post and hitch.

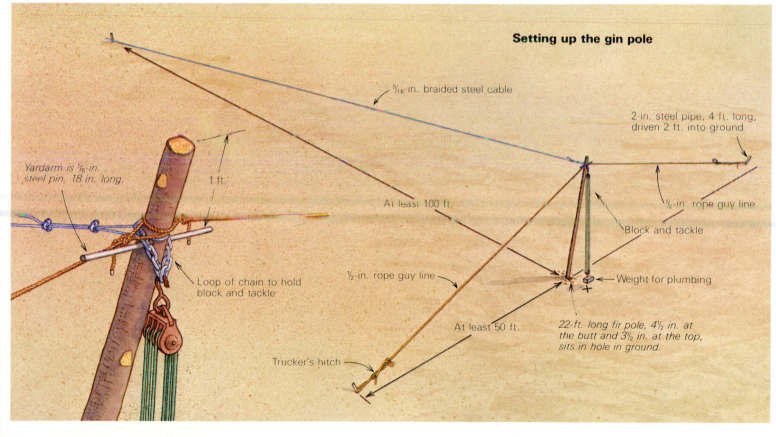

Setting up the gin pole

⁵⁄₁₆-in. braided steel cable

2-in. steel pipe, 4 ft. long, driven 2 ft. into ground

Yardarm is ⁵⁄₈-in. steel pin, 18 in. long.

1 ft.

At least 100 ft.

¼-in. rope guy line

Block and tackle

Loop of chain to hold block and tackle

½-in. rope guy line

Weight for plumbing

At least 50 ft.

22-ft. long fir pole, 4½ in. at the butt and 3½ in. at the top, sits in hole in ground.

Trucker's hitch

How strong?   A civil engineer calculated for us some of the forces working on the gin pole and rigging. He considered a 3½-in. diameter pole 20 ft. long leaning at an angle of 77°. The load on the block and tackle is 1,000 lb. The main line, which is 100 ft. long, keeps the pole from bending toward the load and has to resist a force of 288 lb. The resultant force of the cable and the load on the pole is calculated to be 1,088 lb. The force trying to kick the pole out of its chock is about 270 lb. The force on the side guy lines is negligible, but exists. Thus the gin pole carries most of the burden and will continue to do so unless force surpassing the buckling strength of the wood is applied. The buckling point for our clear fir pole is 2,145 lb., and theoretically it could be used to lift timbers as heavy as 1,800 lb. It might work, but when we raised the 32-ft. 9x18 ridge beam weighing around 1,400 lb.—I hauled on the block and tackle with my '51 Plymouth—the gin pole twanged like a freshly plucked guitar string. To lift heavier loads a stouter pole and stronger rigging are required. A surfaced 6x6 of clear-grained fir 20 ft. long, for example, has a buckling strength of 22,000 lb.   —*T.L.*

Illustrations: Roland Wolf

Roofs that seem to hover. The gazebo roof shades a large deck (top), and the open tower acts as windbracing along the length of the house. This view can be seen only by skirting the steep drop-off on the east side of the butte. The house looks tall and imposing from the road (bottom left), but the view from the west on the top of the butte (center left) emphasizes the 105-ft. length of the structure and its huge, single-gable roof.

Hidden entry. The breezeway (center, right) shows a silhouette of the gazebo roof, and leads the visitor from the open courtyard through the width of the house to the entry on the other side. The strong Japanese influence is apparent in 8-ft. deep, cedar-clad eaves and precise stone paths (bottom, right).

At the Top of the Mountain

Architect Paul Schweikher used a spectacular setting, a massive post-and-beam frame, and Japanese-influenced detailing to build his own house

by Paul Spring

The house sits on the very top of a butte. For the red rock country of Northern Arizona, it isn't a very impressive butte, but it offers a 360° view of the surrounding red sandstone ridges and canyons. From the main road a few hundred feet below, the windowless gable end of the house and the massive, open patio roof stand side-by-side in silhouette (photo facing page, bottom left).

Architect Paul Schweikher, 80, designed this house for himself and his wife Dorothy in 1972, after a career of more than 50 years that included a long and successful practice in Chicago and top posts in the architecture departments at Yale and at Carnegie Institute of Technology, now Carnegie-Mellon.

Schweikher is known for his simple, graceful detailing using just a few basic materials—in particular, wood. He also likes to expose the structure of his buildings, and this house is no exception. The massive fir post-and-beam frame is the primary source of decoration, and its success depended on the architect's sense of how things should be scaled and related to each other. There is a strong Japanese influence in the design that shows in the clear relationship between house and site. Schweikher didn't attempt to make his house look Japanese, but instead, let his appreciation for Japanese forms and textures spill over into his own Western design.

The plan—Once you reach the top of the butte, the house appears to be all roof. Over 105 ft. long, it is an uninterrupted single gable that is pierced by two large metal fireplace flues (photo facing page, center left). Eight-foot deep eave overhangs along much of its length make the house appear considerably wider than its 17 ft., and bring the roof closer to the ground. They also keep the glass walls, which are outside the supporting posts of the frame, hidden in shadow. This immense roof plane seems to hover off the ground.

The approach to the house is up a short driveway of crushed red sandstone that widens out immediately into a court. Directly ahead, the house is divided into two distinct parts by a breezeway. On the right is the studio, with the garage underneath. On the left, the main living space of the house sits on the same level as the studio. A duckboard path leads to the breezeway, which shelters a series of small decks. These are stacked like giant blocks, and serve as steps up through the breezeway. An enclosed bridge, which is really a small room lined with bookshelves, is tucked up into the peak of the roof above. It's seldom noticed from below.

As soon as you walk up the steps of the breezeway looking for the entry, you discover that you have already passed through the width of the house, and you are outside again gaping at a 180° panorama of sculpted sandstone that couldn't be seen before because of the house. In the foreground, crowded out near the edge of the butte at the end of a wooden walkway, is the covered patio, which Schweikher calls the gazebo. Like the house, it is a huge gable roof (photo facing page, top). But here, the gable ends are left open, with the exception of a horizontal beam and a kingpost. Supported by just four corner 8x8s, which are well back from the eaveline, it looks like a huge tent canopy.

As you turn around, still looking for the entry, you see a singularly spectacular butte, Courthouse Rock, framed in the breezeway that you just passed through. Only then do you see the stone path on your right, bordered in red gravel, that leads to the entry. It parallels the glass walls under the eave and ends at the acrylic sliding door of the main house. Even when you are facing the house,

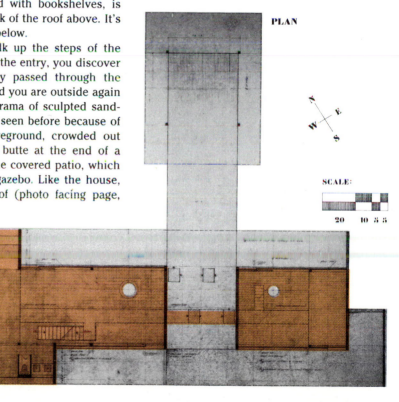

PLAN

SCALE:

20 10 5 5

LONGITUDINAL SECTION

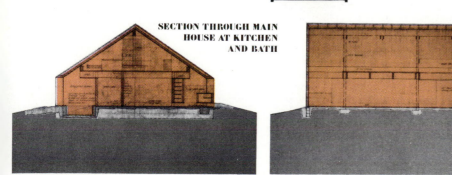

SECTION THROUGH MAIN HOUSE AT KITCHEN AND BATH

Dining area. A view down the length of the main house from the living room (top) shows the kitchen pass-through on the right, and sliding acrylic screens for the sunken bath, lavatory and water closet on the left. The catwalk in the upper foreground leads to the loft.

Kitchen. Built out under the eaves, the kitchen (left) is 24 ft. long with only a 3-ft. wide walkway between the storage cabinets on the right and the black linoleum-covered counters on the left. A 24-ft. run of glazing uninterrupted by mullions (above) makes the room seem much larger and shows off the view.

Living room. The huge living room of the house (facing page) is a good example of Schweikher's use of the exposed frame as decoration. The pairs of 3x16 cross beams, the cedar battens on the underside of the rafters, the catwalk, and glass walls and deep overhangs all make the room appear much wider than its 17 ft. The 36-in. steel tube fireplace, which helps heat the house, is a strong vertical element in the design.

walking along this path, the view plays a cat-and-mouse game with you. Because both long walls of the house are glass, you either see red sandstone vistas by looking through the interior and beyond, or you get a reflection of the mountains off the near glass.

The main house is essentially one big room, with a large loft above its northwest end. An open-stringer stairway of natural fir on one side leads to a wood catwalk suspended in the peak of the roof. It connects the breezeway bridge with the loft.

The floor throughout the main house is 4-in. by 8-in. red quarry tile, set in a running bond with natural-color grout. The underside of the roof is covered entirely with roughsawn cedar battens. At the long walls on each side of the house, both the quarry tile and the cedar paneling continue in a single plane from one side of the plate glass to the other with no interruption. All 8 ft. of the eaves beyond the glass are wrapped with the cedar, and the tile extends outside more than a foot. There are times, depending on the angle of the sun entering the room, that the glass walls just don't seem to be there, and the distinction between *out there* and *in here* is almost lost.

On the northwest end, where the house jogs out from 17 ft. to 31 ft. by expanding to the edges of the overhangs, there are two interior walls running along the length of the house (photo top left). One is the shower wall of the sunken tub. This is part of a bath complex that includes a water closet and a washing sink. The area is screened for privacy with sliding acrylic panels—one of only three interior doors in the entire house. The other wall, solid except for a pass-through and a doorway, divides the kitchen from the rest of the house.

The kitchen is a 24-ft. long galley, with only a 3 ft.-wide walkway between floor-to-ceiling storage on the interior wall, and the counters and cooktop across from it (photos bottom and center left). Although it breaks all the rules of kitchen design, the linear plan works well for Dorothy Schweikher, who doesn't like help getting meals. Because of the unobstructed glass above the counters, the kitchen gets plenty of light and feels bigger than it is.

While the studio uses the same pattern of windowless endwalls and glass sidewalls as the main house, it is much smaller. Even the views are smaller in scale. Bushes planted close to the house on one side create a foreground, and a tall bookcase partially obstructs the view from the other window.

The floor in the studio is end-grain wood block. The room has a fireplace and drafting table, with a sleeping loft overhead served by a stair ladder. The Schweikhers use the loft as their bedroom, and have built closets into the eaves along a short catwalk that connects the loft with the bridge over the breezeway. Like the rest of the house, the master bedroom is spare to the point of being Spartan.

Using the frame—During the later years of his practice in Chicago, Schweikher watched a dramatic change in the skyline of the Loop. He traces his fondness for the strong joints

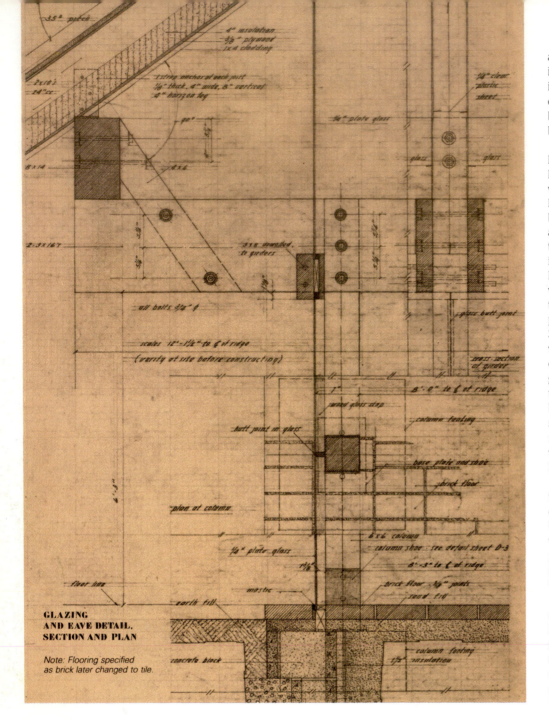

**GLAZING
AND EAVE DETAIL.
SECTION AND PLAN**

Note: Flooring specified
as brick later changed to tile.

and long spans of wood post-and-beam framing to watching the high-steel workers riveting together skyscrapers from his office in the city. He feels that exposing the structure of a building lends it a kind of honest beauty, based on its function.

The post-and-beam frame of the Schweikher house, which can be seen most clearly in the living room, is designed to span the 17 ft. width of the house. The carrying beams are huge gluelams—the ridge beam and shoulder beams at the eaves of the house on each side are all 8x14s (drawing, left). Their size allows the 6x6 vertical posts that hold the entire roof in the air to be placed 16 ft. apart inside the long glass walls on the northeast and southwest. What is even more remarkable about this system is that the shoulder beams are not posted to the ground, but sit on top of pairs of 3x16 Douglas fir cross-beams that span the width of the living room. These pairs bolt to either side of the 6x6 posts just inside the glass walls, and cantilever beyond to pick up the shoulder beams. This puts the shoulder beams 4 ft. outside the glass, rather than inside the house where you'd expect them. The rafters that bear on top of them are 2x10s with level-cut tails, 24 in. o.c.; and they cantilever yet another 4 ft. beyond.

However, the rafters don't figure as a part of the exposed structure. Like the inside and outside of the walls, they are wrapped with ⅜-in. plywood from eave to ridge. The plywood is covered with 30-lb. builder's felt and paneled vertically on the underside with 1x4 roughsawn cedar boards, their edges spaced ⅜ in. apart to let the black felt show through.

The detailing of the glass, and how it intersects the structural frame, is kept simple. Unlike most post-and-beam houses, the plate-glass panels on the long walls of the studio and main house aren't infill, but one continuous plane. There are no jambs, mullions or sills. The ¼-in. plate is butted together with a ⅛-in. bead of clear silicone. Since the glass

Paul Schweikher, Architect

One of Paul Schweikher's favorite stories about his career was told to him by a client, who threw a party when his house was completed in Scottsdale, Ariz. The guest list included Frank Lloyd Wright, Mrs. Wright and others from Taliesin West. The new house owner approached Wright after most of the other guests had gone home and said, "Mr. Wright, you've spent the entire evening here, but haven't told us what you think of our house." After musing for several moments, Wright swept the room with a huge gesture, "You're very lucky to have such a fine house . . . by such a poor architect."

Although Schweikher's work has received wide attention, students in architecture survey courses will probably never be required to memorize his name. Architects become famous by establishing a style. Talent is necessary, but showmanship also helps a lot. Wright is nearly as famous for his hat and cape and his high-handed, imperious manner as for his designs, and Mies van der Rohe was almost as well known for his fat cigars and his cryptic comments as for his buildings.

Paul Schweikher has no such personal affectations. His designs aren't easily pigeonholed either. But they do convey some of the same resolution, balance and wholeness as the buildings designed by architects who are required reading.

A 50-year career—Schweikher's work spanned a period of great change in American architecture. In 1928, he went to Chicago and worked for David Adler, who was known for designing baroque "great-houses" for wealthy clients. Flipping the pages of a book on Adler's work, Schweikher points out his first assignment as one of many nameless architects hired to draw details—a small but incredibly ornate balcony.

In 1933 he formed his own partnership. He won the grand prize in General Electric's house competition in 1935, and he began getting regular attention from national journals. Schweikher recalls these days as his happiest.

In 1937, Schweikher built his house and studio in Roselle, Ill., a rural area west of Chicago. It

helped Schweikher establish a reputation for long, low houses with wide overhangs and simple wood detailing that took up where the Prairie School style left off. He was designing in a city that was home to many of the new century's great architects in what was called the First Chicago School. By the late 1930s, Mies van der Rohe had introduced the steel structural frame and begun what would become known as the Second School. In the meantime, a rich local tradition for innovative residential architecture established by Wright and others inspired a new generation of architects like Schweikher, George Fred Keck and William Pereira.

Schweikher continued practicing in Chicago after World War II. But in 1953, after three years as a passes outside the 6x6 posts, the only support it gets against wind loading is at the top and bottom, and from a 1x2 cedar vertical bedding strip nailed to the outside of the post.

Instead of a sill where glass meets floor, the panels rise from a narrow aluminum channel set flush with the quarry tile. These panels of glass are 8 ft. high and are capped at the top with a 3x8 glazing beam that runs between the bottom edges of the cross-beams. Above the glazing beam, more glass carries to the roof. The cross-beams, which are the only members to pierce the glass, are dadoed to accept it. The space directly above the beams is filled with a ¼-in. thick acrylic panel that meets the glass on each side with a silicone butt joint.

Wind bracing

One of the most difficult problems that Schweikher had to deal with was wind that often tops 60 mph. With glass on two sides and unusually deep overhangs, his house is especially vulnerable to uplift and racking. Although the design helped create this weakness, the sturdy connections of the post-and-beam frame and the plywood diaphragm behind the cedar paneling are also a large part of the solution. The paneling detail—walls and roof sheathed (shear paneled) on both sides—creates tremendous rigidity.

Across the narrow width of the building, the diagonal braces of the main frame, in the form of short lengths of 6x6s, resist racking effectively with their large surface area and steel connectors. They are bolted between the cross-beams and the shoulder beams at the eave, and from the cross-beams to the posts that support the ridge beam in the center of the room. All of these connections are made with ¾-in. bolts, and plate-steel connectors were used to resist uplift forces where they could be hidden from view.

Schweikher refers to the third major device for stiffening the house merely as wind bracing, but it's easier to imagine it as the lone bell tower of an old Spanish mission (photo,

Functional decoration. The steel-tubing fireplace (drawing) and the garage-door counterweights (photo) contribute mechanically and aesthetically to the house.

top of p. 74). It is built out from the south side of the gable end of the studio and garage, creating an offset of 8 ft. between the two halves of the building's end. The open structure is divided by horizontal 4x14 beams into three identical open squares that reach the full height of the gable. The cross-bracing in each of these, and the deep footing below them, work to keep the house rigid along its length.

Exposing function

Schweikher left much of his house's functional machinery as exposed as the structural frame. The fireplace in the living room is a good example. So are the garage-door counterbalance weights in the eaves of the studio. Each has an aesthetic as well as a functional role to play.

The fireplace is a black painted steel tube 36 in. in diameter (drawing, right). The cylinder rises from a recessed tiled circle in the floor that is ringed with steel edging, and continues to the roof without changing size. It is supported in the center by a short length of 2-in. steel pipe welded to a flange at the base of the cylinder. A semicircular opening was cut away and fitted with a simple horizontal grate to form the firebox. The damper, a huge flat plate, is suspended in the tube and operated by a steel rod outside the cylinder.

The garage-door mechanism (photo right) is another example of functional decoration. Normally, the scissor hinges on pivoting garage doors are fitted with very stiff springs for counterbalancing. Instead, Schweikher suspended black cylindrical weights under the eaves to do the same work. Each of the two doors has two 20-lb. weights. They are made of 6-in. steel pipe filled with concrete. The weights hang from taut ropes that run through 6-in. pulleys, which hang from the 8x14 shoul-

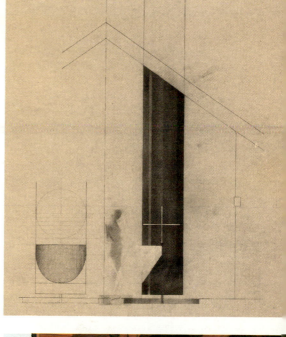

visiting critic at Yale University, he became the chairman of its architecture department. He was admittedly naive about how sensitive egos can be in the charged atmosphere of a school receiving constant national attention. After three embattled years, he left Yale to become the head of the architecture department at Carnegie Tech, where he stayed until he retired from teaching 11 years later.

A matter of style—Schweikher has many boyish qualities—an easily kindled enthusiasm, a quick grin, and an almost deferential politeness. He isn't aggressive or pretentious, and he is bewildered by people who are. He's a reductionist who insists on seeing the world in simple, almost

idealized terms. Sometimes this makes him appear naive; at other times it's refreshing.

Schweikher doesn't like being part of the crowd, and in a gentlemanly way he is something of a rebel. When I asked him why he's not a member of the AIA, he said that he had joined twice, certainly enough for any man. The first time was as a young architect in Chicago. He didn't renew his membership when he found the local chapter was reluctant to take stands on controversial political issues, even when they involved the architectural community. He tried again years later when officials at Carnegie Tech pressured him to join. This time, he found the whole thing "a colossal bore," and soon resigned.

Schweikher doesn't see himself

as having a style, or even a philosophy of design. He recalls the day that Mies van der Rohe told students at Carnegie Tech to "find a philosophy and stick with it, as Paul has done." Schweikher regrets not having interrupted to find out what his own philosophy was. "I spent my life looking for a style," he says. "I copied a lot, there's no doubt about that, and maybe more than I needed to, but I did it honestly."

When I asked him if his designs had been influenced greatly by the work of any of his contemporaries, he replied that the influences were largely negative. So many of the basic approaches to design had been previously explored by others. He admits to backing off from an idea more than once because it wasn't in the

mainstream. "Looking back," he says, "the really successful people were the ones that could go straight ahead as if with blinders."

During my visit with Schweikher, I asked him why he had chosen a particular size for a beam or height for a ceiling. He answered in practical terms that I understood as a former carpenter, but that didn't explain why his design worked aesthetically. I later realized that one of the reasons Schweikher's architecture appeals to me is its practical, functional nature. Combined with that is his unfailing sense of proportion and his feel for what works. I suspect these abilities aren't based on hard, rational decision-making. Instead they seem intuitive, sensed even before they are understood. —*P.S.*

Photo and drawings: Paul Schweikher

der beam. The other end of each rope is fastened to the garage doors with eyebolts.

Japanese influence—Schweikher traveled to Japan in 1937, and the trip left an indelible impression. He talks enthusiastically about what he saw on this first trip and brought back with him. "Foremost was the pristine concentration of geometric order that was everywhere," he says. Some of that same order is obvious in his Arizona house—the spaced 1x4 cedar battens inside and out, and the repeated pattern of the quarry tile that covers the floor of the entire main house. The red gravel driveway and court are patiently raked in diagonal patterns each day.

The bathroom sink (photo below) is an adaptation of basins used in Japanese country inns. It is a long narrow trough with 8/4 maple sides and a black marble bottom and backshelf. Angle-iron ledgers keep it suspended between two walls that are a little more than 4½ ft. apart. Only the waste pipe for the drain shows below the 8-in. high maple front panel. The acrylic privacy screens for the bathroom, which are fixed in narrow cedar frames and slide in wooden tracks in the floor, are a more durable version of Japanese *shoji*.

Hindsight—Paul and Dorothy Schweikher say that the house works as well after 11 years as it did on the drafting board—no mean accomplishment. But Schweikher still regrets not being able to design a frame with more sophisticated joinery because of the restraints of money and inexperienced labor. He sees the cross-beams in the house as being clumsy compared to Japanese designs and thinks he might have done something with trusses to make the beam ends lighter and give them a better sense of closure. He criticizes the catwalk for being too imposing. Had he made it a single, narrow box beam, he feels he could have diminished its presence.

The single biggest failure in the house was the corrugated metal roof. Schweikher specified 18-ga. metal, but could only get 22 ga., and this distorted somewhat in installation. More important, he had problems getting paint to bond to the metal, and painted it three separate times before giving up and having it shingled recently. Squinting against the sun, he speculates on how the roof would have looked if he had specified a weathering steel, which is made to rust on the surface. And he worries out loud that the scale of the cedar shingles is a bit too small. □

This trough-like lavatory, made of 8/4 maple and marble, echoes the basins found in Japanese country inns. Suspended between the cedar-covered walls, the lavatory hardly blocks the view.

The evolution of a design

In Paul Schweikher's view, style is a result of the design process, not its starting point. This isn't a new philosophy for him. Interviewed by *Architectural Forum* in 1939 with his partner, Theodore Lamb, Schweikher put it this way: "If we solve the vital problems of satisfying the true requirements of the client, creating a simple workable structure, orienting the structure to sunlight, to prevailing winds, and to the physical character of the property and adjusting these to social and economic influences, we find little need for serious discussion of the building's style."

With himself as the client, he didn't see things any differently. The house he built in 1972 doesn't conform to any one style, yet it isn't just a collection of mechanical decisions.

After spending several days in the house, I found myself curious about how the design evolved. Schweikher's architecture doesn't feel forced, and I wanted to know how the lines got on the paper. The same question occurs to me when I hear a song I particularly like. He began answering by using my musical analogy.

Schweikher likens the design process to composing at the piano. At first what comes out are small snatches of melodies and leftover notions of things you've always wanted to try out and never have. As each of these is exposed to the constraints of rhythm and harmony, it is refined or discarded or both. This is at once a process of elimination and an amalgamation of thoughts into a final form.

The constraints that Schweikher put on his house when he began designing in 1970 included a construction budget of $100,000 and the realization that he and Dorothy didn't need a huge, elaborate house at this point in their lives. As he began talking to contractors about his plans, he found that there weren't many craftsman in the area at the time who could handle the difficult joinery he wanted to use.

On the facing page are a few of Schweikher's early design sketches for his house. He began with a rectangular module. In the first series of drawings, he was trying to separate the confined spaces with avenues or courtyards to bring the outside in. The second series is based on juxtaposing storage spaces, an idea borrowed from Louis Kahn, who was a visiting critic at Yale with Schweikher in the early 1950s. This plan soon evolved into a series of projections where the modules lined up diagonally, creating a sawtooth roof.

In the third series, Schweikher tried out the idea of interconnected pavilions all the same size. He based this in part on a Japanese Shinto shrine he had visited. But by the time he began sketching the elevations, Schweikher realized that the concept was more appropriate to Japan than to the Arizona butte he had chosen to build on.

In the fourth series, Schweikher got bolder about using the natural slope of his building site. This plan, which concentrated on the motion of up and down, was a favorite of Schweikher's, but was priced by a local contractor at $250,000. The fifth series is much closer to the final design. It's based on the Native American longhouse. Schweikher likes big spaces, and still has a soft spot for the solid barns raised by German farmers west of Chicago, where he built his first home.

In the final design, Schweikher simplified the roof into one unbroken line. He dislikes roofs that meet at less than 90°; he says they lose their purity. But ultimately, he compromised and set the pitch at a little more than 8½-in-12—just steep enough to incorporate lofts in the studio and the main house. —*P. S.*

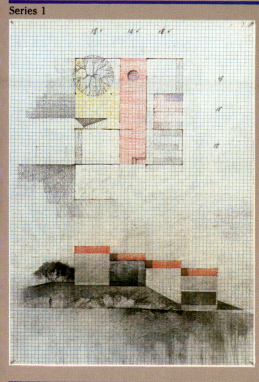

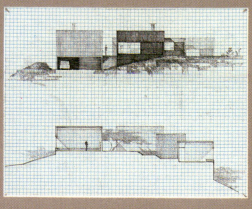

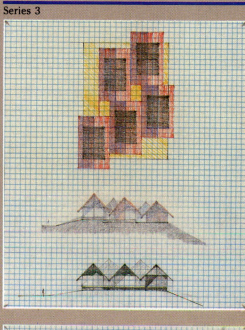

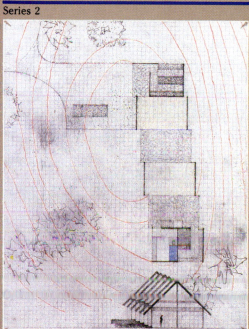

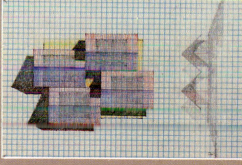

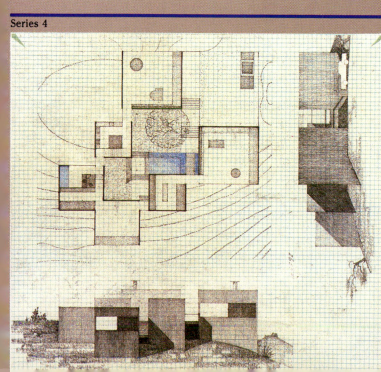

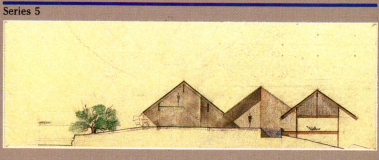

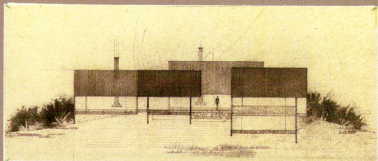

A Modular Home

Japanese-style timber construction in the foothills of the high Sierras

by Chuck Miller

The first design consideration in any Japanese house is the number and size of the tatami mats that will cover the floors. The mats are made of rice straw, tightly bound into a flat plane about 2 in. thick, then covered with a woven skin of reeds that is virtually waterproof. With care, the mats will last 30 years. The mats vary in size from province to province, but are always twice as long as they are wide. The Brackett house is designed around the largest mats (called the Kyoto size); they are 6.3 ft. long and 3.15 ft. wide. Room sizes are described by the number of mats required to cover the floors rather than by square footage. There are half-mat segments to complete the center of spiral arrangements or to allow half-mat size alcoves to project into the room.

An interest in Japan took Len Brackett to Kyoto in 1970. Persistence, dedication and luck landed him an apprenticeship with one of

Japan's foremost temple builders. Brackett spent five years with his master, absorbing the subtleties of the craft. Eventually the desire to put his own house together ended his training in Japan. Brackett and his wife, Biva, owned a small piece of wooded land near Nevada City, Calif.; they set their sights on building the house there and moved into a tiny garage, up the hill from the site, in 1976.

In any culture, budget has a lot to do with design resolutions and it's no different in Japan; as a general rule, the finer the home, the more wood goes into it. Door-frame dimensions and headers, window shapes and sizes, the purlins and rafters, literally every stick of wood in the building is part of an overall scheme of dimensional interrelationships. If there is to be a second story, the posts must be larger throughout the building to convey a sense of effortless continuity. The post dimension is therefore a critical

decision, since all other framing elements will be scaled to the posts.

Lumber is expensive in Japan and appreciated to such a degree that some species are classified by as many as 30 grades. The best grade of a local softwood can cost several hundred dollars a board foot. In California, Brackett had access to an abundance of local trees and the personal skill and energy required to build an expensive Japanese-style house on a shoestring budget.

Because the design module of each Japanese house depends on the owner and the locale, every house has its own measuring rod based on the length of the mat plus the width of a post. This measure is called a *ken* and in Brackett's house is 6.72 ft.—a 6.3-ft. mat plus a 5¼-in. (.42 ft.) square post. The measuring stick, called a *kensau*, is about 2 in. square by roughly 16 ft. long. Its four faces are filled with information denoting such dimensions as post centers, ridge

From *Fine Homebuilding* magazine (August 1981) 4:52-57

rafters and purlins, top plates for walls, and log beams, as well as the placement and size of the many complex wood joints that hold the building together. When the home is finished, the *kensau* is placed in the attic for any future needs.

Elements from both country and teahouse styles are evident in this home. The round windows with reed screens and the mud walls are examples of teahouse rusticity. The interior garden, common to both styles, illuminates the surrounding rooms. Wide overhanging eaves, the two-story firepit room with its open beam structure and smoke hole, and the relatively large size (about 1,300 sq. ft.) are country-house influences. The hipped gable roof is ubiquitous. The glassed-in verandas (photo, facing page) are an untraditional, passive solar feature.

Foundations—Traditional Japanese foundations are composed of large flat stones arranged vertically, like books in a hole in the ground (drawing, next page). Earth is then tamped between the rocks to minimize settling, and a large capstone placed on top. Each post is custom fitted to the irregularities of the stone that bears its load. There are no metal connections. Foundations vary in size according to the mass they are meant to support; the capstone raises the wooden posts above the damp earth.

Today's foundation consists of concrete grade beams with raised stem walls. Where a post-to-foundation connection is a visible element, capstones are embedded in the concrete beams, and a thin layer of earth is raked over the cured concrete to give the stones the appearance of being independent. The posts are still carved to match their individual stone.

The foundation for Brackett's house required 35 yards of concrete. As the trenches were dug, the excavated earth was set aside for use on the walls. Once the forms were in place, six dump-truck loads of sand and gravel were staged on the driveway and a gas-powered mixer brought in (the site has no power lines). Brackett built a concrete chute from an old corrugated roof and invited two dozen hardworking neighbors for concrete duty.

Building the framework—Each member of the post-and-beam framework was shaped in Brackett's shed-roofed shop, 200 yards up the hill from his homesite. The heart of this well-equipped backwoods shop is a 38-in. bandsaw capable of cutting veneer as thin as $\frac{1}{8}$ in. A 350-cc Subaru car engine powers the bandsaw, and the planer and jointer as well. There isn't a standard dimensioned piece of lumber in this entire house, so this mill was critical.

Brackett's prior experience as a lumberjack in Oregon resulted in a network of suppliers who let him know when especially fine logs were available. He selected each tree with a practiced eye and had them rough-cut at a local mill to his specifications. The green boards were then carefully stacked to air-dry. Only air-drying will do; kiln-drying affects the workability of the wood, resulting in a condition that Brackett likens to "drinking flat beer—there just isn't any fizz in kiln-dried wood."

The framing elements are all local softwoods:

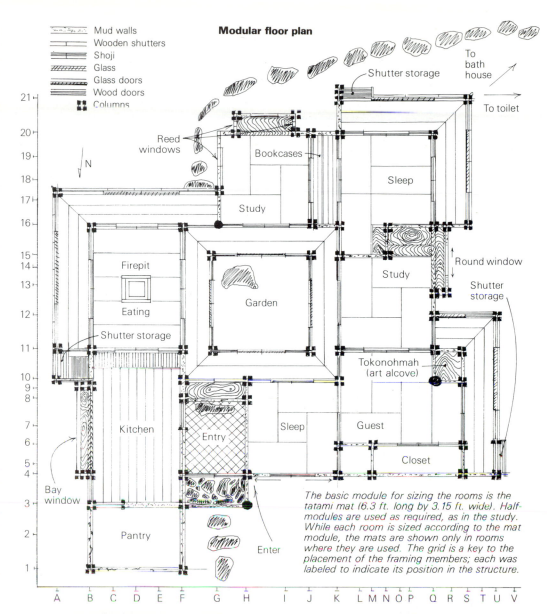

Modular floor plan

Mud walls
Wooden shutters
Shoji
Glass
Glass doors
Wood doors
Columns

The basic module for sizing the rooms is the tatami mat (6.3 ft. long by 3.15 ft. wide). Half-modules are used as required, as in the study. While each room is sized according to the mat module, the mats are shown only in rooms where they are used. The grid is a key to the placement of the framing members; each was labeled to indicate its position in the structure.

Cascading roof planes with wide overhanging eaves are major elements of Brackett's Japanese-style house (photo facing page). Left, veranda eaves seen from below are delicately structured and carefully proportioned. Overlapped cedar shingles, top right, are three deep at the edge. Above right, natural-colored mud walls surround a traditional reeded window. The mud is made from rusty red clay from the site, mixed with sand and straw.

Neighbors help complete forms for the 18-in. stem walls that are 6 in. wide and connect to adjacent grade beams waiting for capstone placement, a contemporary method (see drawing below).

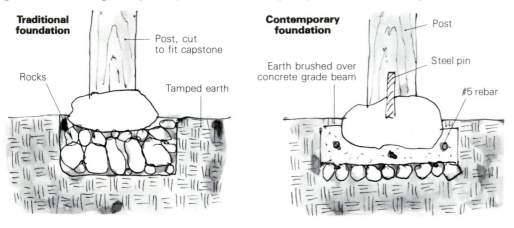

Traditional foundation
- Post, cut to fit capstone
- Rocks
- Tamped earth

Contemporary foundation
- Post
- Earth brushed over concrete grade beam
- Steel pin
- #5 rebar

sheathed and shingled to protect the house for the next two years of interior finish work. The 1x10 incense cedar sheathing, bought in bulk, was carefully inspected for grades. The best pieces were finish-planed and used for the visible roofing elements in the kitchen, firepit room and entryway. The eaves over the verandas are finished with #1 cedar shingles, three deep at the edge. Copper flashings protect the cedar sheathing. The atrium eaves are also finished in cedar shingles without flashing at the valleys; instead, the shingles are carefully woven together at this confluence. To make the shingles appear the same distance apart when the atrium eaves are seen from the inside, the shingle exposure is increased $\frac{3}{16}$ in. with each lap to allow for perspective. This also puts more shingles where the weather is most harsh and eliminates unnecessary overlap below the overhanging eaves.

The other roof surfaces were finished with asphalt-based three-tab shingles over 30-lb. roofing felt. Eventually these roofs will be covered with reddish high-fired interlocking tiles, tied to battens and counterbattens for ventilation, directly over the asphalt shingles.

Walls—Earth removed from the foundation trenches was used to finish both interior and exterior walls. For the base coat, this heavy clay soil, rich in iron and rusty red in color, was mixed with straw and applied with a trowel to a hefty lath structure of Port Orford cedar strips $\frac{3}{8}$ in. thick and $1\frac{1}{2}$ in. wide, milled from scraps. The strips run both horizontally and vertically, leaving 1-in. square voids between. Grooves cut into the posts and plates accept the laths at each end as they are sprung into place. A 4d galvanized nail secures them at the ends. In the middle of each lath network, braces cross to provide further support for the delicate cedar strips. Before the mud is applied, oil-impregnated sisal twine is wrapped around intersecting laths, 1 ft. on center, to bind the members. The 2-in. thick base layer of mud is clay soil sifted through $\frac{1}{8}$-in. screen, and 4-in. pieces of straw, cut from the bale with a chainsaw (if the straw is too long it will wad up during mixing). The measured ingredients were piled in a mound, blended with a rototiller and mixed with water and a workable consistency. This pure mud and straw wall cracks as it dries, creating fissures for the second coat to lock into. The $\frac{1}{2}$-in. thick second coat contains a lot of sand to prevent the wall from cracking; but too much sand will make the wall flake away. The recipe for this particular soil was 17 square shovels of soil to 34 square shovels of sand to 18 gallons of 1-in. long straw. The straw was cut to length in a garden mulcher, and the parts mixed in a boat by hand with a hoe.

Doors—The post-and-beam structure allows long spans, unbroken by load-bearing walls, to be filled with sliding doors. Each sliding door can be easily removed from its track. Special closets on each veranda can house the doors when they are not in use. Various combinations of room shapes and sizes are therefore available when needed, making the house truly elastic. Brackett's house has 104 sliding doors. Each door frame is of Port Orford cedar, with double

Douglas Fir, ponderosa pine, sugar pine, and Port Orford cedar. Port Orford cedar is a rare and treasured wood, highly workable, strong, rot-resistant, and possessed of the spicy aroma associated with hope chests and broken arrow shafts. The pieces used in this house were deadfalls collected in the Oregon woods, victims of the vast Tillamook forest fire of the 1930s. The other favored structural wood is sugar pine. It is easy to work and, most important, dimensionally stable. The Douglas fir in Brackett's area can twist to an alarming degree as it ages. One of the large top plates of Douglas fir torqued to the point where the ends were as much as 30° out of square with one another, resembling a giant propeller, and requiring heavy persuasion to come into place as the pieces were assembled.

When the air-dried wood was ready, each framing element was rough-cut and marked with ink into a gridwork drawn on the floor plan. Alphabetical reference points run down one axis of the building, and numerical down the other. This system keyed the hundreds of separate parts to one another as each was labeled according to its position in the framework. The ink labels always went on top of the posts and the top of the tree always pointed up, just as it did in the forest. The roughed-out pieces were then finish planed and covered with a temporary pro-

tective layer of butcher paper glued with watered-down wallpaper paste.

The three basic joints in the framing are the dovetail, the swallowtail and the mortise and tenon (drawings, facing page). Each is subject to variation as the need arises, and there are about 50 distinct modifications in this house. There are some metal connections in the frame-work, like the 30d nails that tie the rafters to the purlins, but most of the binding elements are unseen wood joints, a system a thousand years old.

Assembling the frame—Brackett chose a local wood, incense cedar, for the sill plates and cut each 5¼-in. by 6-in. piece from the heart of the tree, because the heartwood is exceptionally rot-resistant. The sill must be this massive to accept the 5¼-in. post tenons designed to resist lateral loads. Joints in the sill are dovetailed, and the entire sill is bolted to the stem walls with ⅝-in. J-bolts, 4 ft. o.c. Prior to placement, the sill was painted with two coats of creosote.

Sill completed, the neighborhood work force was again summoned for the house-raising. Stacks of finished posts, plates, rafters, purlins and beams were moved to the site from the shop, and in three days the pieces were installed according to their location on the gridwork plan.

When the framework was done, the roof was

mortise-and-tenon joints held by cedar wedges. The "bones" of the gridlike *shoji* screens, also of cedar, are notched together with an alternating half-lap system to avoid torquing; each bone is tenoned to the door frame. The grid is then covered with mulberry paper, which comes in rolls about a foot wide. The paper is applied like shingles, from the bottom of the door up, each lap centered on a horizontal bone. The glue is a blend of one tablespoon of cornstarch to a cup and a half of water, which is boiled to a jelly-like consistency and then brushed on. When all the individual paper shingles are in place, the entire door is lightly misted with water; this shrinks the paper slightly, ensuring a tight, smooth finish. The paper is surprisingly durable, but will occasionally tear and require patching. In this case, a circle of paper, large enough to overlap the torn area, is cut with pinking shears to resemble a chrysanthemum and then glued over the rip. As a time-honored proverb observes: "Where children grow, a thousand flowers will bloom."

The same cedar door frames are used to hold ⅜-in. thick redwood panels for closet doors, and for the wood-and-glass panel doors in the firepit room. Bandsawn from large cants, the panels are numbered and used adjacent to one another in neighboring doors. The glass panels are held in place by press-fit moldings, easily removable should the glass ever need replacing.

Brackett has taken advantage of a local wood's slick characteristics in constructing the door runners. Grooves cut directly into the floor plates hold inlaid strips of hard and slippery madrone, allowing the door bottoms to slide more easily. For further ease in sliding, the top track, cut into the belly of the upper lintel, is about ¼ in. higher at midspan than at the opposing posts. This barely perceptible arch between posts adds a subliminal quality of weightlessness to the entire assembly, and is accomplished by hanging the upper lintel in midspan from one of the heavy eave beams.

The veranda doors are each fitted with a heavy tempered glass panel. To allow smooth sliding, two stainless steel ball-bearing sheaves are mortised into the bottom rails of each door; they run on narrow brass tracks, nailed to the tapered threshhold. Glass is inserted through a slot in the top rail, and can be removed just by turning the door upside down.

Mechanical systems—This house is five miles from the nearest electrical power hook-up but still has electric lights and duplex outlets in every room. The source? Two deep-cycle 12-volt marine batteries designed to take recharging are linked parallel to provide low volt/high amperage service. Twelve-gauge Romex wire connects the principal circuit, supplying power to all rooms. The lights are fluorescent fixtures requiring a modest 1.8 amps per hour each. A second circuit, with only one outlet, comes off an inverter to supply the kitchen with standard 120-volt AC power requirements. This system isn't designed to run toasters and convection ovens, but used prudently, it can easily maintain the lights, the stereo and occasionally the electric mixer. An Arco photovoltaic cell mounted in a tree on the south side of the house recharges the batteries on sunny days at a maximum of 2½ amps per hour. The cell cost about $400, but the

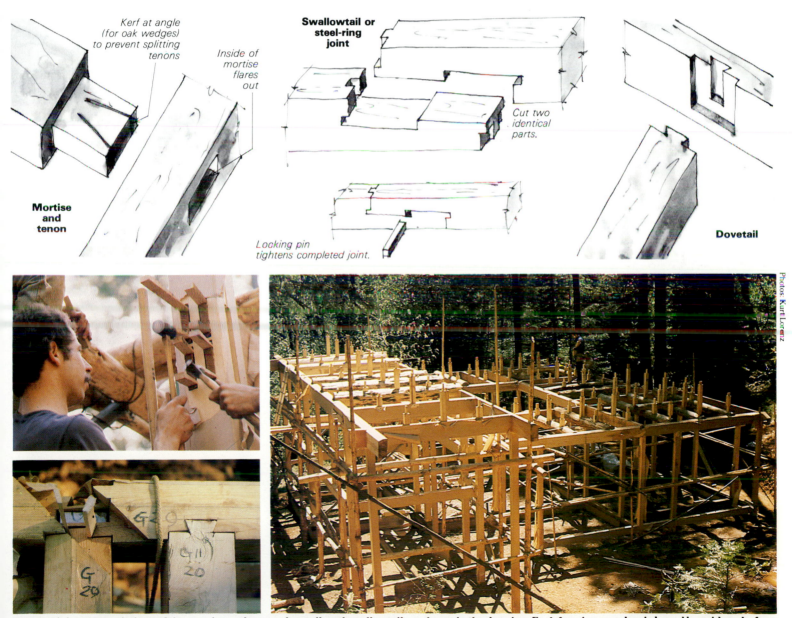

Framing joints are variations of the mortise and tenon, dovetail, and swallowtail, as shown in the drawing. Each framing member is keyed by gridmarks from the original plan. At gridmark G29, above left, beams are joined to posts with dovetail and tenon. The head of the lower dovetail on the beveled beam matches the shoulder dimension of the female counterpart. The post tenon has yet to receive its wedges. The diagonal notch picks up the hip rafter. The empty dovetail slot will hold a short cap beam. Top left, Brackett drives a wedge. Right, tenoned king posts await ridge beams and purlins. Wedged kerfs in top of beams prevent the logs from checking on the opposite (ceiling) side.

A view down the atrium hallway toward a gridded screen *(shoji)*; the atrium garden is at left and the firepit room at right. Glass panels are removed and stored in special closets during the warm months. The low windows in the firepit room are for looking out when sitting on the floor.

cost is partially offset by state and federal tax credits. Brackett likes the idea of a home power company and hopes someday to add more cells.

Another backwoods innovation is the house sprinkler system. Far from any fire hydrant, in an area that is prone to summertime blazes, the sprinklers are a realistic last line of defense. The heart of the system, an 1,800-gal. concrete tank buried 200 feet up the hill, provides water at 90 psi distributed by 1½-in. pvc pipes. The sprinklers are set to go off at 165°F in every room except the firepit room where the gauge is set at 212°F. Each bedroom has a sprinkler in the center of the room, and the closets contain a sprinkler slightly above ceiling level. The plastic pipe filled with water would melt only at extreme temperatures, but Brackett notes if that happens it will be too late anyway.

Floors—The entry and the kitchen are the only rooms in the house where shoes are allowed. Brackett chose Pennsylvania slate for the floors in these rooms; the square slates carry on the angular motif, and their blue-black color harmonizes with the wood tones. The slates are set into mortar applied to a 4-in. thick concrete slab.

The atrium hallway (photo, facing page) is Port Orford cedar, matching the cedar posts and rafters. In this focal point, the foresight in lumber selection is most evident. The pieces are magnificent boards, 1¼-in. thick and 21 in. wide, secured to the floor joists from below using hooks that remain invisible from above. Floorboards are splined together, at ends and sides. The wood, polished by each passing sock, is acquiring a luster that will improve with time.

The bedroom, study, and guest room floors are done in tatami mats on a 6-mil vapor barrier over the 1x10 subfloor. Rigid Styrofoam boards add insulation under the entire house.

The entryway and guest room hold special significance in the Japanese home; they confirm the value of human relationships, and they display the most careful details and finely patterned woods. The *tokonohmah*, or art alcove (photo bottom right), is the keystone of any traditional guest room. The alcove is a platform about 3 ft. square projecting into the room from the wall at right angles to the veranda. It is raised a few inches above the mats and visually anchored by the *tokobashira*, a natural post extending from floor to ceiling. Brackett selected this post for a gently contrasting curve, and removed the cambium layer with a concave bamboo scraper to reveal the first layer of sapwood. Inside the alcove rests a treasured object, usually a vase or an incense burner, and on the back wall hangs a picture scroll. The alcove floor is myrtlewood, splined and dovetailed together, and finished with varnish.

This house is both a showplace and a laboratory for Brackett. With it he has brought to this country a style of building that can trace its origins back 1,400 years and yet be contemporary in its use of common materials and a flexible floor plan. He hopes to build many more such homes, carefully integrating exemplary craft with Western needs. In the workshop up the hill his log decks are stocked with choice cedar and pines, waiting their turn. □

The massive sliding entry door. The slate in front of the door carries inside to the vestibule, which along with the kitchen, is the only room in the house where shoes are worn.

The atrium, left, viewed from Brackett's studio. Downspout chains at each corner direct rain runoff to stone trenches. Right, the art alcove *(tokonohmah)* is enclosed by mud walls over lath. Varnished myrtlewood floor is adjusted from below with oak wedges to compensate for expansion or contraction.

In the Japanese Tradition

Japanese and Western framing techniques blend in a hybrid farmhouse design

by Dennis Tucker

I first visited Japan in 1969, a wide-eyed 19-year-old student. I ended up staying for more than nine years. My wife, Yuko, is a native. Although I went to Japan to study Zen Buddhism and later, medicine, I became fascinated with the beauty and vitality of Japanese buildings. The basic components of wood, paper, stone and clay are proportioned to form a unity of fabric and structure that is starkly beautiful. Hand-planed wood, highly finished natural clay walls, intricate sliding paper-panel doors and windows, tightly woven straw mats and the frequent use of rounds and naturally curving wood form an environment that seems to improve with age.

After living in some large extended-family thatched-roof farmhouses, in several tile-roofed single-family dwellings and in a number of magnificent old Buddhist temples, I was determined to learn as much as I could about how these different structures were designed and built. During my last two years in Japan, I was fortunate to become the apprentice of Isao Ogura, a traditional rural carpenter who lived outside Kyoto.

One truth that emerged from my years in Japan was that although the Japanese house is assuredly a thing of beauty, it is also cold, drafty and dark. Its walls are acoustically transparent, and personal privacy is a cerebral, rather than an architectural, matter. Of all that has been written (particularly in the West) on traditional Japanese architecture as an aesthetic ideal, there has been little mention of the practical problems it poses. Because this architectural aesthetic and the precise carpentry that gives it life have become so highly formalized, it is difficult to imagine how to apply them to the conditions and demands of the 20th century.

In fact, very few Japanese houses are being built these days using the traditional materials or form. Japanese cities are filled with plastic, stucco and ferro-cement structures, because just the cost of wood makes a traditional Japanese house prohibitively expensive. Without the labors of temple carpenters and a few "old-fashioned" builders like Ogura-san in rural areas, this exacting work would be in danger of extinction.

It was this problem of how to adapt a highly stylized building tradition without violating its spirit that my wife Yuko and I puzzled over as we left Japan for 20 acres of heavily wooded land on the western slope of the Sierra Nevada mountains. We had less than five months to build our house before the rains came, no electricity within miles of our land, and all the constraints of a back-to-the-land budget.

We were fortunate that our land was densely forested. When I bought the acreage on a trip back to California three years before, I'd spent some time clearing timber and brush for a house and garden site. I had hoped that this would yield enough native wood for the house and outbuildings. After a good bit of felling, hauling to local mills, stickering and waiting, we ended up with a three-acre meadow in the middle of our land and about 30,000 bd. ft. of local hardwoods and softwoods.

The design—We began designing our house by examining the shortcomings we'd experienced in traditional houses in Japan. These homes excel in summer with their long overhangs, openness and cross-ventilation, but they are cold in the winter, chiefly because

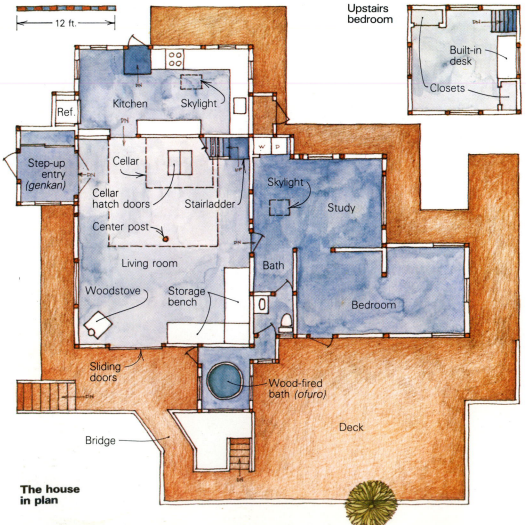

The house in plan

Upstairs bedroom — Built-in desk — Closets

Kitchen — Ref. — Skylight — Step-up entry (genkan) — Cellar — Cellar hatch doors — Center post — Stairladder — Living room — Woodstove — Storage bench — Sliding doors — Bridge — W D — Skylight — Study — Bath — Bedroom — Wood-fired bath (ofuro) — Deck

12 ft.

From *Fine Homebuilding* magazine (December 1984) 24:60-64

the cracks between the posts and walls and at window and door openings let warm air out and cold air in. This infiltration, along with uninsulated floors and the high open-beam ceiling in the typical farmhouse kitchen, makes it clear why the Japanese traditionally use small charcoal hibachis to warm themselves instead of trying to heat whole rooms or the entire house.

Our decision to heat with a single wood-stove and our desire to make the house feel bigger than its 1,400 sq. ft. determined a more open floor plan (drawing, facing page) than is typical of most Japanese houses. As a result, we greatly exceeded the usual eight-mat limit in the living room (straw mats, or *tatami*, which are approximately 3 ft. by 6 ft., are the traditional modular measure of Japanese rooms). We did adopt the central pole *(di-koko bashira)*, common to Japanese farm-houses (photo above right).

Above this central support, we designed a second-story room that would take advantage of the views and leave the rest of the roof radiating away in all directions as is traditional. Access to this room would be through a stair opening small enough to prevent overheating in the winter. The stair ladder that reaches up to this opening was one of the many places in the house that naturally curving rounds were to be used.

Although our house plan incorporated the traditional Japanese lower-level entry *(genkan)* (photo below right) with the intention of creating a shoeless interior space, we also decided to use hardwood flooring for its durability and ease of maintenance rather than *tatamis*. All of the door and window openings are Western style, although we made some of the French doors into simple wooden-track sliders. We also used a good deal more hand-planed interior paneling than is traditional. For added light, we incorporated several skylights and borrowed from temple architecture by using plaster rather than earth-colored walls. I used button board for my lath, and found that system as easy and quick as gyp board in the small, infill spaces that I had to deal with.

Post and beam—The frame that would support all of this was to be ponderosa pine (for the largest structural beams) and incense cedar (for posts and lesser beams). Because our

Upon returning from Japan, the author and his wife had less than five months to build their house before the winter rains. The roof framing is Western, but they maintained traditional Japanese forms by using a central half-story with shallow hips radiating out from it (facing page). Instead of the traditional Japanese scheme of small interconnecting rooms, they needed a more open plan in order to heat the house with a single woodstove. The traditional central post *(di-koko bashira)* served to open up the living room (above right). The flooring is 12-in. wide 4/4 tan oak, harvested on the site. You step up into the living room from the *genkan*—the traditional Japanese entry (right). The kitchen pass-through can be seen at left, and the ladder to the upper bedroom is ahead.

Keeping the joinery simple

Japanese temple carpentry is known for its intriguingly complex joints, but the author chose some of the simpler versions, shown below, from traditional farmhouse construction. Where two roofs converged (photo, below), he used a cross-lap joint to mate the corbel and gable-end beam, and he seat-cut the 4x gable-end rafter and the 2x barge rafter to fit over the top.

¼-in. taper

Lag bolt set at 45°

Non-traditional tapered joint

This very strong joint is held with a hidden lag bolt and was used frequently for joist-to-beam connections that had to deal initially with shrinking green timbers, and later with seasonal wood movement.

Last 6 in. of beam slightly tapered

Ai-gaki (cross-lap joint)

This cross-lap joint can be used anywhere beams intersect, whether it's over walls or in the ceiling.

Koshikake-ari-tsugi (dovetail lap joint) and koshikake-tsugi (simple lap joint)

These two lap joints were used to splice beams together along a wall.

Hira-hozo (true mortise and tenon)

This classic joint was typically used to connect the cedar posts to pine beams they supported.

Working with rounds

Natural log poles, or rounds, are used extensively in Japanese carpentry. Structurally, a downward-curving round acts like a truss when used as a header or an exposed roof member. Peeled rounds are also central to the Japanese aesthetic, as expressed in tea-house carpentry or the elegant recess (tokonoma) in the main living area used to display scrolls and art objects. Madrone, which is common in the Sierra foothills, works well for these applications if you take the time to find the right pieces.

Rounds can also be used as a quick, inexpensive source for framing members where they won't show, or where their rustic appearance is appropriate. Although I used milled floor joists under my house, the large expanse of deck surrounding it is supported entirely on incense cedar rounds 6 in. to 10 in. in diameter. These fairly straight poles were simple to limb and buck to length. As joists, the rounds were kept long. I used a 6-in. power plane to flatten them on the top for the decking, and then cut out a rough mortise every 8 ft. to accept the log posts that support them. The log joists were set in place with a water level to get their flat top surfaces all at the same height. The posts were then chamfered at the top with a chainsaw to fit the mortises, cut to height individually and set on their concrete pier blocks. This makes a sturdy deck, and yet requires few tools and goes quickly. It took me just two days to frame up the entire structure ready for decking using only the planer, string, two squares and a water level.

The drawings at right illustrate a simple method for establishing a flat surface on any round. Start by taking a few passes with the planer set to a maximum depth. This will create a fairly wide flat. Then fasten a string along the length of the round to find any dips or swales by sighting underneath the string from the side. For things like decks and the

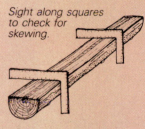

Check beneath taut string for dips.

decorative pole joists in the kitchen, a ¼-in. variation in 16 ft. was accurate enough. A few more selective passes with the planer will flatten the surface end to end.

You also need to check that the surface you have created isn't twisted or skewed. The easiest way to do this is by placing a framing square at each end

Sight along squares to check for skewing.

of the log. By sighting down the length of the round across the tops of the squares (and by gradually moving them together), you'll be able to see any twists and correct them. —D. T.

---

design was an open one and the rooms were considerably larger than their residential counterparts in Japan, we had all of the structural members milled to the heavier temple proportions: 5½ in. square for the posts, 3 in. by 5½ in. for half-posts to frame openings, and 6x8 and 6x12 for most of the beams. We also used the temple interval of six *shaku* (about 6 ft. o. c.) for the posts. In general, the Japanese use the beam or header at the top of the wall at the full dimension, and then reduce the remaining members in ⅛-in. to ½-in. increments from the top to the bottom, and from the outside to the inside. This ensures that no edges remain exposed and that these beam faces will be inset from the chamfers on the posts they butt.

I centered 2x3 (actually, 1½-in. by 2¾-in.) horizontal nailers between the posts every 2 ft. or so vertically. I glued and nailed more of these nailers on the inside of the posts and beams to complete the grid and to eliminate the problem of wall-to-post separation. This also gave me room to stuff the wall with fiberglass batts. I used plywood shear panel on the outside of the nailing grid at key spots in the frame, with cedar board and batt siding or stucco panels as an outer covering.

In the open-beam kitchen of traditional thatched-roof farmhouses (wari buki), the interlocking log joists are visible, but the typical Japanese roof structure is a hidden marvel. A Western roof, however, is much faster to build, and better braced. For these reasons, although our roof design is a composite of traditional

Japanese elements, the understructure is standard frame construction using 2x6 rafters. For rafter tails, we found the Western fascia well enough suited to the Japanese house.

Preparing the frame—At first, the only electricity we had on the site was a gadget that produced 110 AC-DC when hooked up to the generator of my old ¾-ton truck. This was sufficient to power my 6-in. Japanese portable planer when we had to reduce the size of a beam or post. The rest of the time I used hand tools. Since my only experience in building had been in Japan, I used my Japanese tools and the methods I'd learned from Ogura-san. I laid out the beams from their center using the Japanese inkpot (whose closest Western relative is the chalkbox), a bamboo pencil and an angle square. Centerline measurements are usually used in Japanese carpentry, as they are in American log building, so milling and planing won't affect the layout. I've used feet and inches in recent additions to my house, but back then I was measuring in Chinese feet.

Early on, we discovered that the small local mills to which we had dragged our lumber three years ago had been less than conscientious in milling the timbers to our specs. Every beam required some serious remilling. We organized this process as best we could by waiting until we had a number of members to do. We would then rev up the old truck, with Yuko in the cab to keep the throttle going, and I would plane like there was no tomorrow.

Most of the joinery is mortise and tenon,

dovetail, or simple lap joints (drawings and photo, facing page). By staying with the more basic joints and using heavy Douglas fir dowels or ⅜-in. lag bolts to prevent movement and separation of the still-green beams, we ended up with a tight and very strong structure. With the exception of temple construction, using hidden metal fasteners to strengthen critical joints is quite common in Japan today, even among carpenters who still build traditional Japanese houses.

All the structural members were milled, cut to size, mortised for joints, hand-planed, wrapped in paper and assigned their letter-number designation on a sectional grid on the plan in the traditional manner. We kept the protective paper on until the finish coat of plaster was applied. I had added a liberal coat of Watco Natural to all the wood before wrapping to protect it further. The amount of attention each beam received at this stage might seem inordinate to someone used to stud framing, but it goes remarkably fast when set up in an assembly-line manner. Yuko and I cut and planed all of the structural components for the house in two months.

The day before the raising, a friend and I assembled almost the entire frame flat on the subfloor of the house in a dry run. There were major differences in the width of many beams and posts, and we had a frantic last day of preparation for the raising. Things went well—the main portion of the house, with the help of six neighbors, went up in six hours. The traditional house raising (muneage) is

Illustrations: Frances Ashforth

The study is one of two gable-roofed additions to the original house. Tucker used Japanese temple proportions that call for 6x posts and beams. Remaining posts and lintels are reduced in size in increments of ⅛ in. to ½ in. from the top down, and from the outside to the inside of the wall. The unmilled header on the left is a madrone log. The surfaces of all the finish materials in the house are hand-planed.

an exhilarating experience, not much different from a barn raising or timber-frame raising in North America. Once the final joint is driven into place with a large wooden mallet called a *kakiya*, a party follows at which a liberal amount of sake is drunk and everyone takes a turn at traditional folk songs. Ours was no exception. The next day, the winter's first storm hit us. It lasted a week.

Interior finish—In the case of a Japanese house, the initial ease with which it goes up is somewhat deceptive; another year-and-a-half elapsed before our house was truly complete. There seems to be a common misconception about Japanese carpentry that a great deal of this time is spent hand-planing the finish materials. In fact, a very small amount of my time was spent in this pleasant activity, even though every interior surface, including wall paneling, posts, beams and ceilings, was hand-planed. I spent far more time hand-joining and laying the tan oak floor in the living room and the madrone floor in the kitchen. These woods aren't commonly used for flooring, so it was a calculated risk to have them milled in the first place. With their ends painted, the boards were stickered under the enormous weight of all of the posts and beams in an uncovered lumber pile for three years. They then spent another six months indoors before I laid the flooring. The boards were milled at 4/4, and ran 12 in. wide on the average. I laid them over ½-in. plywood with 2½-in. ring-

shank nails that we set deeply and then plugged with maple dowels. But planks that wide still move, and the floor shrank about ⅛ in. per joint the year after it was installed.

Without a power pole outside our door, we have used a variety of sources for energy, and they've worked out well. For our domestic hot water, we use a system of solar panels in the summer, and a convection heating unit (Holly Hydra Heater, made by Suntronics, PO Box 864, Petaluma, Calif. 94953) inside the woodstove in the winter, with a conventional propane hot-water heater as a backup. Our *ofuro* (Japanese bath) is also heated by a combination of solar energy and the woodstove, as well as by a small Japanese wood-fired heater made for just this purpose.

Our electrical needs break down into two systems as well. Our 12-volt house current draws on a bank of batteries that have a 600-amp/hour storage capacity. The electricity is supplied by photovoltaic cells on the roof and an on-demand propane-gas generator located in an outbuilding. The generator does double duty by running our 110-volt appliances at the same time it's charging our 12-volt system. In the time it takes to do a wash, we can be using the floor buffer, pump water from our well into the holding tank, and be assured of another two days of 12-volt electricity from our batteries. Our "utility bill" runs around $30 per month year-round. Progress marches on, however, and the power poles will soon be running past our land.

Final approval—By using modified Western framing techniques to build the walls and roof, we not only saved a lot of time but also achieved the original objectives for our house: good year-round thermal qualities, spaciousness and increased natural light. Most important to us, we attempted to make these modifications without losing sight of the aesthetic. Although the use of Western-style doors and windows and the hardwood floors make the house decidedly un-Japanese, the classical structure, proportions, finishing techniques and colors, textures and materials are generally traditional.

After completing most of the house, we returned to Japan in 1981 for a short visit. Wondering how my old carpentry teacher would react to our efforts, my wife and I drove to the remote village in the central highlands of western Honsho, where I'd lived for six years. Disappointed at not finding Ogura-san at his shop, we dropped pictures off with a note and drove on to meet someone else. That night, Ogura-san and his wife surprised us with a visit. He was dragging a huge magnum bottle of sake and grinning from ear to ear. He declared our hybrid "a real Japanese house." Although that may be true in spirit only, I owe Isao Ogura my thanks for his patience in sharing a beautifully refined answer to the question of shelter. □

Dennis Tucker is a doctor of acupuncture practicing in Nevada City, Calif.

Cobblestone Cottage

There's a hybrid structure under its roof

by Don Price

Dave Menefee is an agile mason, with one foot in the twentieth century and the other in Elizabethan England. I've worked with Menefee off and on for ten years or so in southern Michigan. During one joint venture in 1985, I'd seen Menefee draw many versions of a Cotswold cottage on his breakfast placemat. Six months later, he asked me to take a look at the concrete-block foundation of a Cotswold-style cottage that he was building near Ann Arbor.

But work on the cottage began long before Menefee invited me to look at its foundation. The owner of the cottage, Jamie Valen, had been thinking of building a house for several years. By 1984, she was anxious that the cottage exist somewhere rather than just in her imagination, and asked Menefee to work with her in developing the details and building the house.

Hammering out the plan—Although Valen wanted the look of a cottage for her house, she needed considerable room for a painting studio. And should she ever move, she wanted a house with reasonable resale value. For these reasons the house had to be larger than mere cottage status would imply. A steep roof would allow the house to look one-story yet hide a second floor.

At $100,000 or less, Valen's construction budget was tight for the region and size of the house, and it called for the judicious use of materials. Valen had lived in a house built of concrete block and liked the material for its inherent solidness. Menefee, who is also a timber framer, agreed that a masonry house with a stone veneer would look most natural, but thought that timber framing would add to the house's Elizabethan quality. Timber framing the entire house could be too costly and time-con-

suming, so Menefee came up with a hybrid solution of timber framing, concrete-block masonry and conventional wood-stud framing, all with a stone veneer. The house would have the appearance of a centuries-old stone cottage and the energy performance of a modern one.

Siting of the house was as important as the use of materials. The site is bordered by woods on the north and east, and slopes down to the woods on the east. To take advantage of view and sun, living and dining areas would have a southeast exposure. The kitchen would be on the northeast corner, avoiding summer sun. Roof overhangs and deep-set windows would keep out the worst of the summer sun, but would allow the winter sun to warm the downstairs bedrooms, which would face southwest.

The floor plan is L-shaped. One leg of it—the great room—is where the timber-frame

From *Fine Homebuilding* magazine (June 1989) 54:83-87

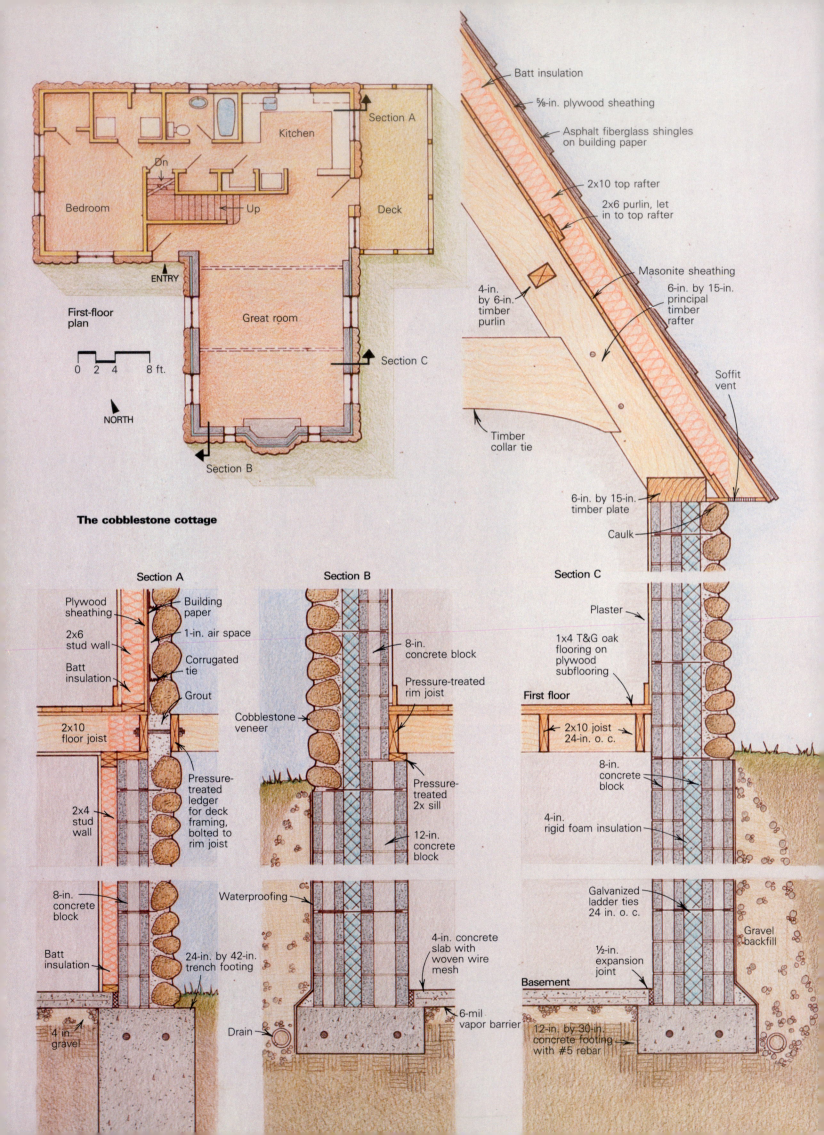

First-floor plan

Bedroom

Kitchen

On

Up

ENTRY

Great room

Deck

Section A

Section C

Section B

0 2 4 8 ft.

NORTH

The cobblestone cottage

Batt insulation

⅝-in. plywood sheathing

Asphalt fiberglass shingles on building paper

2x10 top rafter

2x6 purlin, let in to top rafter

Masonite sheathing

6-in. by 15-in. principal timber rafter

4-in. by 6-in. timber purlin

Soffit vent

Timber collar tie

6-in. by 15-in. timber plate

Caulk

Section A

Plywood sheathing

2x6 stud wall

Batt insulation

Building paper

1-in. air space

Corrugated tie

Grout

2x10 floor joist

2x4 stud wall

Pressure-treated ledger for deck framing, bolted to rim joist

Section B

8-in. concrete block

Pressure-treated rim joist

Cobblestone veneer

Pressure-treated 2x sill

12-in. concrete block

Section C

Plaster

1x4 T&G oak flooring on plywood subflooring

First floor

2x10 joist 24-in. o. c.

8-in. concrete block

4-in. rigid foam insulation

8-in. concrete block

Batt insulation

24-in. by 42-in. trench footing

4 in. gravel

Waterproofing

4-in. concrete slab with woven wire mesh

6-mil vapor barrier

Drain

Galvanized ladder ties 24 in. o. c.

Gravel backfill

½-in. expansion joint

Basement

12-in. by 30-in. concrete footing with #5 rebar

structure is most evident (floor plan, facing page). The rest of the house, containing kitchen, bathrooms, bedrooms and studio, would be more conventionally framed. Valen often uses crutches as an aid in walking, due to a childhood bout with polio. Although she negotiates stairs in a quick manner, she thought a ground-floor bedroom would be in order, leaving the upper spaces for guests and art projects. A second-floor studio would overlook the great room, borrowing space from there to enlarge its own perceived size. The slope of the site would allow the northeast part of the basement to be a walk-out, below a first-level wooden deck. The basement would have plumbing stubbed out for future expansion.

Hand-dressing the timber frame—In the fall of 1984, Menefee took delivery of 6,800 lb. of red oak for the timber-frame roof structure of the great room, feeling some trepidation at the lumber's great bulk.

Working at a measured pace, Menefee took his time with the timbers, first using a broadax and adze to remove the mill markings and to give the surface a scuffed, hewn look. That same winter and spring, he cut and joined the frame in the open field. Hand tools were the rule of the day (top photo, next page). A 2-in. dia. auger provided a rough opening for the 2-in. mortises; and handsaws, drawknives, chisels and slicks were used to shape both mortises and tenons and to make peg stock.

The design of the frame was inspired by traditional curved framing, with two curved braces and a two-piece curved collar tie (middle photo next page). Menefee used a 6-in. by 10-in. timber for the top half of each tie and cut a curve into the bottom of a 6-in. by 14-in. timber for the lower half, leaving 4 in. at its narrowest point. The 6-in. thick curved braces were hewn from 7-in. by 20-in. stock. He hewed two pairs of principal rafters, each a substantial 6 in. by 15 in., and cut common rafters and purlins to 4 in. by 6 in. Plates for rafters were cut to 6 in. by 15 in.

Readying the timber roof was good winter work. With the help of a backhoe, Menefee and his crew lifted the trusses onto plates leveled on the ground, placed the purlins, then snugged the assembly together on a temporary base of loose block. Later on, a crane would lift the entire roof into place atop the finished block walls. In place of a last set of principal rafters at the gable end would be concrete-block wall, to be built after the roof was in place. Looking stout in the extreme, the assembled timber roof sat at grade to the side of the foundation, awaiting spring and the masonry walls.

Block walls, double-thick—Although I knew of the plans for the cottage from an early date, I was still surprised when I saw Menefee laying double wythes of block on the south part of the house during my visit to look at the foundation (photo above right). He spaced the wythes 4 in. apart and tied them together with ladder ties spaced at 2 ft. o. c., fitting two lay-

On the gable-end wall of the great room, the 12-in. inner wythe of the two-wythe block foundation allows bearing room for floor joists next to an 8-in. block first-floor wall. Four-in. block makes a continuous wall where the firebox foundation angles out. At the two side walls, the inner wythe is 8-in. block, which will continue to 8 ft. above the finished floor.

The outer wythe of 8-in. concrete block drops with the grade towards the basement walk-out. A 4-in. gap left between wythes is room enough for two layers of Styrofoam insulation. Ladder ties for the stone veneer are laid in the inner wythe at 24-in. o. c.

ers of 2-in. rigid Styrofoam board between the wythes as he went (section drawings B and C, p. 94). Menefee followed the angled foundation for the fireplace using the same method. I thought this looked both labor- and material-intensive, but when Menefee described the use of the two wythes, his logic became clear.

The inner wythe of the foundation for the south leg of the house continued up to form the great-room walls and to support the timber-frame roof. The outer 8-in. wythe would support an 8-in. stone veneer. Eight-in. block was used in the inner foundation walls that are parallel to the floor framing (section drawing C, p. 94), but to provide a ledge for the floor joists at the end wall, Menefee used 12-in. block (section drawing B, p. 94). Where the grade drops and the basement wall is exposed, the stone veneer continues to the footing and is backed by an 8-in. block wall (section drawing A, p. 94). It was fairly tricky to follow the dropping grade with a stepped outer wythe (bottom photo, previous page).

Menefee asked me one day if I thought his grandfather would have liked this house. F. N. Menefee, an engineering professor at the University of Michigan, had built his own version of an English cottage in Ann Arbor in the 1920s. The elder Menefee's cottage, published in the September 1927 edition of *Building Age and National Builder*, was built from stucco-covered rammed earth (compressed with pneumatic tampers) in an attempt to bring an age-old building process back into use for modern houses. I visited the rammed-earth house with Menefee and thought it had held up well, and I allowed that Grandfather Menefee would approve of his grandson's own blend of traditional and modern building techniques.

Topping it off—In the spring, Menefee completed the block work for the timber-roofed great room. A crane was used to lift the entire frame and place it on the interior 8-in. block wall. Great care was taken to lower the roof uniformly to keep the walls from being stressed. All went smoothly. The 15-in. wide timber plates were set on the block wall to allow a wide overhang on the outside—enough to top the 4-in. space between the block and the stone veneer—and a fraction of an inch on the inside (section drawing C, p. 94). Later, when the house was closed in, Valen found a coating to finish the block wall and bring it level with the edge of the timber plate. The coating, a premixed cement product called Thoro-Stucco (Thoro System Products, Inc., 7800 N. W. 38th St., Miami, Fla. 33166), adhered uniformly to the block, hiding the mortar lines satisfactorily.

To provide insulation for the timber-frame roof structure, a second roof frame was added using Masonite sheathing, 2x10s and batt insulation. A Cotswold-style slat roof was beyond Valen's budget, so the roof was finished with diamond-shaped asphalt shingles from a local roofing-supply company.

Framing the house. In the photo above, David Menefee hand-dresses commercially milled timbers before joining them to make the roof structure of the great room. All timbers were ordered in 7-in. widths and dressed down about an inch. Both dressing and joinery were done on the ground, and the assembled roof sat at grade on a temporary foundation of loose concrete blocks while Menefee laid the block foundation and first floor of the house. The roof structure was then hoisted by crane and set in place on the great-room walls (photo left). Principal rafters are 6 in. by 15 in., common rafters and purlins are 4 in. by 6 in., and the curved tie is made up of two 6-in. wide timbers. The 15-in. wide plate overhangs the wall slightly on the inside and will be flush with a plaster wall finish. The outside overhang of the plate accommodates the cobblestone veneer. In the photo below, the house is almost completely framed. The great-room roof structure, right, is covered by a second structure of 2x10s, allowing for the addition of batt insulation. The remainder of the house is conventionally framed with 2x6 walls and 2x10 rafters. The pocket shed dormer allows light into the second floor under the steep roof.

Stonewalled—Menefee and Valen had both considered cut stone as a veneer, but to save dressing charges, they settled on cobblestone, a naturally rounded stone left in abundance by glaciers. Fifty tons would cover the house. But Menefee wanted to use cut limestone for window sills and for quoins in the endwall. Valen objected to the cost, and this difference of opinion brought the project to a standstill after the shell was complete. The loss of momentum provided a needed break while everyone rested over the winter and resolved the remaining issues concerning finishes. Valen and Menefee finally agreed that limestone was too expensive and that cobblestone would serve for sills, and concrete block would be used for quoins on the chimney.

When work commenced in the spring, Menefee laid up the stone veneer, tying it to the block by ladder ties and to the stud walls by corrugated ties. He raked the joints deeply and evenly, making strong shadows and giving the wall a well-ordered texture that changes with the light (photo p. 93). The deep-set joints occasionally resulted in a stone falling from the top level after a day's work, but it was replaced the next day and stayed put after the mortar cured. Somewhere in these walls is a loose stone—a place to keep the house key. Even with some looking, I haven't been able to find it.

Concrete-block quoins—It was agreed that limestone was not in the budget, but the edges of firebox and chimney still needed the crisp definition of quoins to keep them from blurring with the cobblestone. Menefee decided to use manufactured angled concrete block as quoins and to give them a coating that would mimic stone.

Menefee concocted a recipe made up of one 50-lb. bag of Thoro-Stucco, a 25-lb. bag of silica sand (a clean, sharp sand often used for sandblasting), three shovels-full of air-entrained portland cement, one 3-lb. box of light-buff mortar tint and 1 gal. Acryl 60, an admixture that improves cohesion and adhesion (Akryl 60 is made by Thoro System Products). This amount was enough to feed the three-dozen hungry concrete blocks that make up the quoins and the top of the fire box. Menefee mixed the materials with a little water into a very stiff batter, then allowed it to "fatten" in the mortar box. Before applying the mixture to the block, he wet the block thoroughly. He applied the mixture to the block with a plastering trowel, using a redwood float to drive the mixture into the voids of the block and to bring fines to the surface. The sand gives the surface a limestone-like finish. The result was a sharp-looking chimney (photo p. 93), and the budget was still intact.

Modern comfort inside—Although the timber frame is a handsome sight, the visual focus of the living room on a cool day is a crackling fire in the fireplace. Its cast-in-place concrete mantel is tied to the cobblestone surround with reinforcing. Menefee formed the

The timber frame and thick, beveled window jambs add to the English character of the cottage. The Rumford-style cobblestone fireplace has a tinted cast-concrete mantel.

mantel early in construction and tinted the concrete to give it a softer color. His first batch took on a heavy red color and was quickly discarded in the footing trench, but the second batch was a success and had the color of a faded, fallen maple leaf.

Menefee normally would have applied his mason's frown to any chimney placed on an outside wall, both for historical and energy reasons. But the thoroughly insulated double-wall construction took care of any heat loss.

Many owner/builders, in a burst of self-reliance, often overlook professional advice in window placement. Valen, though, did extensive research on her own, and the use of ventilation and light in the cottage is successful—especially important for a stone building that could otherwise appear cold. The jambs in the

thick walls are beveled inward to help bring light to the interior (photo above). Cross-ventilation was a major concern, so each room has openings on at least two walls. The Marvin windows (Warroad, Minn. 56763) with true divided lights are not only sympathetic to the style but they scoop in the breeze on warm days.

The mass of the walls helps to stabilize temperature swings, winter and summer. Even without air-conditioning, the inside of the house is 10° to 15° cooler than the outside temperature during warm weather. After Valen's first winter, the heating bills were much lower than expected for a house this size in Michigan. □

Don Price is a builder in Ann Arbor, Michigan. Photos by Jamie Valen and David Menefee except where noted.

Building with Stress-Skin

Laminated, insulated panels offer new ways to build economical, energy-efficient houses

by Alex Wade

Many of the clients I work with are owner-builders who want livable, energy-efficient houses for as little money as possible. The post-and-beam designs I've come to specialize in are meant to be built quickly and economically, with special consideration given to the local climate and available materials, as well as to the skill of the builders. Over the last 15 years, I've been able to improve the speed, economy and quality of this kind of construction by using stress-skin panels to enclose simplified post-and-beam frames.

Stress-skin panels are rigid sheets (usually 4 ft. by 8 ft.) made from foam insulation and various sheathing materials such as plywood, waferboard and drywall. The sheathing is bonded to both faces of the foam (see *FHB #24*, pp. 58-59 for information on how stress-skin panels are made), producing a laminated panel that has unusual shear strength and insulative value.

Laminated building panels had been used for years in commercial construction before a handful of timber framers recognized their suitability for enclosing finely joined frames some 10 years ago. Stress-skin panels gave these traditional-style framers a fast, effective way to fill the space between timbers with insulation, exterior sheathing and drywall (see *FHB #24*, pp. 54-58). It hasn't taken very long for stress-skins to catch on, and they have uses that reach far beyond timber frames. In fact, stress-skin panels and low-cost construction go hand in hand.

Stress-skin construction—To understand how stress-skin panels affect the economy and strength of a building, let's consider an analogy based on the evolution of auto designs. The traditional oak timber frame with its pegged, tight-fitting mortise-and-tenon joinery can be likened to the heavyweight chassis of an old-fashioned, full-size automobile designed with a separate body and frame. The often ornate body parts fastened to this gas-guzzling structural system weren't expected to make it stronger. In similar fashion, the traditional oak timber frame is massively sized, and then strengthened further with knee braces. Joined together properly, the frame can stand on its own perfectly well, so the

Builder Kevin Berry and crew tilt a stress-skin panel into place against a frame designed by the author. Revising construction details to take advantage of stress-skin's strength, size and insulative qualities will lead to a new generation of economical, energy-efficient houses.

From *Fine Homebuilding* magazine (February 1985) 25:42-46

Types of stress-skin construction

Enclosed-frame designs call for nonstructural stress-skin panels (one face of the foam core is clad with drywall) to be fastened to the outside face of a timber frame with spikes and adhesive caulk. Even nonstructural panels have enough shear resistance to replace the many knee braces used in most traditional timber-frame buildings. As a result, frame joinery can be simplified, cutting lumber costs and speeding erection time. In the frame shown above, major posts are 4x4s, and simple lap joints are used where girts meet over posts. Temporary braces hold the frame plumb and square until the stress-skin panels are applied.

Structural stress-skin panels must have plywood or waferboard bonded to both faces of the foam core with construction adhesive rated for structural use. Structural panels also have to be joined together edge to edge more solidly than non-structural panels, usually with wood splines. Once trucked to the site, these panels are simply tilted up onto a footing, subfloor or slab and joined with splines and spray-on adhesive to form the walls of the building (photo above right). Rough openings for doors and windows can be cut before or after wall raising. With cross-bracing (usually floor or ceiling joists) to keep wall panels from bowing out, structural stress-skins can also be used for the roof.

Hybrid stress-skin panel designs borrow construction details from structural-panel systems and enclosed-frame designs. In the design shown in the drawing, less expensive non-structural panels can be used in 4x8 size. Horizontal and vertical 2x6 splines tie panels together, supporting the stress-skin walls and also the ledger board to which the floor joists are fastened. Interior loads are carried by the ledgers and a single girder that is supported by 4x4 posts. The simple girder-and-post arrangement is the subframe in the hybrid design. It runs parallel with the ridge, supporting the floor joists and a second beveled girder at the roofline. —A. W.

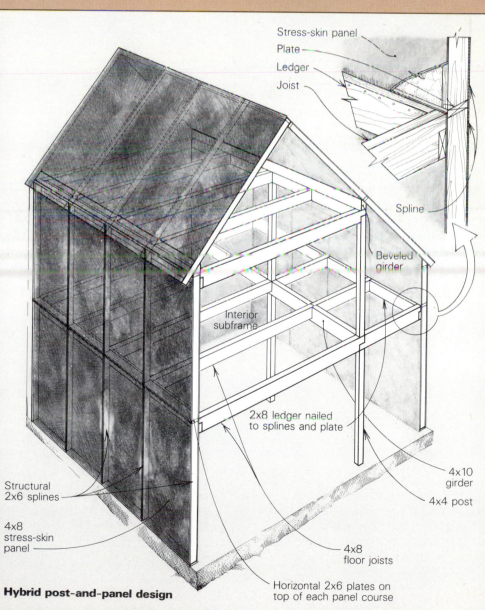

Stress-skin panel
Plate
Ledger
Joist
Spline
Beveled girder
Interior subframe
2x8 ledger nailed to splines and plate
4x10 girder
4x4 post
4x8 floor joists
Structural 2x6 splines
4x8 stress-skin panel
Horizontal 2x6 plates on top of each panel course

Hybrid post-and-panel design

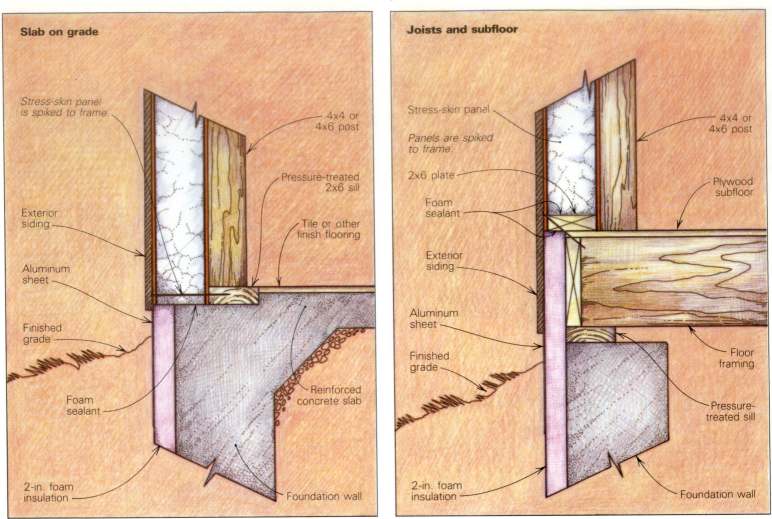

Slab on grade

Stress-skin panel is spiked to frame.

Exterior siding

Aluminum sheet

Finished grade

Foam sealant

2-in. foam insulation

4x4 or 4x6 post

Pressure-treated 2x6 sill

Tile or other finish flooring

Reinforced concrete slab

Foundation wall

Joists and subfloor

Stress-skin panel

Panels are spiked to frame.

2x6 plate

Foam sealant

Exterior siding

Aluminum sheet

Finished grade

2-in. foam insulation

4x4 or 4x6 post

Plywood subfloor

Floor framing

Pressure-treated sill

Foundation wall

Frame enclosure details. Stress-skin panel dimensions should be a major factor in the frame design. Above, frame and foundation detailing are integrated with panel thickness to create a flush finish at the base of the exterior wall. Both designs shown above provide a solid ledge for the panels' bottom edges. The width of the ledge aligns the sheathed exterior face of each panel with the foundation insulation.

rigidity and shear resistance provided by the stress-skin panels are quite superfluous.

In their quest for better fuel economy, auto manufacturers have since learned that by combining the structural qualities of body parts and the chassis (called *unibody* or *monocoque* construction) they can reduce curb weight (and also manufacturing costs) without adversely affecting the overall strength of the car. Steel ribs and stiffeners are designed into floor pans, fender walls and other body parts, integrating the car's structure with its interior and exterior skin. Similarly, stress-skin panels can be used as stand-alone structural members.

Many mobile-home manufacturers use structural panels, but so far only a few companies use structural stress-skins for site-built houses. Delta Industries (1951 Galaxie St., Columbus, Ohio 43207) and J-Deck Inc. (2587 Harrison Rd., Columbus, Ohio 43204) are the two most successful structural stress-skin builders that I know of, and Neilsen-Winter Corp. (Main St., West Groton, Mass. 01472) has recently developed a structural panel system. Delta Industries has even had success in using structural stress-skin panels clad with pressure-treated plywood for below-grade foundation walls.

Hybrid stress-skin designs can be even less expensive to build than either a structural panel house or a lightweight frame design that's enclosed with non-structural panels. The use of structural splines between inexpensive non-structural panels and a small subframe for interior loads give this type of system a great potential for simplicity and economy in a small house design. Hybrid panel systems could easily compete in cost with factory-built prefab houses, and they offer more in the way of energy efficiency and aesthetics. In order for this to happen, though, building codes and especially building inspectors will have to change.

Stress-skins and the unbraced frame—At this stage, small-scale contractors and owner-builders generally favor using some kind of exposed frame with stress-skin panels. Building officials are likely to put more faith in structural systems that they can see, and the exposed timbers in a frame house have a definite aesthetic appeal. In addition, non-structural 4x8 panels have become widely available, and competition among panel manufacturers continues to drive prices down.

Even though panels faced with drywall on one side aren't rated to stand alone, they still perform like torsion boxes when spiked and glued to the outside of a frame. The foam core and the adhesive bond between core and sheathing materials provide the racking resistance. This means that the post-and-beam frame doesn't require corner braces. In fact, I've slimmed down my post-and-beam designs spe-

cifically to take advantage of the racking resistance that stress-skin panels provide.

Apart from saving time and timber, the unbraced frame (especially in a small house) looks cleaner and offers far more freedom in locating windows and doors. There's no need for complex timber joinery either. Where traditional timber framers use housed dovetails and pegged tenons, I usually specify nailed lap joints reinforced with metal truss plates that are eventually hidden beneath panels or flooring. Kevin Berry and Jeff Seeley, two builders I work with frequently, are often able to put together one of these simplified frames in just two days. The cost for a completed shell, with windows and doors installed but without finish siding or roofing, is usually around $15 per square foot.

In most cases, all the joinery for a simplified frame can be cut on site. Whenever possible, we try to get a good price from a nearby mill on roughsawn lumber (usually hemlock), and I try to hold the thickness of all framing members to no more than 3½ in. so that most of the joints can be cut with a skillsaw.

In houses that use a light post-and-beam structure, panels are spiked to the frame with either ringshank or hot-dipped galvanized spikes that penetrate 2 in. or more into the timber. The interior face of the panel should be seated in a thick bead of caulk where it rests against the frame. Where panels join vertically, the joint is

Illustrations: Elizabeth Eaton

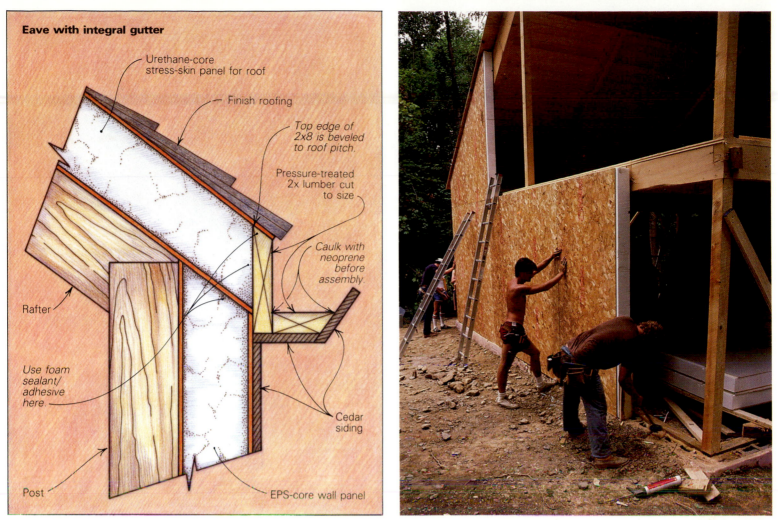

Eave with integral gutter

Urethane-core stress-skin panel for roof

Finish roofing

Top edge of 2x8 is beveled to roof pitch.

Pressure-treated 2x lumber cut to size

Caulk with neoprene before assembly.

Rafter

Use foam sealant/adhesive here.

Cedar siding

Post

EPS-core wall panel

Above, eliminating eave overhang and incorporating a wood gutter are economical roof-construction details that also look good on the finished house. Above right, a scrap 2x6 pad and a hand sledge are used to close the tongue-and-groove joint between two wall panels. The posts and girts in this frame are located to provide nailing surfaces along panel edges.

usually a manufactured tongue-and-groove that is bonded with site-applied aerosol foam. Horizontal joints between panels are usually butt joints if they fall over solid backing. Otherwise, a 2x spline is necessary. In either case, the joint is sealed with spray-on foam.

In order to save time and money building a post-and-panel house, you have to plan post and girt locations carefully so that the panels are easy to install and waste from panel offcuts is minimal. I locate posts on 8-ft. centers. This way, wall panels can be installed vertically, and every other vertical panel joint lands on a post. Girts between perimeter posts should be located on vertical 8-ft. centers to provide a nailing surface for panel edges.

Because the stress-skin panels provide the wall's shear resistance in this type of design, the unbraced frame needs temporary braces to hold it plumb and level until the panels are nailed up. We temporarily brace posts to girts and to the ground as the frame is built. These braces stay on until the stress-skin wall is applied.

I've seen all sorts of arrangements tried at the base of the wall, where the frame, panel and foundation all converge. Many of them aren't very attractive, and not all of them are as easy or as economical to build as they could be. I prefer the details shown in the drawings on the facing page because they're uncomplicated and because the finished appearance unifies the insu-

lated foundation with the insulated wall. The frame shown in the left-hand drawing has a pressure-treated 2x6 sill bolted atop a 10-in. block wall that extends just a few inches above finished grade. This sill location leaves the outer 4½ in. of the foundation's top edge exposed, and this is where the 6½-in. thick stress-skin panels are set. The panel overhangs the foundation by 2 in.—just the thickness of the foam foundation insulation coming up from below. The outer face of the panel is flush with the foundation insulation. Kevin Berry likes to flash this grade-level joint with low-cost aluminum roll-stock before nailing up the exterior siding (photo below left, next page). Alternatively, you could parge on stucco finish over wire mesh. The cheapest designs have poured-concrete ground floors. But with some modifications, you could achieve the same flush-fit appearance with a conventional subfloor (drawing, facing page, right).

The roof—I recommend urethane-foam insulation for the roof—either in the form of stress-skin panels or rigid foam board installed over decking. Urethane provides more insulative value per inch than expanded polystyrene (EPS), and it's also a more effective vapor barrier. If EPS panels are used on the roof, they usually have to have 7½-in. thick cores, and the inner drywall face of the panel has to be sealed with

vapor-barrier paint (in the Northeast, where I do most of my work).

The nicest eave detail that I've seen on a stress-skin house incorporates a site-made gutter and fascia board in the first course of roof panels (drawing, above). To build this type of eave, you have to bevel-cut both the roof panel and the fascia. I use only pressure-treated 2x lumber for the back and bottom of the gutter, and cedar for the front side, since it's a better matching wood for roughsawn siding.

It's possible to let panels overhang by about 1 ft. at eaves and gables, but remember that neither the drywall nor the foam edge can be left exposed to the weather. For the sake of economy and ease of construction, eliminating overhangs altogether makes the most sense.

Windows and doors—Windows are easy to install in stress-skin houses if you've got a small chainsaw or a 16-in. circular saw. Either one of these tools has sufficient depth of cut to saw the rough opening from inside the house. Otherwise, the opening has to be cut from both sides of the panel. Either way, it should be sized about ¼ in. larger than the window frame.

Since the wall panels we use have 5½-in. thick cores, window frames have to have extension jambs made for 2x6 stud-framed walls. Though some builders recommend letting in 2x6s around the rough opening, we've found

Corner construction. Leaving the corner open when panels are installed provides access to electrical raceways routed in the interior face of the panel's foam core. As shown at top left, a 2x6 panel edge has to be notched in line with the raceway before it is let into the panel and secured with caulk and drywall nails. Once both corner panels have been spiked to the frame, above right, plastic-sheathed cable can be run through the sill from the service panel. Then the cable is snaked through panel raceways down the wall to outlet-box locations cut at raceway height inside the house. Above left, the corner is enclosed when wiring is complete. Proper sill and post location allows the sheathed face of the panel to align flush with the foundation insulation. Roll aluminum, installed beneath the siding, extends below grade as a low-cost but nice-looking finish detail.

that the rigidity of the panels eliminates the need for this extra framing unless you're installing a large window or a door.

To install the window or door, you shim it plumb and square in the opening, nail through the exterior trim and into the sheathing, and then fill the shim space with aerosol foam. This foam spray expands and bonds wood to foam, securing the frame. You'll have to trim off some foam squeeze-out before installing interior trim.

The open corner—Most builders who use stress-skin panels to enclose frames overlap panel edges at the corners. The open corner design that I use (photo above right) saves the 6½ in. of panel width lost to the overlap and also provides a very workable raceway for electrical wiring. Electrical wiring has been the bane of stress-skin systems since their development. Some wiring schemes call for custom-made hollow baseboards, while others demand that the electrician be on site as panels go up in order to snake wiring between panel joints. Both of these approaches can be costly and troublesome.

With open corners, neither corner panel ex-

tends beyond the face of the corner post that it's nailed to. This creates a 6½-in. by 6½-in. open area that is later boxed in and insulated. Before this happens, though, the open corner provides access to the wiring raceways that run the full lengths of both walls once all panels have been installed. The raceways are small channels that were routed along the inside face of the foam core before the drywall was glued on. The panels shown here have raceways cut 18 in. from their top and bottom (4-ft. wide) edges. This is a convenient feature, because panels can be flipped without misaligning raceways and because each wall can have outlet locations near ceiling and floor. Not all panel manufacturers are set up to incorporate raceways in their panels, so this could be an important consideration when deciding which supplier to use.

Using this open-corner detailing requires that you let in a 2x6 along each 8-ft. panel edge that will face the corner. This strengthens the panel edge and provides a nailing surface for filling in the exterior corner once the wiring has been run. As shown in the photo top left, the 2x6

edge board has to be notched out to give access to the panel's two raceways. Then it's let into the panel edge and secured with sealant and drywall nails.

Once all the panels are up, plastic-sheathed cable (Romex) is run into the corner from the service panel through a slot or hole made in the 2x6 sill. Using a double sill lets you drill out this hole with less risk of running your bit against masonry. Inside the house, the electrician can locate the raceway simply by measuring 18 in. up from the base of the panel. Holes for outlet boxes are usually cut with a utility knife right at raceway height.

Electrical cable can be run toward the center of the wall from one or both corners, depending on how your circuits are mapped. And by continuing the open corner above the first course of panels, upper floors can be wired the same way. Stud-frame partition walls inside the house are wired conventionally. □

Architect Alex Wade's Guide to Affordable Houses *is available from Rodale Press (33 E. Minor St., Emmaus, Pa. 18049).*

Wiring in Stress-Skin Panels

It's not as tough as you think

by Jeff Arvin

Stress-skin panels are no longer the construction oddity they once were. They're used these days on projects ranging from handcrafted timber frames to factory-built modulars. Many people think, however, that wiring a stress-skin house is a difficult process. Quite to the contrary, we're finding that it's not really difficult, just different.

We make our own panels with ⁷⁄₁₆-in. oriented-strand board (OSB) as the outside surface, then 5⅝ in. of EPS foam insulation, another layer of OSB and finally ½-in. fire-rated drywall. The standard sizes of panels are 4x8, 9, 10 and 12, but I've seen panels as big as 8x28. Stress-skin panels may be built differently by different companies, but most, if not all, of the wiring hassles related to panels can be eliminated with good and thorough planning. There will be some situations best dealt with as the panels are being installed. At other times, the wiring should be done as the doors and windows are being put in place. Your ability to take advantage of these situations depends upon a thoroughly planned electrical scheme, as well as a knowledge of the specific details.

In at least one respect, a stress-skin home is exactly like any other home—any penetration of the exterior wall requires the removal of insulation and opens avenues for air infiltration. It's wise, therefore, to minimize the number of openings in panels.

A professional tradesman will probably find little difference, compared to standard construction, in how much time the wiring takes or in how much it costs. As for building codes, we've had no problems in getting approval for any of these methods (locally, we're under BOCA codes). It wouldn't hurt to check them with the code officials in your area, though. Under certain conditions we can cut holes and pull the wiring through, but generally an electrician does the work.

Using a built-in wire chase—We make our wall panels with a 1½-in. by 1½-in. wire chase already built into the panel (drawing at right). It runs the full 4-ft. width of the panel, and is usually about 14 in. above the subfloor. Wiring can be threaded through the chase as panels are being installed, or pulled through later on. By cutting an opening for an electrical box directly above or below the chase, it's easy enough to feed wire into it. We've had good luck cutting the openings

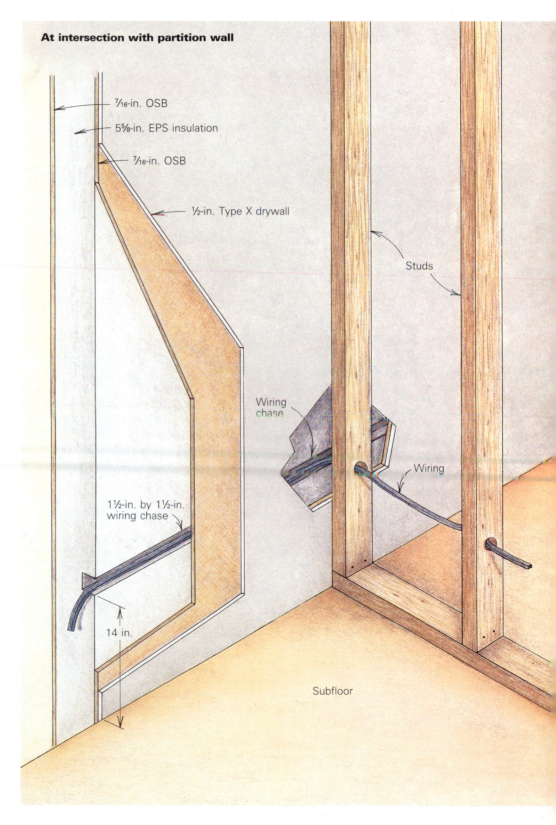

At intersection with partition wall

⁷⁄₁₆-in. OSB

5⅝-in. EPS insulation

⁷⁄₁₆-in. OSB

½-in. Type X drywall

Studs

Wiring chase

Wiring

1½-in. by 1½-in. wiring chase

14 in.

Subfloor

with a jigsaw, then levering the waste out with a screwdriver or prybar. Sometimes we'll just drill a 2-in. hole for the wire and let the electrician cut for the box. In either case, take care to remove only enough foam to make way for the box, and never remove so much that you create a skin-to-skin pocket.

We use two methods for installing the boxes, depending on which one the electrician prefers. We sometimes use *old work* boxes. Designed for remodeling work, these have metal wings on the outside of the box that can be tightened against the inside of the panel to hold the box in place. The concept is similar to the way a toggle bolt works. The second method employs metal *madison straps* that fold around the box to anchor it.

Gaining access to the chase after putting up all the panels is no problem. This is most easily done at the point where an interior partition abuts a stress-skin wall (drawing on previous page). Drill through any studs at the

end of the partition wall and into the chase to open the pathway. Form a loop at the end of the electrical wire, then poke it through the studs into the chase and fish it out from one side of the panel or another by hooking the loop with a length of stiff wire.

You can also get to the wire chase from above or below the panel, as when you're routing wire through the basement, crawl space or attic. To make a small, vertical channel in the foam that will connect with the main wiring chase, poke a stiff wire or rod through the foam, just beneath the surface of the inside skin. A length of rebar or metal conduit will also do the job. To make the going easier over the long vertical run down the panel, use a propane torch to heat the end of the metal and it will pass through the foam like a hot knife through butter. If the channel is coming in from the bottom of the panel, remember that it must go behind any baseboard nailer (these are sometimes let in to the base of panels that don't have an interior

skin of OSB). Another trick is to use a 1-in. nut tied to a length of light-gauge copper wire. Heat the nut with a propane torch, slip it into a starter hole in the panel and let gravity do the work. One of our subs recently used this technique to make a 40-in. long channel from a box to a wiring chase. Any "heated metal" technique will work only with EPS and thermoplastic foams, however, and not with urethanes or polyisocyanurate.

As the panels are being installed, it's sometimes possible to route wiring in the small gaps between them. The gaps are only ⅜-in. wide, but run skin to skin. Later on, we fill them with an expanding foam sealant to eliminate air infiltration. We use Fomofill Sealant (Fomo Products, Box 1078, Norton, Ohio 44203).

As a last resort, you can simply cut a vertical channel through the inside of the stress-skin panel in order to connect with the wiring chase. Short, vertical cuts in the panel won't hurt it, and if you strip away a bit of

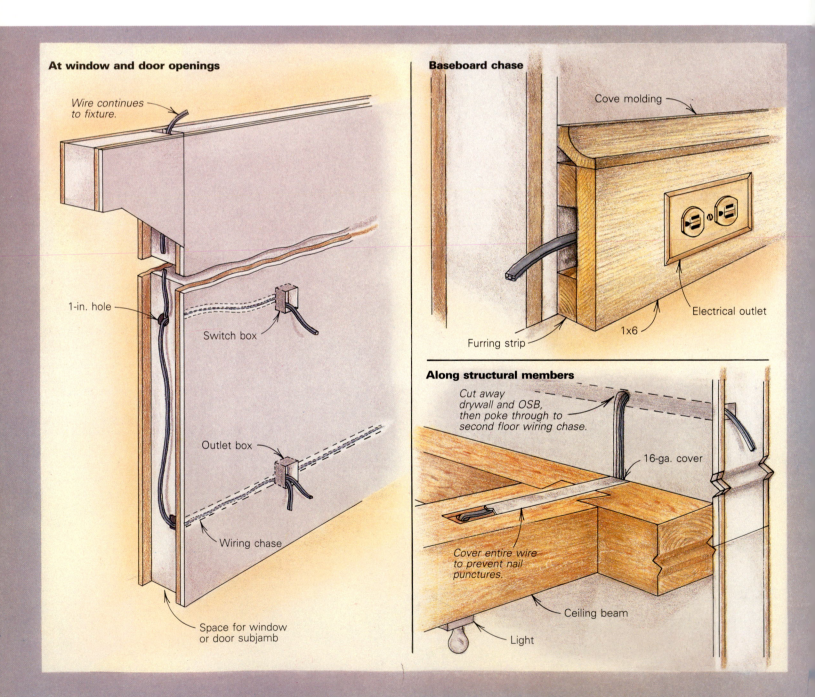

At window and door openings

Wire continues to fixture.

1-in. hole

Switch box

Outlet box

Wiring chase

Space for window or door subjamb

Baseboard chase

Cove molding

Electrical outlet

Furring strip

1x6

Along structural members

Cut away drywall and OSB, then poke through to second floor wiring chase.

16-ga. cover

Cover entire wire to prevent nail punctures.

Ceiling beam

Light

drywall and a little foam in the process, the damage can usually be patched with tape, drywall compound and a minimum of effort. Work neatly, though—don't create more work for someone else later.

Baseboard chase—There will be places where it just isn't feasible to route electrical wire through the panel itself. In those cases, you can run it through a baseboard chase (drawing facing page, upper right). The technique here is simple. We use 1x1 furring strips to space a 1x6 baseboard away from the wall. Various moldings can be used to cover the resulting shelf, but cove molding works quite nicely. You can vary the depth and height of the raceway, but it should have consistent dimensions throughout the project if you want to avoid some tricky detailing problems.

Switches and wall-mounted fixtures—Running wiring for switches and fixtures takes more effort, but it's not difficult. In some in-

stances, you can pull the wiring through a chase and then run it in the recess created for the subjamb around doors or windows (drawing facing page, left). The subjamb is 2x stock let in to the foam around openings and provides a fire stop as well as a base for nailing in the finish window and door jambs and casings. Access to the switch box can be made with a 1-in. auger bit. This is a neat method, but it must be done before the door or window is installed .

If it's not practical to reach a switch or an outlet box for a fixture from a door or window opening, you can get at it as the panels are being installed. After the first-floor walls are up (but before the second floor begins), poke a vertical hole along the inside face of the panel down to a hole cut for the box (top drawing, this page). It's a good idea to mark the path of the channels on the inside wall because it's easy to forget where they are. It's possible to continue the hole down to the wiring chase. We use a length of rebar, bent

into a gentle curve, to poke down through the insulation from the box. The curve allows us to slip the rebar into the hole created for the box and slide it along the inside face of the OSB.

Ceiling-mounted fixtures—The simplest way to install ceiling-mounted fixtures is to attach them directly to an exposed timber. Getting the wire out there, however, takes some planning. We find it easiest to use a router to cut a groove in the top surface of the wood, running it from the wall to a point just above the fixture (drawing facing page, lower right). At that point, we drill a 1-in. hole down through the timber in order to gain access to the fixture. It's important to cut the grooves as straight as possible so that you'll later be able to avoid the wiring when nailing down flooring or sheathing from above. As an additional precaution against dangerous nail punctures in the wiring, fasten a 16-ga. sheet-metal plate over the entire length of the groove. You might even consider running these wires in metal conduit.

I do *not* recommend cutting into stress-skin panels used on the floor or on the roof. In these instances, the sheathing on one side of the panel is likely to be in compression or tension, and any cut can seriously affect the structural integrity of the panel.

Wiring the second story—Above the first floor, wire can be run into stress-skin panels through interior partitions, as previously described, or in a couple of other ways. As the panels are being installed, wire can be placed in the seams between panels or through a gap left where the corner panels meet (bottom drawing). In the latter case, the wire should be stapled to the post before the second panel is installed. Later on, the gap can be filled with expanding foam.

Surface wiring—If you just can't figure out a way to conceal the wiring within the panels or within the frame, or if you didn't plan ahead and find yourself in a real jam, it is possible to surface-wire portions of the house. Various companies make metal channels and connecting pieces that can be run along surfaces. Wiremold (The Wiremold Company, Electrical Division, 60 Woodlawn, West Hartford, Conn. 06110) is one company that has lots of products in this area, including surface-mount electrical boxes. Such systems are rarely our first choice, however.

I'm sure that there are other ways to run wiring in stress-skin panels, but the methods noted above should cover most of the situations you're likely to encounter. As you're doing the work, it's a good idea to make a map of all circuits, fixture locations and the locations of any channels. That will make it easier to add or extend circuits later on.   □

Jeff Arvin teaches and writes about timber-frame construction for Riverbend Timber Framing in Blissfield, Mich.

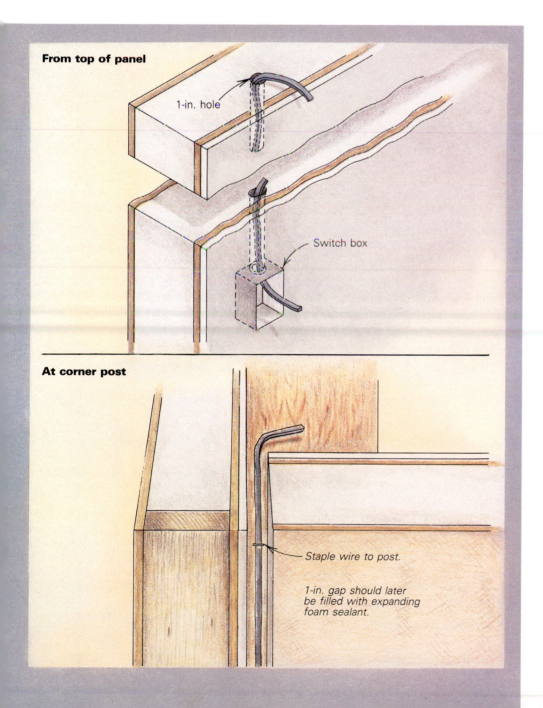

From top of panel

1-in. hole

Switch box

At corner post

Staple wire to post.

1-in. gap should later be filled with expanding foam sealant.

Foam-Core Panels

A survey of the products available, how they're installed and the controversies surrounding their use

by Steve Andrews

While most new synthetic building materials tend to draw mixed reviews in the building community, foam-core panels are simultaneously gaining favor with the most traditional and the most progressive builders in the U. S. (photos facing page). Popular with timberframers for years, the panels are now being used by builders of conventional homes to construct energy-efficient houses that are a cross between custom-made and factory-built. Panels are now available for walls, roofs, floors and even foundation walls. In fact, manufacturers now offer everything from individual panels to packages that include an entire building shell installed by the manufacturer.

According to the builders I've talked with, it's high time to consider seriously the merits of foam-core panels. They say the panels combine high R-values with the right amount of factory prefabrication to speed up their construction schedules. They're also impressed by the products' design flexibility and structural integrity. While admitting the materials cost more than those used in standard stick framing, they claim the savings in labor costs and the high quality of the finished product offset the extra cost.

Surveying the market in early 1988, I found that 18 of the approximately 75 companies now in existence reported manufacturing panels for 12,000 housing units (including condos and apartments)—with well over half of the panels used being unfaced panels (unsheathed panels consisting of rigid foam and integral structural framing members) for the Canadian market. While this represents a small fraction of the total housing market, individual companies have grown impressively over the last three years.

Types of panels—Though most builders and many manufacturers refer to foam-core panels as *stress-skin* panels, the former term is technically the more accurate. According to the Forest Products Laboratory and the American Plywood Association, true stress-skin panels consist of plywood skins glued and nailed to both sides of a wood frame, resulting in a unit

Foam-core panels can be structural or nonstructural. These structural wall panels are faced with oriented strand board.

that's much stronger than its individual components. When subjected to loading, a stress-skin panel performs like an I-beam. The skins (like I-beam flanges) resist tension and compression, while the frame, or core (like an I-beam web), resists shear and prevents the skins from wrinkling. True stress-skin panels aren't necessarily insulated and, conversely, not all foam-core panels are stress-skinned. To avoid confusion, I'll use the term *foam-core* panels to refer to the whole realm of faced and unfaced rigid-foam panels on the market.

Foam-core panels can be either nonstructural or structural. The nonstructural panels preferred by most timberframers typically consist of a rigid core of expanded polystyrene (EPS) or polyurethane insulation sandwiched between a layer of oriented strand board (OSB) on one side and drywall on the other. The panels are designed to support lateral loads only, and not compression loads (in other words, they won't replace studs, posts or rafters). Structural panels, on the other hand, support loads without the need for additional framing.

Structural panels can themselves be subdivided into two types: sandwich panels and un-

faced panels. Sandwich panels consist of two structural-grade facings, such as OSB, laminated to a foam core (photo left). Depending on the manufacturer and the application, these panels may or may not include framing members within the panel itself. Framing members typically consist of 2x splines joining adjacent panels or of integral studs, and may carry specific point loads or carry the whole structural load. In the U. S., sandwich panels substantially outsell unfaced panels.

Unfaced panels, most of which are made by two manufacturers in Canada (NASCOR, Inc. and Insul-Wall, Ltd.) and one in the U. S. (RADVA Corporation), combine framing members on either 16-in. or 24-in. centers with a rigid-foam core (see p. 111 for manufacturer addresses). Interior and exterior finishes are applied on site. Unfaced panels look like stick framing with foam insulation instead of fiberglass between the studs. But there are two wrinkles: framing members contain a thermal break (a layer of foam in the middle that prevents conduction of heat through the framing members), and RADVA Corporation uses metal studs instead of wood studs.

Panel recipes—All foam-core panels are insulated with EPS, urethane or polyisocyanurate foam. The latter two are chemically similar, so I'll lump them together as urethane here.

EPS, or *beadboard*, was first used in this country in 1954, and is the most common type of foam used in structural panels. To make an EPS panel, fabricators typically apply a structural-grade adhesive (usually a urethane) to both sides of a foam core, place the coated core on a clean facing and place another facing on top. A stack of panels is then put under continuous pressure—as high as 10 psi—for about an hour. After the panels cure for 24 hours, they're either pre-cut in the factory or shipped directly to a job site. Size varies from 4-ft. by 8-ft. panels that weigh about 100 lb. to 8-ft. by 28-ft. panels that must be craned into place.

Urethane panels are either glue-laminated

From *Fine Homebuilding* magazine (August 1990) 62:52-57

like EPS panels or foamed in place. Foaming in place is the more complicated operation, but it's quicker and eliminates the need for adhesives. One method calls for the spraying of liquid urethane into a hollow panel. The urethane expands rapidly and sticks to the facings, curing in 20-40 minutes and cooling fully in three to four hours. Manufacturing can either be continuous (involving a pneumatic pressing device and a moving assembly line) or by the batch (six to 20 panels at once).

As to which foam is best, neither is the clear-cut winner. EPS is inert, resilient, doesn't feed microorganisms, is non-toxic (though it does give off carbon monoxide and other toxic gases when burned) and is cheaper than urethane (about 30% cheaper per R). It's also easy to cut with a hot wire, limiting dust problems. Urethane, on the other hand, has a higher R-value per inch than EPS (R-6 or R-7 as opposed to R-4), is nearly twice as strong in compression and doesn't melt into a flammable liquid like EPS does (EPS melts at temperatures of from 200° to 300° F). Urethane also has a perm rating of less than one, which technically qualifies it as a vapor barrier (EPS typically has a perm-rating of from 1 to 3 and may require the use of a polyethylene vapor retarder or a vapor-retarder paint such as Glidden INSUL-AID).

Though urethanes don't melt, they ignite at temperatures between 800° F and 850° F, and they emit toxic smoke when they burn. Also, most urethanes incorporate Freon gas, a CFC that can leak from the foam and contribute to global warming and damage to the ozone layer, reducing the foam's R-value in the process (more on flammability and CFCs later). On the job site, urethane isn't as easy to plow out of a panel (for installing nailers and electrical boxes) as EPS is—the use of a special router or grinder is required.

Whichever foam is used, most manufacturers offer a number of options for facing materials (except, of course, for unfaced panels). The most common materials used are OSB, CDX plywood, waferboard, ½-in. plywood and 24-ga. to 26-ga. sheet metal. Other facings include T-111 plywood siding and T&G pine. Pond Hill Homes, Ltd. offers panels with fir, pine, cedar, steel, stucco or OSB on the outside and primed, galvanized steel on the inside to which drywall can be screwed. About 25% of the panel manufacturers sell panels with pressure-treated plywood skins and pressure-treated splines to allow installation below grade (bottom photo, p. 110). Advance Energy Technologies, Inc. sells its foundation panels sheathed with either 14-ga. galvanized steel or 16-ga. stainless steel. For use around pools and in other humid areas, Harmony Exchange, Inc. sells panels coated with a virtually impermeable, latex-base elastomeric coating.

Most manufacturers mold conduit into their panels or provide raceways horizontally and vertically to allow for easy wiring. Some will rout these raceways, or even channels for plumbing stacks, in specified locations within the panel on request. In most cases, though,

Photo courtesy of J-Deck Building Systems, Inc.

Long associated with cookie-cutter factory-style housing, foam-core panels now match stick framing with their versatility. The house pictured above is a timberframe clad with J-Deck EPS panels. Winter Panel Corporation's Bow Cape house (photo at right), is built of structural urethane-core wall panels and the company's patented curved urethane-core roof panels, which measure up to 14-ft. long. The house pictured below features structural unfaced panels made by RADVA Corporation. The panels have integral metal studs.

Photo courtesy of Winter Panel Corporation

Photo courtesy of RADVA Corporation

plumbing is best run in interior walls so that it doesn't compromise the strength and insulative value of the panels. A few manufacturers recommend installing wiring behind baseboards and moldings (for more on panel installation, see the sidebar at right).

Costs and services—The simplest way to price panels is by the square foot of panel area. You'll find that prices vary dramatically, ranging, for example, from $1.75 to $2.75 per sq. ft. for structural sandwich panels with 5⅝-in. EPS cores and double OSB skins. Substituting T-111 plywood siding for OSB on the exterior face of a panel will typically bump its price up another $.45 per sq. ft. The cost of urethane structural sandwich panels with a comparable R-value (which equates to a thinner panel) ranges from $2.30 per sq. ft. for high-volume buyers to $3.25 per sq. ft. for everyone else.

But pricing by the square foot of panel area doesn't tell the whole story. Manufacturers usually sell packages, not just individual panels. The least expensive package is uncut sandwich panels for walls and roofs, which are shipped with splines and compatible adhesives. Panel sizes typically measure from 3½ ft. to 8 ft. wide, 8 ft. to 28 ft. long and 3⅝ in. to 12 in. thick. Prices range from $4 to $9 per sq. ft. of finished floor area, depending on panel thickness and other variables.

The next step up is precut panels, for which most sandwich-panel manufacturers charge from $8 to $13 per sq. ft. of floor area. This service includes the cutting out of rough window and door openings and angle cuts on gable-end walls. Manufacturers of unfaced panels concentrate on this type of package, and their prices are almost always lower than the cost of precut sandwich panels.

Still more expensive is the complete shell, installed by the manufacturer on the builder's foundation for a cost of between $16 and $22 per square foot. This package typically includes everything in the shell except windows and doors. The top of the line is the turnkey package, which is a complete home including windows, doors, siding, roofing, carpet, cabinets, stairs, heating and plumbing fixtures, along with other features. The cost ranges from $50 and $75 per square foot, excluding land and improvements. Some outfits offer custom design as an option.

A word of warning: don't shop price at the expense of quality. Ask if the manufacturer warrants its panel products. If the lower-bid manufacturer doesn't have a track record and a good quality-control program, keep shopping. And don't ignore service. Call a builder who has used the product you're considering and ask about the level of consulting assistance provided by the manufacturer during the design phase, contractor training prior to panel delivery, timeliness of panel delivery, condition of panels as delivered and whether factory personnel are present on site during the erection of the shell.

Also, while a large number of structural-panel

Installation options

Most structural sandwich wall panels come with the foam cores notched top and bottom, allowing the panels to straddle a 2x bottom plate nailed to the deck and to be stiffened up top with a single or double 2x top plate. Panels are typically nailed and glued with construction adhesive to the plates (top photo, below). Corner panels are spiked together or joined with metal connectors supplied by the manufacturer.

Adjacent wall panels are connected with one of several different splining systems (drawing facing page). The cam-locking system and systems using a single or double 2x spline offer the quickest installation, while double OSB splines and thermally broken studs offer superior energy efficiency. In most cases, joints between panels are sealed with expanding foam, caulk or construction adhesive (keep in mind that some solvent-based caulks and adhesives dissolve EPS). Nonstructural panels, such as those used for timberframes, usually rest on a sill or ledger and are spiked to the timberframe with annular-ring nails for softwood frames or with spiral galvanized nails for hardwood frames.

Unfaced panels made by RADVA are installed much like sandwich panels, except that adjacent panels interlock with shiplap joints that are screwed together with self-tapping metal screws. Panels made by NASCOR Inc. are toenailed to a 2x bottom plate and splined together with wood and

Drawing: Vince Babak

foam splines, while unfaced panels made by Insul-Wall Ltd. are simply toenailed to the deck.

Most roof panels are either structural clear-span panels (bottom photo, facing page) or non-structural panels designed to be spiked to rafters or purlins. Depending on snow loads, clear-span panels may be joined with single or double 2x splines the thickness of the panels, which serve as structural members. Large panels are usually placed by crane and spiked to the ridge beam and top plates (wedge-shaped 2xs at the top plates provide extra bearing for roof panels).

Typically, for windows less than 4 ft. wide in sandwich panels, rough openings can be cut with a chainsaw anywhere in the wall, including through a panel joint, without the

need for a header. Openings over 4 ft. wide require installation of a header. Some manufacturers, including Enercept, Inc., sell pre-engineered insulated headers, though conventional headers and cripple studs will also work. Perimeters of rough openings, roof perimeters and the ends of corner panels have to be recessed 1½ in. on site (unless the panels are prenotched at the factory) to accommodate the installation of 2x nailers. Urethane foam is notched with a special router or grinder (a dust mask is a must); EPS foam is cut with a hot knife or wire (these tools can usually be purchased from the panel manufacturer). Of course, for cutting whole panels (facings included), these tools won't work. In this case, a beam saw is probably the best bet.

In some cases, the use of metal strapping, connectors and other hardware is required to connect wall and ceiling panels (as many as ten per panel). Check to see that your manufacturer sells these; otherwise you might have a hard time finding, for instance, 12-in. galvanized screwshank nails for nailing thick EPS panels to ridge beams.

Wiring and plumbing of sandwich panels, even those supplied with precut chases or conduit, tend to take more time than with conventional framing (for more on wiring in foam-core panels, see pp. 103-105). Some panels come with cavities that allow installation of electrical boxes; others have to be recessed on site. With plumbing, the secret is to plan ahead so that as much of it as possitble is kept out of exterior walls. — S. A.

Some panel-joint options. *Here are sections of 10 different panel-joining systems. The top two splining details are used by several manufacturers; the rest are offered by the manufacturers shown. Faced panels are typically clad with OSB, plywood, drywall, sheet metal or rough-sawn wood. Panels are typically nailed or screwed together, then sealed with expanding foam, caulk and/or construction adhesive. Walls are typically reinforced with standard 2x plates top and bottom. The thickness of the panels varies according to the insulation requirements.*

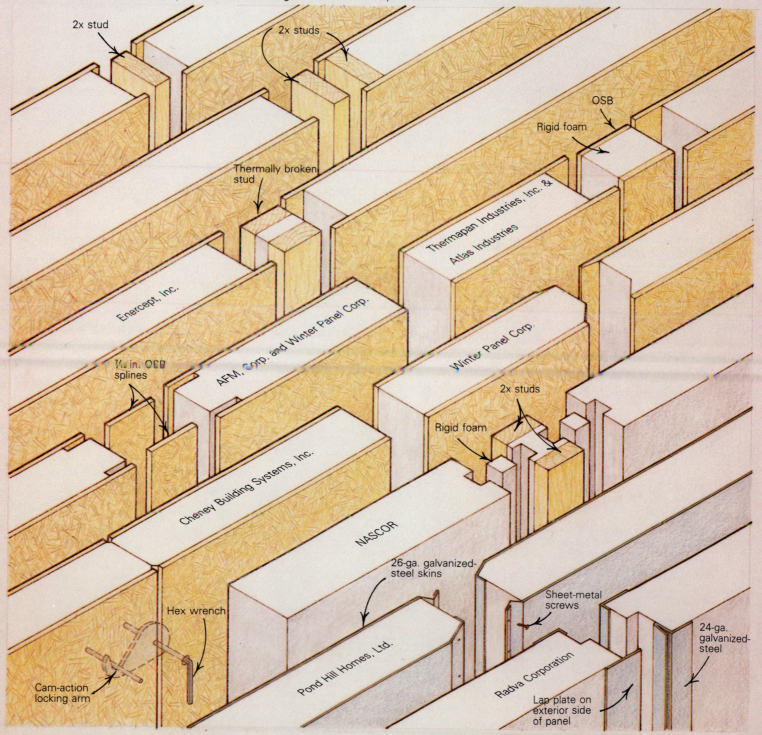

manufacturers have submitted their products to BOCA, ICBO or SBCCI, few have actually received compliance approval. Associated Foam Manufacturers (AFM Corp.), a group of 20 independent manufacturers who make R-Control brand EPS panels, and RADVA Corporation are among the manufacturers who have received a compliance notice from all three model building-code organizations. Code compliance may eliminate problems with local building departments. If such problems exist, urge the manufacturer to handle that headache for you.

Foam panels and fire—The fire-safety issue of foam-core panels could be the focus of a long article or even a short book. EPS and urethane manufacturers don't help their case by throwing stones at each other. Here's the bottom line: rigorous tests by independent laboratories, including Underwriter's Laboratories (UL), substantiate the fact that properly designed and installed urethane and EPS foam-core building systems are safe. They will not contribute unduly to the fuel supply or to the toxic gases present during a house fire.

Though a small amount of cyanide is released when urethane panels burn, researchers say the risk is minimal. In a paper presented at the 1985 Society of the Plastics Industry annual meeting on polyurethane foam, J. R. Mehaffey of the National Research Council of Canada pointed out that it's usually carbon monoxide that presents the principal toxic threat to life in house fires. Mehaffey reported that there is no definite proof that urethane insulation augments toxic hazards that already exist in a burning home. He also said that foam applied behind drywall presents no greater hazard than fiberglass insulation or no insulation at all in a preflashover fire (before gases in the air combust).

But the true test of any foam panel is how it responds to fire in a structure built to code and to manufacturers' specifications. Several EPS panel manufacturers have submitted their products successfully to a "Room Corner Test" (UBC 17-5 or UL 1715) as well as a fire-endurance test under loaded conditions (ASTM E-119). AFM sells a videotape of R-Control panels undergoing fire testing; it's $25.

Nevertheless, for added insurance against fire, some manufacturers use *type-M* beads in the manufacture of their EPS foam. EPS modified with these beads demonstrates improved smoke-test and flame-spread ratings and won't burn when the source of a flame is removed. According to the Fischer Corporation, a manufacturer of EPS-core panels, the use of type-M beads adds about 29¢ to the cost of a 4-ft. by 8-ft. panel.

Lab testing costs manufacturers anywhere from several thousand dollars for a single test to as much as $100,000 for a full battery of tests. Not surprisingly, a manufacturer who has performed many tests will have to recover some of those costs through higher prices. You'll have to decide how much that's worth to you.

Incidentally, if you're worried about outgassing of formaldehyde from foam-core panels, don't be. There is no formaldehyde in either EPS or urethane, and softwood plywood, OSB and waferboard (the most common facings used for foam panels) are made with phenol formaldehyde adhesives, not the urea-formaldehyde adhesives that cause allergic reaction to products such as particleboard.

Coming unglued—A sandwich panel will delaminate if the bond between the facings and foam fails. This can be caused by poor quality control or by selection of the wrong type of adhesive by the manufacturer (which is much less of a problem than it used to be). It can also be caused by loading a panel beyond its engineered design load.

Make sure the manufacturer you select has a comprehensive structural testing program

A number of asphalt-shingle manufacturers won't warrant their shingles if they're installed directly over unvented roofs, including roofs built of standard foam-core panels. One solution to this problem is to install vented roof panels. The EPS-core panels pictured below are manufactured by Branch River Foam Plastics. *Photo courtesy of Branch River Foam Plastics, Inc.*

Several panel manufacturers sell panels with pressure-treated plywood skins and pressure-treated splines to allow installation below grade. The photo above shows a basement wall built out of structural EPS foundation panels manufactured by Thermapan Industries, Inc. All foam-core panels must pass specific burn tests, including ASTM/E-119, to achieve the hourly wall rating required by the major model building codes. *Photo courtesy of Thermapan Industries, Inc.*

(including testing-to-failure of one panel from every large run of panels) to ensure that panels meet code requirements. Also make sure that there's someone in the plant whose primary responsibility is to oversee quality control, or that the company employs an outside agency such as UL to provide third-party inspection and oversight of the in-house quality-control program.

If you think you might lie awake at night worrying about the failure of the bond between the foam core and sheathings in your structural panels, you can choose a structural-panel system that includes integral framing members, such as that offered by Concept 2000 Homes. Admittedly, adding more wood framing back into a panel decreases its insulating value, but only by 2% to 4% for the total shell.

Working out the bugs—Carpenter ants love EPS and urethane foam. In rural areas especially, the building-construction process can wipe out an ant colony's home so that once the foam-core panels are in place, the ants become early tenants. They don't eat the stuff, but there are some notorious cases where ants have pillaged whole panels in both structural-panel homes and panel-clad timberframes.

The problem is treatable, but it can cost thousands of dollars to eliminate a full-fledged ant colony in panels. So wherever carpenter ants are suspected, prevention is the primary defense. Check with the manufacturer for his detailed recommendation (if he plays dumb about ant problems, cross him off your list).

The Winter Panel Corporation has been very open about the carpenter-ant problem, with the result that they've gathered and published the most comprehensive ant-combat strategy I've seen (they'll send you a copy of their Technical Information Sheet No. C-3 on request). Recommendations include treating the foundation before backfilling and treating its perimeter after backfilling with a residual-acting insecticide. They also recommend installing a termite shield under the sill, using pressure-treated lumber for the sill and for other high-moisture areas and, in those wooded areas where carpenter-ant infestation is highly likely, treating the panel sheathing with long-lasting insecticides. Winter recommends that contractors hire a licensed exterminator for all insecticide treatments.

If all this sounds hopelessly complicated (not to mention toxic), here's the good news. Winter Panel Corporation has just introduced a borate-impregnated urethane panel that it claims will prevent infiltration by ants and other insects. In addition, the borate may actually increase the R-value, structural integrity and fire-resistance of the panels (though that has yet to be proven conclusively). Likewise, AFM has introduced R-Control panels containing TIM-BOR, a borate-based wood preservative. In independent tests, carpenter ants and termites died when force-fed the foam.

Shingle durability—In 1987, the Asphalt Roofing Manufacturers Association (ARMA) reported that installing asphalt shingles over foam-core panels (or rigid-foam insulation) may reduce the fire rating of a roof assembly as well as reduce the lifespan of shingles because of overheating. According to ARMA, in cases of fires external to the roof, the foam insulation may inhibit heat dissipation from the underside of the roof, causing an increased rate of flame spread on the surface of the roof. Regarding shingle overheating, a number of asphalt-shingle manufacturers, including Georgia Pacific, won't warrant their shingles if they're installed directly over foam-core panels.

One solution to the problem of overheating shingles is to purchase vented roof panels (top photo, facing page), which are offered by Branch River Foam Plastics (EPS) and Cornell Corporation (urethane). Some shingle manufacturers appear to be accepting this compromise (check with the manufacturer or with ARMA). An alternative is to continuously vent the roof by installing furring strips and ½-in. plywood over the panels. This is an expensive proposition, but one worth considering in a hot climate, especially if you plan to install a radiant barrier in the vent space. Finally, you can ask your panel fabricator for a list of shingle manufacturers who warrant the use of their shingles over foam panels. For example, Elk Corporation has notified AFM that after successful in-field testing they would warrant their Prestique product line when used on R-Control panels. If you go this route, I would stay away from dark-colored shingles as a matter of simple prudence.

CFCs and the ozone—In response to global warming and damage to the ozone layer, there's a move afoot among industrialized nations to significantly reduce production of CFCs within the next decade. That could have a serious effect on the cost and availability of urethane foams. But at least one urethane panel manufacturer—Winter Panel Corporation—is aggressively moving to cut its use of CFCs as an insulation-blowing agent. Their current strategy of combining the use of Freon with that of carbon dioxide has already produced a 35% reduction of CFCs in their foam, with the ultimate goal of eliminating CFCs altogether by 1991.

According to the company's president, Amos Winter, alternatives must not reduce the R-value by more than 5%, must still retain a Class 1 fire rating and must add little to the cost of manufacture. So far, Winter is on target with all three criteria. □

Steve Andrews is a residential energy consultant who writes about energy-efficiency technologies. He is the author of Foam-Core Panels & Building Systems: Principles and Practice Plus Product Directory *(Cutter Information Corp., 37 Broadway, Arlington, Massachusetts 02174-5539). Photos by author except where noted.*

Sources of supply

There are more than 75 manufacturers of foam-core panels in North America, too many to list here. Following is a list of manufacturers mentioned in the text. For a more comprehensive list, see Steve Andrews' book, *Foam-Core Panels & Building Systems* (address at end of article) or *The Timber-Frame Home*, by Tedd Benson (The Taunton Press, Inc., P. O. Box 5506, Newtown, Ct. 06470-5506; 800-888-8286). Also, you might want to contact the newly formed Foamcore Panel Association, a panel-manufacturers' association that consists of nine charter members. Call Amos Winter at (802) 254-3435.

- AFM Corporation, R-Control Div., P. O. Box 246, Excelsior, Minn. 55331; (612) 474-0809
- Advance Energy Technologies, Inc., P. O. Box 387, Clifton Park, N. Y. 12065; (518) 371-2140
- Advanced Foam Plastics, Inc., 5250 North Sherman St., Denver, Colo. 80216; (303) 297-3844
- Atlas Industries, 6 Willows Rd., Ayer, Mass. 01432; (508) 772-0000
- Branch River Foam Plastics, Inc., 15 Thurber Blvd., Smithfield, R. I. 02917; (401) 232-0270
- Cheney Building Systems, Inc., 2755 S. 160th St., New Berlin, Wis. 53151; (414) 784-9634
- Concept 2000 Homes, 3003 N. Highway 94, St. Charles, Mo. 63301; (314) 947-7414
- Cornell Corp., P. O. Box 338, Cornell, Wis. 54732; (715) 239-6411
- Enercept, Inc., 3100 9th Ave. SE, Watertown, S.D. 57201; (605) 882-2222
- Fischer Corporation, 1843 Northwestern Parkway, Louisville, Ky. 40203; (502) 778-5577
- Harmony Exchange, Inc., Rte. 2, Box 843, Boone, N. C. 28607; (704) 264-2314
- Insul-Wall Ltd., 11 Mosher Dr., Dartmouth, Nova Scotia, Canada B3B 1L8; (902) 465-7470
- J-Deck Building Systems, Inc., 2587 Harrison Rd., Columbus, Ohio 43204; (614) 274-7755
- Marne Industries, Inc., P. O. Box 465, Grand Rapids, Mich. 49588-0465; (616) 698-2001
- NASCOR Inc., 7803P 35th Street S. E., Calgary, Alberta, Canada T2C 1V3; (403) 279-1966
- Pond Hill Homes, Ltd., Westinghouse Rd., R. D. 4, Box 330-1, Blairsville, Pa. 15717; (412) 459-5404
- RADVA Corp., P. O. Box 2900, FSS, Radford, Va. 24143; (703) 639-2458
- Thermapan Industries Inc., Box 479, Fonthill, Ontario, Canada L0S 1E0; (416) 892-2675
- Winter Panel Corp., R. R. 5, Box 168B, Glen Orne Dr., Brattleboro, Vt. 05301; (802) 254-3435

Island Victorian

Stress-skin panels lock up a post-and-beam weekend house

by Don Price

On a clear day in May my friend Charlie Reeder and I boarded the ferry for Mackinac Island, intent on our upcoming building project. The blue of the sky and the blue of the lake were fused, with only the island in the distance breaking the color. The captain, his spirits lifted by clear weather, took to the intercom to say, "No man is an island. Only an island is an island. There is Mackinac, your destination of 19th-century tourism. No cars, lots of fudge. Beware of the leg-hold tourist trap. They *are* ready for you. Don't forget to buy a guide book on sale at the pilot house."

Don Price is a builder in Ann Arbor, Mich.

Land of the Great Turtle—Mackinac Island (pronounced "mackinaw") is located in the Straits of Mackinac, where Lakes Huron and Michigan converge and Michigan's two peninsulas are joined by the spectacular Mackinac Bridge. The island is turtle-shaped, with high bluffs and inland hills (hence its Indian name, Michilimackinac, Land of the Great Turtle). Mackinac's elevation and location made the island an important military outlook during the Revolutionary War and the War of 1812. Mackinac's winter weather is so severe that a style of heavy woolen coat carries its name.

The high bluffs and proximity to the mainland appealed to early cottage builders in the

1850s and to swarms of summer naturalists in the 1870s. As with the Adirondack Park in New York State, the cottage builders on Mackinac succeeded in convincing the state to buy the remaining land to avoid unregulated tent camping and other "democratic tendencies." It was a wise decision, at least as viewed today, since much of the island is covered by woods, riding trails and carriage paths instead of wall-to-wall cottages. An early decision to prohibit automobiles was a further stroke of genius. Except for firetrucks and ambulances, there are still no cars for transportation on Mackinac, only horses and bicycles.

Cape Cod meets Victoriana—Charlie Reeder and I were on our way to Mackinac to build a weekend and vacation house for our families. We had found a small lot outside of town on the western bluff of the island. You can look out over the water to a breathtaking view of the Mackinac Bridge and the tip of the Upper Peninsula. Victorian styles dominate island architecture, so subdivision restrictions required us to build a Victorian design with a minimum area of 1,500 sq. ft.

I'm a contractor with a historical bent and an interest in timber framing. I have had success building houses using plans from Alex Wade's book, *30 Energy Efficient Houses...You Can Build* (Rodale Press, 1977), so we decided to adapt one of Wade's pole-construction plans called the Gummere House (revised in Wade's *Guide to Affordable Houses* (Rodale Press, 1984). We wound up doubling the size of Wade's design, then added an octagonal tower as a third floor and altered window placement and siding details to give the saltbox shape more of a Shingle-style Victorian character. Architect Marc Rueter of Ann Arbor sketched some early variations and did the final drafting of the plans (drawing on facing page).

We wanted to make the house look like an older structure that had been carefully remodeled. The two-story east facade is Cape Cod in nature, and the west facade has a saltbox silhouette. The Victorian tower takes over the southwest corner. We found inspiration for the tower from the octagonal lantern on a nearby lighthouse, and from the Fort Mackinac tower, which cantilevers from a narrow base. Our hybrid Shingle style seems to work well here. The tower continues the

A towering cottage. The author combined colonial and Victorian shapes and details to make a weekend house for two families. An octagonal deck mimics the geometry of the tower.

From *Fine Homebuilding* magazine (April 1988) 46:80-83

Floor plans

Storage/workroom

Living

Up

View of Mackinac Bridge

Dn

Deck

Dn

Kitchen

Dining

N

First floor

Open to below

Sitting/sleeping
Alternating tread stair

Up

Dn

Bedroom
Octagon room above

Bedroom

Storage

Second floor

Scale in feet

0   4   8   12

line of the bluff, and the colors and texture of the exterior finishes blend with the surrounding woods (photo on facing page).

Taking advantage of a stable economy—
Building a house on an Island without the use of cars or trucks does present a challenge. Most of our materials were brought to the island by ferry. At the dock, they were loaded onto dray wagons pulled by teams of horses. As a result, the materials were handled quite a lot. The stress-skin panels had some rips in the drywall paper owing to numerous transfers. Rips were easily dealt with later, but the extra cost of handling was something of an issue—it added $1.80 per sq. ft. to the project. Carrying bricks on boats and horse-drawn wagons is expensive because weight is the measure for billing.

The horse-drawn wagons proved quite maneuverable on the heavily wooded site in all kinds of weather, and we never had to wait long for materials. It often happened that supplies traveling on the same ferry as I did made it to the site by wagon before I could get there by bicycle or horse-drawn taxi. After the ferry stopped running in the fall, we took to the air. Pilot Paul Fullerton made many deliveries for us, including an 8-ft. Corian slab that he carried in the aisle of his six-passenger airplane. The local people are used to the transportation problem, and rarely does it stop them. I wish I had a photo of the plumber, a sturdily built, soft-spoken fellow, with our new toilet in the basket of his bicycle.

Post-and-beam framework—We built most of the house using a post-and-beam structure, with conventional rafters. Although most of the pine framing members were milled in central Michigan, we thought it a nice touch to use wood from the site, so we hewed four 6-in. by 12-in. beams—two 24 ft. long and two 11 ft. long—from red pine growing on the bluff. (These pine timbers were kinder than the many oak timbers I've hewn.) Two hand-hewn beams flank the dining room and kitchen (photo right), and two are upstairs.

We worked the timbers and built the conventional stud framing for the octagon side by side, then raised the timbers in a few hours with the aid of a crane that was on the island for use in building a new water plant. With the timber elements in place, we set the octagon on the southwest corner of the second floor astride one bay of the timber frame.

Cam-locking panels—I have found that a timber-frame and stress-skin panel system is economical and simple because the preassembled panels cut down on labor. The frame for our Mackinac house has no corner braces, but gets its rigidity from the urethane panels that sheathe it. We ordered these panels called Chase Thermo-Panels, from Cheney Building Systems (2755 S. 160th St., New Berlin, Wis. 53154). The panels have a 3½-in. core of urethane foam (with raceways for wiring formed into the foam) between an outside face of ½-in. plywood and an inside face of ½-in. drywall (photo next page, bottom

One of the hand-hewn pine beams runs left to right, in the photo above. Cabinets and shelving are finished with beaded fir—known locally as 'cottage board.'

left). This composition isn't unusual, but what makes these panels different is how they are joined to each other.

One of the toughest jobs in installing stress-skin panels is fitting the panels together smoothly. To make a strong, interlocking wall, the Chase panels have metal cam-lock devices formed into the urethane every 30 in. along the sides. These cam-locks work together as a pair, with a hooked cam in one sleeve and a fixed pin in the opposing sleeve. Sleeves with pins are cast into one

Sections through cam-lock panel

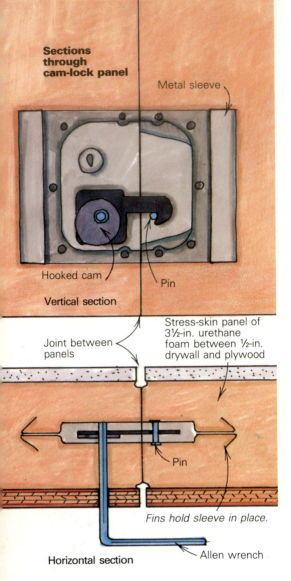

Metal sleeve

Hooked cam

Pin

Vertical section

Joint between panels

Stress-skin panel of 3½-in. urethane foam between ½-in. drywall and plywood

Pin

Fins hold sleeve in place.

Allen wrench

Horizontal section

side of a panel while the sleeves with cams are cast in the other side (see drawing left).

Thanks to factory precision, it was no problem to line up opposite pairs of cam-locks during the wall assembly. After we raised the panels and nailed them to the framing at top and bottom, we inserted an Allen wrench into the cam from a predrilled hole on the plywood side of the panel and gave a turn, causing the cam to hook over the pin in the adjacent panel. The panels fit so tightly that only minimal urethane caulking was needed to seal joints between panels. I wish we could have built a roof using the Chase Thermo-Panel cathedral panel, which has T&G wood strips bonded to the urethane. Unfortunately, the complex relationship between the tower and the main roof tipped the scales in favor of a site-built roofing system using rafters, standard insulation and ceiling details.

These cams are not really new. They have been used in the commercial cooler market for many years. One Sunday after the panels were up, an older gentleman on a hike stopped by and introduced himself as the owner of a pub in downtown Detroit. As he looked around the house, he examined an exposed corner of the panel and announced without surprise, "Freezer panels. Nice touch." Our pride was only slightly deflated. Nowadays, it's often only new uses of old materials that seem original.

Shingle-style details—Exterior walls are shingled in white cedar from the Upper Peninsula, the corners woven—instead of butted to cornerboards—to get a Shingle-style edge.

Red cedar shingles are more resistant to the weather, so we used ⅜-in. thick red cedar to shingle the roof and the side walls of the octagon. Although shingles on most Mackinac houses are painted, we let these shingles weather naturally. The overall texture of the shingles led us to call the house "Seabird" to indicate the salt-water origin of the Shingle style on the East Coast.

We built windows on site from pine barn sash. In keeping with the Shingle style, we built small-paned operable sash for the inner windows, but used a single pane for the storm windows. These double-glazed windows don't have true insulated glass but allow some air infiltration to balance the airtightness and energy-efficiency of the wall panels. This contrasts with the standard method of building inefficient walls and very tight windows.

The windows worked fine except that water sometimes passed the storm window at the head. To remedy this problem we turned roughsawn cedar boards into window hoods (photo below right), similar in shape to those shown in A. J. Downing's *The Architecture of Country Houses* (1850, reprinted in 1981 by Dover Publications, Mineola, N. Y.). As further protection, the storm windows received copper V-shaped weatherstripping.

Cottage finishes—The open-plan interior is small but feels spacious, with lots of windows for views of the surrounding woods and water. We finished the interior simply. Window trim is pine to match the window casing and the post-and-beam frame. The

The author and crew raise the two-story cam-lock stress-skin panels (above). Metal cam-locks are formed into the panels 30 in. o. c., seen here as slots on the panel edges. After the panels are nailed in place, they are locked together by tightening the cam-locks with an Allen wrench. The windows of the cottage (right) reflect the Mackinac Bridge. Waterproofing tricks include window hoods and copper flashing at the deck rail.

kitchen cabinets are made from narrow fir boards, a popular material on the island since the 1890s and locally called "cottage board." In its original use as interior paneling, the material allowed tall balloon-framed houses to be made more rigid. On Mackinac, where skilled plasterers were hard to find, cottage board also made an easy-to-install and easy-to-maintain finish.

The cost of cottage board varies from $.40 to $.60 per lineal foot, so we used it sparingly compared to older Mackinac cottages, where it is used on just about every surface imaginable. On this project, it appears on shelving, risers and closets and as skylight trim and shower surround. We made the vanity and kitchen cabinets from the same material and topped them with Corian. In the smaller bedroom the ceiling is finished with cottage board as though it were simply a porch ceiling. Most other ceilings are finished with lap-joined 1x8 pine.

Towering over it all—Since we designed it as a summer room, the octagonal tower is not insulated, and the rough pine framing in roof and walls is visible (photo, upper right). Only the two walls next to the chimney are insulated and finished with cottage board (photo, middle right). The floor of the tower is insulated to isolate it thermally from the rest of the house, and the hatch door to the second floor is insulated with urethane foam. During warm weather, we lift the door and hook it out of the way to allow light and air to pass from floor to floor. There's a pleasing contrast between climbing the steep, alternating tread stair and entering the large, light tower room.

When we use the tower in cold weather, we fire up a Nova Scotia fisherman's stove, which vents into the chimney behind it. We cooked our Thanksgiving chicken in its oven. Ringing the stovetop is a rail that prevents pots from sliding when in nautical use—a nice reference to the island's former reliance on fishing. The tower has been a favorite of every visitor, and the view does not disappoint. I have noticed that conversations started in the octagon go on longer than they do downstairs. We may build in bench seating to encourage the tendency to linger.

After our first snowfall, a large horned owl flew up from the bluff to sit in a tree next to the house. The bird was 20 in. tall, grey with some white seasonal camouflage. It suddenly occurred to me that the shape of the house and its tower greatly resembled the owl. We had cocked the octagon to turn to the Mackinac Bridge, like the rotation of an owl's head left to right. And the shingles would change color with the weather, just as the bird does.

Getting the building tight to the weather—I spent the fall of 1986 getting the building ready for winter. The roofing went slowly, largely because of the fancy flashing around the tower and chimney and because of the height of the tower. While fitting cap shingles to the octagon roof in late October, I watched

a bat try to push under a shingle nearby. The bat, sensing the approach of winter, was looking for shelter. When the animal could not fit under the crack, it walked down the roof showing considerable displeasure. As I turned on the scaffold for another shingle, the bat's sonar triggered a quick exit. We both had the same goal: to get ahead of the weather.

One weekend in early 1987 as I was finishing the last of the drywall, the cottage received the test I had been waiting for. On Saturday the thermometer read −10°F and the wind blew out of the west at 35 mph. The house held steady at 70°F with just a small fire in the woodstove behind the fireplace.

Garbage in, topsoil out—If you build on an island, it's important to work with locally available materials. One local builder and developer told us early in the project, "Don't throw anything away." As we graded the site for landscaping, we saw the truth in that statement. The soils on the island are generally limestone and gravel, with only the thinnest veneer of topsoil. To avoid having to haul away excavated gravelly soil, we spread yards of it over the site. We needed to cover the gravel with topsoil but had only a small stockpile of it and couldn't afford the expense of bringing in more by ferry and dray wagons. We had to find a source of topsoil on the island.

The Mackinac Island landfill is run in a most progressive way. Michigan's bottle bill, with its ten-cent deposit for return, helps extend the fixed life of this small landfill. Composting helps, too. Both residents and businesses separate their refuse into recyclable material, compost material and paper. The paper trash—no metal, heavy plastic or glass containers—is shredded and mixed with the street sweepings from the horse traffic. This mixture is stored in windrows and is turned periodically. We used this compost as topsoil, mixed with soil drawn from a nearby golf-course project. Although the material contains an occasional plastic straw, it is very light and rich in nutrients.

True to form—As we cooperated with the local ecology and local economy, I think we also captured a little Mackinac history in the house. Many of the local residents were very skeptical when we started, but warmed considerably as the building took shape. One long-time resident passing by on her horse exclaimed, "Now that's an Island house."

It's a four-season house, with underground city water (above-ground piping was the old standard for summer-only cottages) and a kerosene furnace, in addition to the fireplace and two woodstoves (photos right). The island may be known as a summer resort, but it is a wonderful place during the winter. The lake freezes between the Upper Peninsula and Mackinac Island, and lights from snowmobiles bounce across the ice at night and during the day, when the winter sun is low in the sky. Snow covers the island and there's heavy cross-country ski travel on the hills. An occasional cutter goes past, bells jingling. □

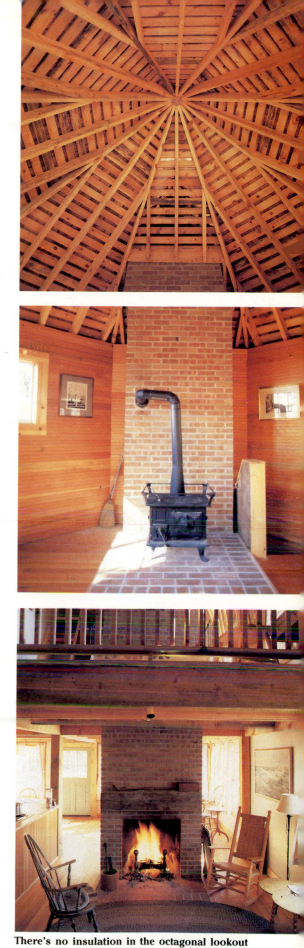

There's no insulation in the octagonal lookout tower (top photo), so its roof framing adds to the view. A Nova Scotia fisherman's woodstove warms the room during cold months (middle photo). The insulated trap door on the right opens to the second floor. A wide brick chimney carries the flue for the Rumford fireplace (bottom photo) as well as two smaller flues from woodstoves on the first and third floors. A railing keeps the sitting/sleeping room open to the living room below.

Framing with Purpleheart

A New England timber framer lands in the Caribbean

by Dennis Darrah

February in Vermont is not exactly the best time and place to practice one's profession as a timber framer, so my initial response to a request to frame in the Caribbean was something on the order of: "It sure beats eating snowballs." Though Entwood Construction, based in Wolcott, Vermont, had framed in the Caribbean before, this was my first opportunity to join the rest of the crew on, as it turned out, their last Caribbean project.

We were hired to frame two hip roofs and one complete timber structure (also with a hip roof) on the tiny French island of St. Barthélemy (about 200 miles due east of Puerto Rico).

Our client appreciated the aesthetic beauty and inherent strength of the timber-framed hip roof, a form with a long history on the island. We got the job because the knowledge and skill required for this type of joinery had fallen into disuse over succeeding generations on St. Barthélemy. Two of the buildings would serve as a garage and workshop, while the third was to house a small office. Later on we were supposed to frame a main house and a guest house, but the project never got that far. Working papers are nearly impossible to obtain, and strict zoning all but shut down construction. In the long run, though, this may be for the best—the island is only about eight square miles in size and can't stand much growth.

A response to the climate—The design for these buildings was derived from the old frames constructed by the 18th-century Swedish and French shipwrights who once inhabited these islands. These timber-framed hip roofs and structures have proven particularly strong over the decades. They have survived numerous hurricanes, including a devastating direct hit in the 1960s. The island is also in an earthquake-prone region, so whatever is built must be properly engineered to survive.

From *Fine Homebuilding* magazine (December 1989) 57:68-70

St. Barthélemy has no fresh-water springs, and consequently, each house sits atop a huge, basement-size cistern. Via roof drains and gutters, the occasional rainfall is channeled into these man made caverns which, when full, can hold upwards of 30,000 gallons of water. These days cistern walls are formed of concrete that has been thoroughly reinforced with small-diameter rebar. The rebar extends from the cistern walls upward into poured-concrete columns, and through the columns into a concrete ring beam supporting the roof. In effect, the houses are post-and-beam frames of reinforced concrete, locked to a foundation full of water. That combination offers maximum resistance to uplift forces.

The spaces between columns and beams are filled in with concrete block and then masterfully stuccoed over. This style of building and the exceptional and plentiful use of steel owes its lineage, as far as I've been able to determine, to the work of the early 20th-century French architect Auguste Perret, one of the pioneers in the use of reinforced concrete.

Working exotic woods—The hip roof is one of the strongest roofs ever devised, and it is a design that has flourished over the years on St. Barthélemy, contributing to the unique charm of the island. The early roofs, and in fact, the complete timber-framed structures before the advent of concrete, were all built of relatively small timbers. Rafters were typically 3x4s milled in South America from whatever hardwoods could be obtained. Most commonly, this was angelique. This wood is both termite- and rot-resistant, and that's why it's also used extensively for dock pilings.

On this job our client decided to go with a slightly larger section of timber than was traditionally used. The rafters are 4x6s, collar ties are 4x4s and the plates are 4x6s laid flat on top of the ring beams. All joints are not only pegged, but additionally some are fastened with stainless-steel bolts, with the bolt heads covered by wooden plugs. The bolts offer an added margin of safety.

Though we did use some angelique in the frame, most of the wood in the structures is purpleheart, which we obtained from French Guiana. It shares the strength and density of angelique (both are approximately twice the density of oak), but offers a beautiful red-purple sheen. Though purpleheart generally keeps its color, the sun is so intense in this climate that the wood turns an ashen gray if left without a finish of some sort. We used liberal quantities of linseed oil on all the timbers.

Without the proper tools, purpleheart is plenty tough to work. Drilling into it for the bolts took a fair degree of determination (photo, below right). To cut the wood, we had sawblades specially made that could rip even a 16-ft. 4x6 without overheating or warping, leaving behind a surface that needed only a light sanding and oiling. We found that Planetor self-feeding drill bits (Rule Industries, Cape Ann Industrial Park, Gloucester, Mass. 01930)) worked well in the hard wood. They can be resharpened and have a replaceable pilot bit.

All the lumber arrived rough from South America, so we also made extensive use of two Makita 6¼-in. planers with carbide blades. These blades are excellent and hold an edge for a long time, but once they dull they seem nearly impossible to sharpen. We have since found, here in Vermont, someone who can do a decent job of it. Before this, though, whenever we nicked a planer blade, we bought a new set—a decidedly expensive solution. We used a 14-in. carbide-tipped blade in our chopsaw, and it left glass-smooth butt cuts on the end of the timbers.

Squaring the timbers—Purpleheart is a particularly stiff wood, and if a timber is at all crooked or hooked, it will be nearly impossible to straighten. A 4x6 purpleheart timber, laid flat across an 18-ft. span, can support the weight of three men without showing any deflection, even after a mortise has been cut out of the middle of it—I can vouch for that.

Fortunately, over the years Entwood Construction developed a system of joinery to deal with the dimensional vagaries one finds in timbers. This system helps us to avoid any problems in fitting timbers, which is particularly important when it comes to working with purpleheart. The technique reduces the end of each timber to an exact, predetermined dimension that is square, parallel to the other end and sized to fit precut mortises in the frame. Usually the fits are so snug that we have to use a 1,500 lb. come-along to ease each piece into its receiving mortise.

To illustrate the way we square timbers, I'll run through our procedure using a very simple example—4x6 joists (drawing next page). Any given 4x6 might actually be 4½ in. by 6¼ in. at one end, and 3⅞ in. by 5⅞ in. on the other end. Once we've checked all the joists and determined the range of sizes, we square and reduce the working ends of each joist to a dimension slightly smaller than the smallest joist end. The joist is only reduced to the depth of the receiving mortise. All the "slop" is on the bottom of the timber and the opposite face, and can't affect either the plumb or the level of the frame. This saves us the enormous effort of having to true and square the entire length of each timber.

A good set of working drawings all but eliminates the need to measure off the frame itself in the course of building. It also brings

Tropical timber. **The structures built on St. Barthélemy included a garage, a workshop and a small office, and blended traditional forms with contemporary construction techniques. Each timber-frame roof (photo left) was hipped to resist tropical storms; the wood is purpleheart, a dense tropical hardwood. Working with purpleheart proved no simple task (photo above). Bits and blades were chosen specifically to hold up during grueling hours of working the material. To keep the wood from losing its color in the tropical sun, it was oiled once a day until enclosed.**

the whole frame into mathematical precision so that even on a building as large as 28 ft. by 40 ft., the tolerances of the finished frame can be held to within ⅛ in. overall.

Figuring the cuts—The calculations for these roofs were aided by a Texas Instruments TI-55 calculator that allowed us to come up with the actual lengths to cut. In framing hip roofs with timbers, you can't ig-nore the width of the stock when doing the calculations because the theoretical line of each jack or hip is actually only true for the center of the piece. In 1½-in. thick stock the accruing error may be negligible, but when the stock is 4 in. wide or more, that error builds up.

St. Barthélemy belongs to France, so we decided to use the metric system for all of our measurements and calculations. When we're working in the states, however, we also use a Jobber II calculator (Calculated Industries, 22720 Savi Ranch Pkwy., Suite A, Yorba Linda, Calif. 92686). It readily translates from inches into metric or decimal and back again. These calculators are an absolute godsend, and if you don't believe it, quick—give me the square root of 5-ft. 11¾₆ in. One of the concrete structures made our figuring even harder—not one of the walls was parallel with another—and there was only one right angle to work with. But all the roofs had to rise at the same 45° pitch, so the TI-55 was indispensable. Of course, the problem and the angles involved must be accurately conceptualized before they can be punched in. But once the numbers have been punched in, the calculator goes blank for about four seconds as it searches its memory for the only combination of trigonometric functions that will fulfill the particular parameters you have given it. Then it will supply the exact dimension you need.

A different view of building—All told, it took three of us about six weeks to complete the framing. We sheathed the roofs with 1x6 T&G Honduras pine boards and covered them with tar paper. The roof was eventually finished off with ceramic tile. Though tin and cedar are used extensively as finish roofing, they tend to flavor any water heading into the cistern.

Above and beyond returning home in March with a glorious suntan, building in the Caribbean was a memorable experience. Working on houses down there forces you to think a little differently about the way a house should be built. The loads on these buildings are the exact opposite of those experienced in New England. Instead of having to build to withstand the downward thrust of a load of wet March snow, one has to engineer a building to counter the enormous uplift forces of a full-blown hurricane. And though we in Vermont take all possible measures to drain water away from a foundation, the islanders try desperately to capture any water they can and funnel it into their basements.

Finally, because of the tropical climate, the inside of a timber frame need not be covered by insulation, drywall or even plaster. Instead, it can be left totally exposed with its chamfered and beaded edges forever available to the admiring eye. In this way the frames will carry the vocabulary of their joinery to some future generation of framers. This, of course, is the ultimate satisfaction of any craftsman timber joiner. □

Dennis Darrah specializes in timber-frame construction and drywall finishing. He lives in Montpelier, Vermont. Photos by John Fagan.

The workshop (photo left) was entirely timber framed, in contrast to other structures which featured masonry wall construction. Joists were fit into mortises in the plates and located as shown in the drawings above.

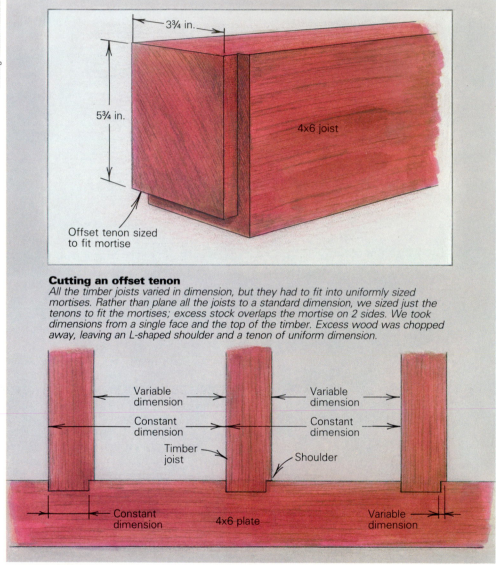

Drawing: Michael Mandarano

3¾ in.

5¾ in.

4x6 joist

Offset tenon sized to fit mortise

Cutting an offset tenon
All the timber joists varied in dimension, but they had to fit into uniformly sized mortises. Rather than plane all the joists to a standard dimension, we sized just the tenons to fit the mortises; excess stock overlaps the mortise on 2 sides. We took dimensions from a single face and the top of the timber. Excess wood was chopped away, leaving an L-shaped shoulder and a tenon of uniform dimension.

Variable dimension

Variable dimension

Constant dimension

Constant dimension

Timber joist

Shoulder

Constant dimension

4x6 plate

Variable dimension

Insulating curtains.

Hung walls filled with insulation can go a long way toward keeping your house warm, but what should you do about your windows, which sit there with a value of R-1 per pane? The typical double-glazed solar house can trace 50% of its heat loss to night radiation and conduction through its south-facing glass. Thermal shutters can raise the windows' resistance value by about 4.

Another approach, and one that's simpler for existing houses, is to use reflective curtains. These can increase the total window system's value to about R-5, cutting window heat loss by about 50%, and the annual heating bill by about 30%. Such curtains, which can be covered with fabric, work in two ways. First, they reflect infrared energy back into the room instead of letting it pass out through the windows. Second, they trap a layer of air next to the window, and inhibit conductive heat loss. They are also good vapor barriers and keep the warm, moist inside air from condensing on the glass. These curtains usually roll down from the top, and one way to seal them effectively is to use 1x3 shutters, which hinge closed and are held with magnets (drawing, below). At the bottom, a 1¼-in. dowel or a metal rod will hold the curtain down snugly. All the materials listed below work well. We've noticed little difference in their performance. —*P.H.*

Glass

Curtain

Magnet

Window coverings: what they cost

Material	Width (in.)	Cost (yd.)	Cost (sq. ft.)
Aluminized polyethylene	58	$ .50	$ .04
Mylar	56	1.20	.09
Astrolon II	56	2.50	.17
Astrolon VIII	54	3.00	.22
Foylon	54	5.00	.37
Warm Window	44	10.50	.95
Window Quilt	custom	3.65	
Window Quilt on rollers	custom	4.40	

Astrolon is distributed by The Shelter Institute, 38 Center St., Bath, Maine 04530. Foylon is made by Duracote Corp., 350 N. Diamond St., Ravenna, Ohio 44266. For information on Warm Window, write 8288 Lake City Way NE, Seattle, Wash. 98115. Window Quilt is made by Appropriate Technology Corp., PO Box 975, Brattleboro, Vt. 05301.

will hang over it. If any leaks develop in the roof, the water will run down the roof poly and outside the wall poly, which should extend below the sill. Your insulation may get wet, but your framing will stay dry, and you won't have any leaks inside.

If, instead of standard transparent or black poly, you use aluminized polyethylene or polyester to double as a heat-radiation barrier, staple it up with its shiny side out, so the house looks wrapped in foil. Then nail 1x3 horizontal strapping 2 ft. on center to create the airspace that is needed for radiation.

The skeleton of the hung wall consists of vertical boards (hangers) attached to the side of each upper rafter tail with 10d nails or split-ring connectors. These hangers are sized in width

for the quantity of insulation you want—in thickness to carry your sheathing, and in length to reach from the rafters down to the sill. Nail 2x6 horizontal blocking on 4-ft. vertical centers between the hangers as nailers for the sheathing. For instance, vertical boards can be roughsawn 1x6s with 2x6s every 8 ft. where the horizontal sheets of sheathing butt.

The tops of the vertical boards should be notched for 2x6 or 2x8 blocking, which is end-nailed through the 2x rafters. These blocks, supported by the notched hangers and the rafters, will carry the weight of the exterior siding. Finish the bottom of the skeleton with horizontal 2x6s.

Insulation goes between the hangers. Rigid foam boards are easy to apply, but they all

aren't chemically stable, and some types may lose insulating value over the years. Fiberglass costs about four to ten times less per R than other insulations, and is a good choice.

We usually use 4x8 asphalt-impregnated (AI) sheathing because it's both permeable enough to let moisture breathe out and soft enough to form a good wind seal when it's nailed to the hangers with 1¾-in. roofing nails. It's also easy to notch around the upper rafters.

Once the AI sheathing is in place, nail vertical board-and-batten or board-on-board siding to the top and middle blocks, and to the bottom 2x6 finishing board. Use 10d nails. The battens or second layer of boards should be nailed with 8d nails, 12 in. on center.

Openings—Windows and doors can be installed individually between the hangers, or grouped and raised into place as a unit. When you're installing individual windows or doors (for more on working with fixed glass, see *FHB* No. 8, pp. 42-43), you have to be sure that the hangers can support their additional weight. We use 2½-in. split-ring connectors to attach the tops of the hangers to the rafters, and bolt 1½-in. angle iron between their bottoms and the 2x8 header, as explained in the box below. If a window has exterior siding below it, the outer 2x6 blocking beneath the sill will carry its weight.

Grouped windows and doors are raised in their framework between sections of hung wall. They can be raised conventionally, with glazing flush to the edge of the house platform. This results in the windows and doors being set in from the siding of the hung walls. Alternatively, their vertical framing members can be notched and hung over the edge of the platform. This brings glazed surfaces and doorways close to the plane of the exterior walls. Both methods work equally well, and the choice between them is an aesthetic one. We have found that indented windows have the effect of bringing the outside in. □

Pat Hennin is the founder and director of the Shelter Institute in Bath, Maine.

Split rings and angle iron

These are two connectors that an owner-builder can fabricate whenever extra strength is needed. A split-ring connector is designed to hold two pieces of wood together better by holding onto more of each piece. We make ours out of ⅛-in. steel tube of various diameters, and usually cut them 1 in. long, with a narrow slice through the wall to accommodate expansion and contraction.

To use a split-ring fastener, cut a ½-in. deep circular groove in both boards with a hole saw and set the ring in it, with half of its length protruding. The other board's groove fits over this projection, a hole is enlarged through the center, and the whole thing is held together with a bolt, a washer and a nut.

Angle iron is great for connecting boards or posts perpendicular to each other. You can get it in 22-ft. lengths from any steel wholesale outlet (check the Yellow Pages). A length of ⅛-in. by 1½-in. by 1½-in. angle iron weighs 27 lb. and costs us $8.66 ($.39 per ft.). We usually use 6-in. lengths as fasteners, so this comes to 44 of them at $.20 each—a real bargain. You can cut angle iron with a $3.50 metal-cutting blade that fits any 7¼-in. circular saw. This process throws out hot sparks, so be sure to wear goggles. —*P.H.*

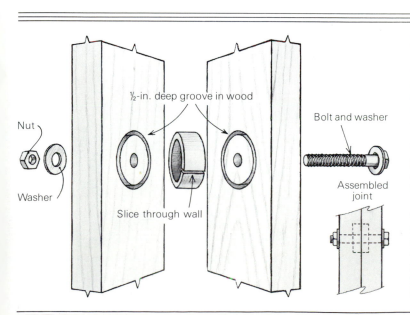

½-in. deep groove in wood

Bolt and washer

Nut

Washer

Slice through wall

Assembled joint

Building Timber Bowstring Trusses

Graceful curves and careful joinery in 5x14 pine

by Glenn Reynolds

New England weather can be harsh, but a house framed with timber holds up well. A timber frame is resilient, and in a storm it may yield slightly but it won't break. On the inside exposed beams and woodwork compose a warm, comfortable atmosphere.

When Kent Kilgore asked Maine woodworker Ron Bracy to build him a timber-frame home with a bow roof, Bracy was doing some finish work in another bow-roof house. The semicircular vaulted roof in that house was created with formed laminated rafters, which would be out of character in a timber frame. In Kilgore's house, Bracy would be faced with the challenge of creating timber-framed bowstring trusses. Drawing on his experience in building boats, Bracy began the project by thinking of the bow roof as an inverted hull.

Framing the house—Building the house took nearly a year (including curing the timbers). The final design called for a two-story main building 26 ft. wide and 32 ft. long, with a single-story 16-ft. by 18-ft. extension centered on one end (photo facing page). The structure was a traditional timber frame with mortise-and-tenon joinery, using northern white pine for the timbers. The main floor was box-sill construction, and the 16 posts supporting the second floor were carved and shaped into traditional gunstock form at Bracy's shop. All timbers were brushed with boiled linseed oil to reduce checking and to protect the wood from the weather as the frame was being assembled. Anyone who has spent time putting up a timber frame knows that accumulated sawdust and dirt, ground together by the constant foot traffic of a construction crew, can lead to trouble later on. Rain hitting an unprotected timber frame makes this goop leach down through the gaps in a subfloor to discolor and streak any unoiled timber.

Basic truss considerations—Bracy chose northern white pine for the trusses because it's a sturdy wood, affordable, available locally and works well. And the wood is relatively light, a quality of no small importance considering that each part of the trusses would have to be hand-carried more than once during the construction process. Because the trusses would be visible inside the finished house, Bracy wanted good-quality stock, which means No. 2 or better. This grade is common, but because the job required many timbers with oversized dimensions and odd lengths, Bracy special-ordered the wood from Joe Putnam's sawmill in South Berwick.

Unseasoned pine is a "wet" wood, which means that in addition to sap, it's also loaded with pitch. Bracy's custom-sawn order came off the truck from Putnam's mill aching to stick to everything in sight. The stock was nearly useless in this condition, so it had to be seasoned to eliminate the undesirable qualities of the green wood. Bracy's crew stacked the timbers out of the weather, away from heat and direct sunlight, in layers separated by 1x1 stickers spaced no more than 3 ft. o. c. The ends of the beams were painted with two coats of oil-base enamel paint to reduce the wood's tendency to check. The beams were stacked in a well-ventilated

barn for about eight months. When Bracy was ready to work the wood, the timbers were dry, straight and much lighter.

Truss design—Since bowstring trusses call for unconventional roof construction and standard roof pitch calculations don't really work, Bracy began with scale drawings. The first thing he had to work out was the ridge height of the trusses. If it was too high, trusses would permit ample headroom near inside edges, but might easily exceed a size that could be practically built. On the other hand, if the ridge height was too low, headroom inside the structure would be diminished.

After a few trial-and-error sketches, Bracy chose a ridge height for the main structure of 15½ ft., with the arc reflecting a 20-ft. radius. The collar tie was located so that its lower surface was 8½ ft. from the floor. These dimensions yield an open and spacious interior, with 6 ft. of headroom only 2 ft. from the side of the room, a gentle bow effect, and a truss that the crew could handle.

Each truss would have a curved outer chord and a straight collar beam, with a "king and queen" post web design (drawing, facing page). The joinery would be a combination of pegged mortise-and-tenon (borrowed from traditional timber-framing practice) and the scarf (from boatbuilding). The scarf was used to join the six separate sections of 5-in. by 14-in. stock that make up each curved truss chord. Bracy used the scarf because it's simple to cut and it affords large surface-to-surface contact between members for screwing and gluing the joints.

Bracy knew from his previous timber-framing experience that placing the trusses 8 ft. o. c. with 4x4 purlins sometimes results in a condition called "saddleback." The wide spacing of the trusses allows the purlins to sag over a period of time, resulting in an undulating roof. Placing the trusses just over 6 ft. o. c. with 4x6 purlins between rectifies this problem. With this truss spacing, the main section of the building would need six trusses and the extension would require four.

Layout of the trusses—Once the timber framework of the house had been installed and decked, an exact, full-scale layout of the trusses was done on the completed second-floor deck of the house, and then transferred to plywood templates. Using a few pieces of 1x3 strapping, Bracy made a compass to swing the appropriate arcs on the deck. The center point of the compass was nailed loosely to the deck, and a pencil was snugly fit into holes drilled at the appropriate radius lengths along the 1x3. Since each half of the truss is a mirror image of the other half, only one side had to be scribed out on the deck. After the arcs for the top chord of the truss were scribed, it was an easy matter to lay out the collar beams and the webs.

Next, templates were made. Lengths of ¼-in. plywood were pieced together to cover the full-size truss drawing, and the desired arcs were scribed on the plywood. Bracy drew match lines so that the pieces could be accurately repositioned, then he lifted the strips and cut the tem-

plates with a jigsaw. Each chord required three templates. Then the collar beam and the webs were scribed onto plywood and cut out.

On the templates, Bracy laid out the joinery that would hold the truss together. The bottom template needed a seat cut, 4x6 purlin pockets 1½ in. deep, and a 20-in. diagonal cut for the scarf joint where this section joins the middle one. The seat cut was really nothing more than a provision for the truss to catch on the frame, and to create an overhang for the soffit. The length of the scarf joint allowed a good amount of contact area between the two parts without being too slender and fragile. It was also the largest amount of overlap possible within the bounds of the plywood templates.

The middle template needed a 20-in. diagonal scarf joint on both ends, a mortise to accept the collar-beam tenon, and purlin pockets. All tenons were 2 in. thick, with varying widths and lengths according to the piece and its application. Since the mortise-and-tenon joints would be drilled and pegged with 1-in. oak pegs, the tenon had to be wide enough to accommodate this process without splitting. The collar-beam tenon, for example, is 2 in. thick by 6 in. wide by 6 in. long. The top template needed a 20-in. diagonal cut, purlin pockets, and a mortise to accept the queen-post tenon. The topmost end was plumb cut at the ridge. Templates for the collar beam, king post, and queen post were shaped in the same way, and their joinery laid out according to the scale drawings.

Cutting the timbers—Cutting curved rafter sections from 5x14 stock was a challenge. Since the pieces were too unwieldy to bandsaw, Bracy and his crew had to shape them with portable power saws.

First, a template was placed over the timber to be trimmed, and its outline was penciled onto the surface of the stock. The template was lifted, and the first pass, cutting about half the thickness of the wood, was made with a portable circular saw equipped with a crosscut blade. Though it sounds awkward, Bracy was able to push the saw slowly along the curved guide lines on the soft pine. Then the beam was flipped over. The template was reversed, set on the uncut surface and aligned to match the kerf on the opposite side with a framing square. A second pass with the saw sheared off the waste, leaving a finished 5x10 timber. Bracy used a 2-in. straight spokeshave to clean up saw marks and to eliminate any mismatch between the cuts. It took two men nearly two weeks to cut all the trusses.

Next came the mortises and tenons. With the aid of a framing square, measurements were transferred from the template to the end grain of the timber. Vertical cuts were laid out 1½ in. in from the inner edges, leaving a 2x6 rectangle centered on the end grain of the arc. Mortises were drilled out with a 2⅛-in. spur bit to a depth of 6 in. and cleaned up with a chisel. The extra ⅛ in. left a small amount of play, which became very useful when fitting the tenon.

When the joinery was complete, Bracy began the work of cutting ornamental chamfers in the edges of the truss pieces. He used a router and a carbide-tipped chamfer bit to form the edges,

Photo facing page: Ron Bracy

From *Fine Homebuilding* magazine (June 1986) 33:44-47

After they were assembled on the second-floor decking, the trusses were lifted into place with a 15-ton crane. The gable end was installed first, and each subsequent truss was spaced from it by knocking the purlins into their respective pockets. A come-along pulled trusses together to ensure snug fits.

and cleaned up any burrs with a spokeshave. The surfaces of the pieces were touched up using a wedge scrub plane with a slightly rounded iron to give the trusses a handhewn look.

Assembling the trusses—The six sections of the arched truss chord for the first truss were arranged on the deck, with a 2x4 spreader to maintain the correct building width between seat cuts. The arcs were snugged with clamps to ensure that the scarf joints fit properly, and all the remaining parts of the truss were dry-fitted and touched up to finish tolerances.

After the truss was fitted correctly, Bracy and his men took it apart once again. Now they were ready for final assembly. First, the chord was made fast. Bracy spread a layer of Sikaflex 241 multipurpose marine sealant/adhesive (Sika Corporation, 875 Valleybrook Ave., Lyndhurst, N. J. 07071) between the surfaces of the scarf joints. He then "tacked" each joint with 20d galvanized spikes, countersunk ⅜-in. by 8-in. galvanized lag screws into the joint, and clamped the assembly to provide reinforcement until the Sikaflex set up.

Bracy used Sikaflex because he was impressed with its use in boatbuilding. It's strong, resilient, waterproof, and even comes in an assortment of colors (tan was used to match the pine). Since

Sikaflex cures to a tough rubber-like consistency, its bond is pretty tenacious, which is particularly important when you're gluing wood that's somewhat green. Excess glue, once cured, may be quickly and cleanly shaved off with a chisel. When the bond had partially cured (about a half-hour), slight disparities in thickness between truss chord sections could be spotted at the scarf joints and trued up using a 6-in. Makita portable power plane.

With the chord sections together, each truss could be completely assembled. Because the king post, queen posts, and the collar beam interlock, they had to be joined simultaneously. All joints received adhesive, and once seated, each tenon was locked into place with a 1-in. oak peg.

Each truss was assembled in this fashion, one on top of the other. With large, unwieldy trusses, advance planning is essential so they can be hoisted without confusion and wasted time. Bracy assembled the trusses in two piles at the building site: the six trusses used for the main structure into one pile, and the four trusses for the extension into another. Since the extension was to be open from first-floor level to ridge, both piles had to be located on the main building deck. The extension trusses were arranged so that the seat cuts faced in that direction, with

the gable-end unit on top. The trusses for the main house were stacked in the same orientation but at the other end of the deck, and with the gable-end unit on the bottom of the pile.

The bottom truss in each pile was assembled flat on 2x6 blocks so a crane strap could be slipped under the truss later on. Then each successive member was blocked and built in place. This strategy allowed the units to be lifted and placed smoothly by the crane, working first at the end of the extension, then toward the middle of the building and out to the other end.

Raising the trusses—A 15-foot crane was brought in to raise the trusses, starting with the gable end of the extension. After it was hoisted into place, it was plumbed and braced with 2x6x16 lumber secured with staging nails. It served as the reference for positioning the next truss. Once the second truss was in place, a few purlins were dropped into their mortises and secured, to space the truss exactly. The third truss was referenced off the second, and so on across the length of the building (photo above).

Everything went smoothly until the crew reached the last three trusses on the main house. Bracy found that in order to have enough room on the deck to manipulate the gable-end truss, the preceding two trusses had to be lifted and temporarily propped against one already up. Once the gable end was up and braced, the odd pair were "walked" into place.

With all the trusses finally up, Bracy and his crew knocked in the rest of the purlins, checked the assembly for plumb and secured the purlins with nails. When Bracy sighted down the truss peaks to check their alignment, he found that some were up a little, and some down. To remedy this condition, Bracy pulled a string taut and level along the ridge line defined by the highest truss peak. Metal joist hangers were then positioned near the ridge by loading them with a 2x10 block representative of the "correct" ridge and leveling the top side of the block against the string. The hangers were then nailed into place, and 2x10s were dropped into place between trusses and nailed.

Sighting down the trusses at the seat cut, where the trusses extended past the girt, revealed a few more slight discrepancies in alignment. A taut string was again employed as part of the solution, this time to locate 1x3 nailers for attaching the soffit material.

Finishing up—To provide a base for the roof sheathing, 1x3 strapping was run 16 in. o. c. from soffit to ridge, and nailed into the purlins. The roof sheathing was 6-in. wide T&G pine, fastened with 8d galvanized box nails. Then 15-lb. builder's felt was stapled to the sheathing, and over the felt extra clear white cedar shingles were applied 5 in. to the weather. Over the top third of the roof slope, the shingle exposure diminishes to about 4 in. Bracy found that at these exposures, the shingles lay along the curve of the roof quite nicely.

Inside the house, Bracy planned for a cathedral ceiling because he wanted the trusses to be exposed as much as possible. To accomplish this and provide for insulation, the underside of the roof was lined with 3-in. thick sections of Celotex insulation that was held in place with blocking (drawing, above right). More 1x3 strapping was run from ridge to eave and again nailed to the purlins, this time to provide a nail base for ½-in. drywall. The drywall easily conformed to the curve of the roof without wetting (photo right).

With a bow roof, ventilation is particularly important but must be handled within the constraints of the structure—standard gable-end vents won't work. But since the outer courses of strapping created channels of open space between the sheathing and the purlins, this provided an ideal ventilation route. Bracy installed a series of small circular vents in the soffit and capped the roof with a commercial ridge vent.

Bracy has since done another bowstring-truss timber-frame home that represents a second generation of the techniques he developed on the first one. The main difference is that no timber purlins were used in the second roof. Instead, Bracy used 2x6 stock, installed on metal joist hangers in much the same way as he installed the ridge of the first house. The system is quicker and more accurate, and since the purlins don't show from the interior anyway, no aesthetic compromise had to be made. □

Glenn Reynolds is a freelance writer.

Drawings: Elizabeth Eaton

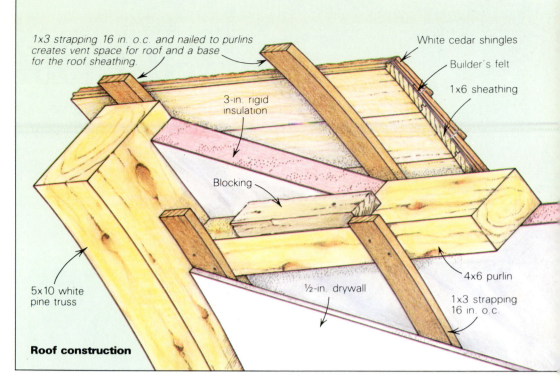

1x3 strapping 16 in. o.c. and nailed to purlins creates vent space for roof and a base for the roof sheathing.

White cedar shingles

Builder's felt

1x6 sheathing

3-in. rigid insulation

Blocking

5x10 white pine truss

½-in. drywall

4x6 purlin

1x3 strapping 16 in. o.c.

Roof construction

The trusses are most dramatic in the kitchen and dining room. Drywall was used to finish the interior wall and ceiling surfaces.

Curved Timber

How one timber framer hews, bandsaws and steambends straight stock into curves

by Ed Levin

The process of turning trees into lumber is largely a matter of turning irregular curves into smooth, straight lines. It's an uphill battle, as any woodworker can tell you. So if straight and square is the lumberman's Holy Grail, why is curved work the highest expression of the woodworker's art? Windsor chairs, Chippendale highboys, the flowing lines of a wooden hull and the soaring heights of a vaulted church all attest to this mystery. The process is fraught with paradox: in order to round the wood, I must first make it straight and square, yet sometimes when working on a curved brace, it seems that I am trying to turn lumber back to a tree again.

The only curved timbers that start out as such are found curves, which are curved trees or limbs that are sawn or hewn along their natural lines. In the medieval heyday of timber framing when elaborate curved work was common, supplying curved stock must have been an established business. Even today, some boatbuilders have a standing order for hackmatack knees—the curved, exposed roots and limbs of larch trees. Found curves are also seen in matched pairs as wind braces or cruck frames (for more about cruck frames, see the article on pp. 66-69).

Curves shaped by hewing—Shaped curves are sawn or hewn from straight stock. These days most of the work done by me and my partners is bandsawn, but once we did hew a curve in a timber, serendipitously. A friend wanted the focus of a timber-frame addition to be a 20-ft. long summer beam, hewn from a tree in his woodlot. We felled and hauled in the only tree large enough to make the required 8x12. After we crosscut and peeled it, the trimmed log was predictably smaller and less straight than it looked on the stump, and it would have made a very waney 8x12. We decided to hew only three sides, leaving the bottom of the beam in the round. After rough hewing the three sides with a 12-in. broadaxe, we shaved them clean with a 6½-in. lipped adze. The completed summer beam was handsome and reasonably square and straight, and we quit for the day well satisfied.

But by the next morning, the tension in the undressed sapwood side had pulled the beam into a curve and the midspan of our formerly straight summer was now displaced more than 2 in. out of line with the ends.

A four-part curved arch joins a hammer post to the hammer beam. Rather than feather into the post, the arch is cut with blunt ends for bearing strength.

Since attempts to straighten the timber by additional hewing would probably only cause it to bend further, we concluded that we'd found a new method for curving timber and had better make the most of it. We raised the joists so that their tops would clear the high point of the summer beam. The counterpoint of the straight joists against the gently curved summer beam gives a slightly domed effect to the room.

Curves shaped by bandsaw—The simplest way to introduce a curve into a timber frame is to use curved wind braces. We first attempted this by cutting a radius only in the inner edge of the brace, then tried rounding both inner and outer surfaces. This was better but still not right. We were looking for a shape that would look both tense and limber. We finally settled on a broken-back brace with the inner face radiused and the outer face faceted (photo facing page). Here, the brace

seems to be flexing its muscles against the load. This shape also works well for a curved collar beam, where the collar strains against the inward thrust of the rafters at midspan.

To make a curved brace, we start with 3x10 stock. We rough cut it with a 14-in. bandsaw, then clean up flat surfaces with a power plane and curves with a compass plane, removing any blemishes with a steel scraper. An alternative to the power plane would be to use a powerful router with a long straight bit, guided by a radiused fence. A well tuned spindle shaper can make a reasonable substitute for the compass plane.

Another curved timber that is easily incorporated into an otherwise straight frame is a flared post. The extra width at the top can accommodate tenons from both the plate and tie beam. Folklore tells us that such posts were cut from butt logs using the natural taper of the trunk to obtain the flare. These days we saw flared posts from oversize straight timbers.

Bandsaw technique—A word about bandsaw technique with heavy timber: You can easily run braces and other light members through a bandsaw, but as the stock gets bigger, you'll have to improvise. Rather than horse around with a giant green timber on your saw table, you might want to consider moving the saw rather than the stock.

You'll need a flat, stiff shop floor and a small bandsaw on casters. Support the stock on sawhorses (it's useful to have three or four because you'll have to shift them during cutting) and wheel the saw through the cut. The beam must be raised above the saw table, or you can remove the table entirely to provide additional clearance for thick stock. Timbers heavy enough to warrant this procedure will not flex under the downward pressure of the saw blade.

For repetitive work like sawing flared posts, we use a portable bandsaw mill. We cut 2x guides to the correct radius and fasten them to the timber. The mill rides on the curved guides. This produces a smooth, accurate cut requiring little cleanup.

A hammer-beam roof—Although we enjoy using curves as accents, we also like the opportunity of building a frame with curved work throughout. My neighbor Dimitri Gera-

From *Fine Homebuilding* magazine (August 1988) 48:44-47

karis began construction of his new blacksmith shop in 1973. For a year he laid stone walls, and we talked about what his roof should look like. We met one evening at the Dartmouth College library, where I was researching carpentry in the Middle Ages. Thumbing through engravings of medieval buildings, Dimitri turned to a section on church roofs. A single look was enough—he would have a hammer-beam roof.

If you were an Englishman building a church in the 14th century and a vaulted stone ceiling was beyond your means, you might have built a hammer-beam roof. Such a roof features brackets that project from the top of the wall to support roof trusses, allowing relatively short timbers to span a wide room (photo, facing page). Often the oak timbers were richly molded, with winged angels on the ends of the hammer beams. This would be a blacksmith shop, not a church, so we built a plain version (no angels).

Curves spring from wall post to hammer beam and flow up through the semicircular arch, which ties hammer posts, principal rafters and collars into a rigid frame. The arch is made up of four segments, each with two long tenons connecting the rafter to post or collar. The curved segments have blunt ends both for bearing and to avoid the weakness inherent in a feather edge in short grain.

One house, many bandsawn curves—Several years passed between the raising of the blacksmith shop and our next major curved work. Steve Manning asked me to design and build a house in Greenwich, Conn. Following his program, I designed a house with curved spaces defined or accented by curved framing. The second-floor landing is defined by a 12-ft. dia. semicircle and is open to both the living room below and the peak of the gable above (photo at right). In order to frame each

of the two quadrants of the curved landing with a single piece sawn from solid wood, the raw stock would need to be 24-in. wide. In addition to the impracticality of searching out such enormous pieces of wood, the resulting structure would be unstable—the curve is so deep that a point load at midspan would torque the ends. We solved this problem by making each of the quadrants from two pieces joined together like halves of a pair of scissors. To avoid the feather-edge problem mentioned earlier, we used a strengthened halving joint. The inside of each quadrant is cut to a 6-ft. radius and the outside face is faceted in the broken-back profile (drawing below).

We also designed a solarium with five arches, each made up of two quadrants sawn from 5x15 stock (photo, next page). The quadrants are fastened into posts, girts and plates, and tenons running the full length of the straight side of each quadrant are shouldered at the bottom for more bearing (drawing, next page). The plate (dubbed the "serpentine plate" because of its sinuous lower edge) receives tenons from three arches and two posts so that it contains a continuous mortise.

Curves shaped by steam—In the spring of 1985, Bill and Tom Webster asked us to design and build a small house with a timber frame that would enclose one large space. We designed a roof formed by two intersecting gables, with windows in the four gable ends and a lantern set atop the crossing (for more on this house, see *FHB #45*, pp. 44-48).

The 24-ft. by 32-ft. open space under the crossing presented a structural problem because we wanted to avoid interior columns. To resist the thrust of the roof and to stabilize the roof frame, we linked the four posts that support the valleys with tie beams and

braces to form an octagon, 10 ft. on a side. The connection between valley posts and rafters was stiffened by the addition of arched braces that join these elements together into the continuous ribs of a cross vault. Pairs of curved wind braces would branch upward from the corner posts and arches would rise from tie beams to collar beams in the gable ends. As we designed the frame, the catalog of curved timber grew un-

The two curved timbers in this floor opening are joined by a strengthened halving joint (drawn below). The post is stiffened by two broken-back braces.

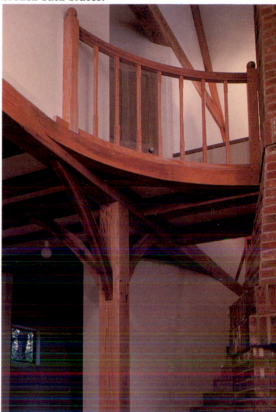

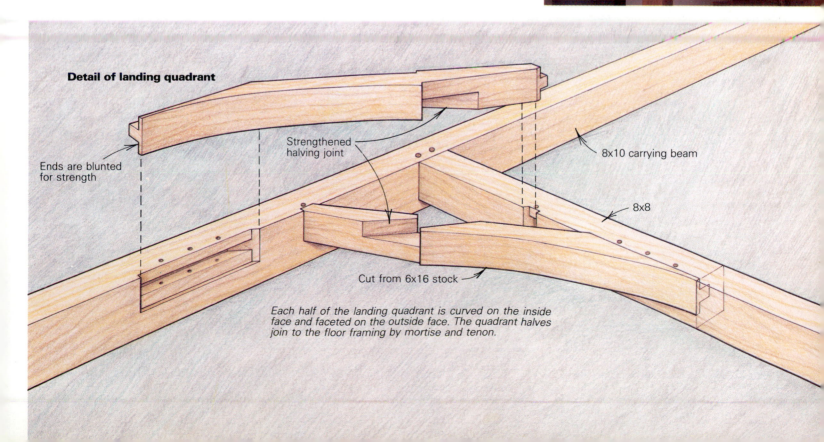

Detail of landing quadrant

Ends are blunted for strength

Strengthened halving joint

8x10 carrying beam

8x8

Cut from 6x16 stock

Each half of the landing quadrant is curved on the inside face and faceted on the outside face. The quadrant halves join to the floor framing by mortise and tenon.

Each arch in this sunroom is made up of two quadrants sawn from wide stock (drawing below). The 5x5 plate waves slightly along its lower edge as it reflects the slope of the arch quadrants. The plate is mortised along its entire length. *Photo by Karen Bussolini.*

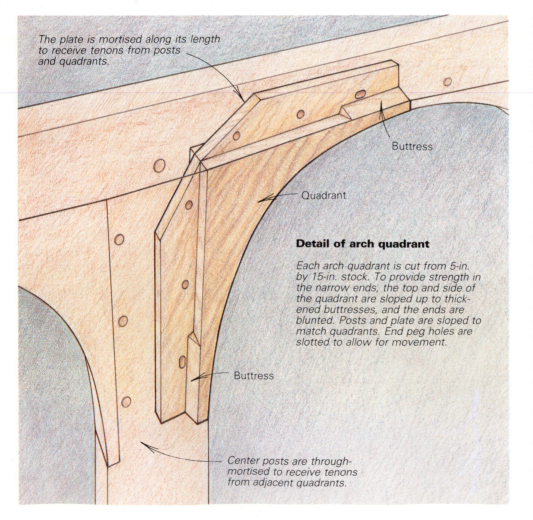

The plate is mortised along its length to receive tenons from posts and quadrants.

Buttress

Quadrant

Detail of arch quadrant

Each arch quadrant is cut from 5-in. by 15-in. stock. To provide strength in the narrow ends, the top and side of the quadrant are sloped up to thickened buttresses, and the ends are blunted. Posts and plate are sloped to match quadrants. End peg holes are slotted to allow for movement.

Buttress

Center posts are through-mortised to receive tenons from adjacent quadrants.

til it comprised one-quarter of the lumber, engendering a crisis.

For some time, doubts had been growing in our shop about the wisdom of bandsawing these curves from oversize stock. First of all, there was the waste. The sizes of stock for this frame ranged from 5x12 to 6x18, most of which would end up as firewood. And the sawn curves would invariably cut through the heart of the tree resulting in unsightly checking as the wood dried out. Finally, the straight-grain pattern would conflict with the curved edges of the stock. On all counts we would be much better off bending rather than sawing our curves.

Taking the plunge, we ordered straight-grained 6x6 oak timbers and got in touch with Ed McClave, a boatbuilder and repairer from Noank, Conn., who, more than anyone, has turned steambending into a science.

The physics of steambending—The most difficult of the obstacles encountered in bending heavy stock are springback and overbend. Under normal conditions wood is an elastic material—it bends in proportion to an applied load and straightens out when the load is removed. Steam performs two functions in bending timber. It heats up and plasticizes the wood fibers so that the stock does not return to its original shape after the bending load is removed. Steam also keeps the wood moist and moderates the effects of too-rapid drying.

But the wood is never completely plasticized (nor would you want it to be for any kind of structural application), and the elasticity left after steaming and bending causes the timber to move partway back toward its undeflected shape. In order to compensate for this movement, or springback, you must overbend. The trick lies in determining the amount of the overbend. Paradoxically, the milder the bend, the more elastic the wood remains, requiring greater overbend. Conversely, for sharper bends less overbend is called for, since the stock is more completely plasticized.

Careful observation over years of boatbuilding, coupled with a strong engineering background, allowed McClave to work out the physics of steambending. He gave us the basis for calculating the correct overbend radius for a given species, stock thickness and finished radius.

Steambending apparatus—We began by building a bending table and steambox. The bending table was a 90° grid of timbers stacked and bolted together. The top layer of beams was closely spaced, then sheathed with ¾-in. plywood (photos, facing page). After screwing down the plywood, we sealed it with two coats of waterproofing primer and marked out the overbend radius, which was about 9 ft. for 5-in. thick stock that we wanted to bend to a finished radius of 11-ft. 6-in. Cleats fabricated out of 4-in. by 3-in. by ¼-in. angle iron were then bolted to each timber to define the inner edge of the curved piece.

Drawings: Heather Lambert

A timber, hot from the steam box, is pulled against a curved form with a come-along and clamps.

Our table could accommodate two nested bends, so we made our steambox large enough to hold two 16-ft. 6x6 timbers.

We set up the steambox, a long, open-ended pine box on sawhorses (photo above) and pitched it slightly toward one end so condensed water would drain. We added sleepers to elevate the stock and allow the steam to circulate, and attached plywood doors and felt seals at each end. The temperature inside the box was monitored by several meat thermometers. We fashioned a steam generator from a 250,000-Btu propane torch set inside an open-topped metal drum that supported a water-filled 5-gal. fuel can. Steam from the can was fed into the steambox through a radiator hose. The water level was maintained through a Rube Goldberg arrangement we devised after a near-meltdown. A garden hose regulated by a toilet float valve fills a bucket with water, which then siphons into the fuel can. At peak output, we converted a gallon of water to steam every three to five minutes, consuming 40 lb. to 50 lb. of gas per day. We also had a backup steam generator on loan from the town road crew, which used it to thaw frozen culverts in the winter. We used it to apply steam to the stock as it was being bent, in an effort to keep the wood from cooling too quickly.

The bending moment arrives—The scene at the first bend, with crew members dressed in protective clothing and ready for fast action, resembled a pitstop at the Indy 500. At the signal, the torch was killed and the doors to the box flung open. We hustled the timber onto the bending table shrouded in great clouds of steam, and each crew member took up his assigned station. Two men worked come-alongs, two others applied the

After the steamed timber was clamped into place on the bending table, Levin hosed it down to keep it from checking.

clamps as the timber came up against the cleats and the last man used the town's antique boiler to play live steam over the stock, once again enveloping us in fog. After a couple of bends, it dawned on us that steaming wood was like working iron in a forge—small pieces heat up and cool down rapidly but large pieces heat up slowly and cool slowly. We realized that we could ease off the frenetic pace and dispense with the secondary steaming, so subsequent bends were more relaxed, workmanlike affairs.

Once out of the protective environment of the steambox, the timber's internal heat would cause rapid drying and would also cause checking. So as soon as a piece was securely

clamped in the bending form, we would hose it thoroughly with cold water, cover it with with wet burlap and keep it wet with a soaker hose until it cooled completely.

As we learned more over the course of the job, we incorporated other improvements. Rather than bending smoothly, the timbers would tend to kink around the clamping stations, so we made a continuous inner form of laminated oak and fastened it to the angle iron cleats. A ⅛-in. by 6-in. sheet-metal compression strap clamped to the outside radius with end blocks let us bend pieces that would not otherwise have held up under the tension of the bend (photo, left). We also clamped the stock to the table vertically to control the tendency of the timber to twist.

Midway through the job, the bending routine was well established. We placed two 6x6s in the steambox at the end of each day, and the first person in the shop in the morning fired up the boiler. Following the rule of about one hour of steaming per inch of thickness, we kept the interior of the steambox at or above 207° F for at least five hours for a 6x6 timber. Just before the new sticks were to come out of the cooker, we would remove the previous day's work from the table. But first, we'd secure and tension each bend with straps and a come-along ("stringing the bow"), then release the come-alongs and clamps holding the pieces to the bending table and tilt the curved timber up off the table. Finally, we nailed stay laths to both sides of each piece, slackened the bowstrings and stockpiled our newest bends. □

Ed Levin is a partner in the timber-frame company, Paradigm Builders, in Canaan, N. H. Photos by Richard Starr, except where noted.

Curved-Roof Bungalow

Boatbuilders and carpenters conspire to make wood bend

by Bonnie Cullen

Home owners sometimes ask their builders to create structures that at first glance appear to have conflicting requirements. Take for instance this house by Washington State builders Duke Rhoades and Gaylord Stadshaug (photo above). Their clients own a forested old farmstead near the northeastern corner of the Olympic Peninsula. Along the northern boundary of the pasture the land is bordered by a long, straight mound, about 10 ft. high, that resembles a levee. The mound buffers the winds that blow here, offering shelter for a home built in its lee.

The clients wanted a long, low house. They also wanted to top the house with a curved roof and ceiling spanning nearly 30 ft. over an open floor plan. This request left the builders juggling seemingly incompatible conditions. For one, they had to keep the house low, yet create enough pitch to allow drainage off a concave surface. The large span suggested a truss of some kind, but a simple triangular truss system would create a headroom problem where the bottom chord of the truss joined low supporting walls. It would also limit the spacious feeling in

the middle of the room and detract from the curved ceilings. Laminating curved rafters seemed like a possibility, but Rhoades and Stadshaug were apprehensive about how much weight they could carry and how long it would take to build them.

Then Rhoades had an inspiration. Recalling some graceful bridges that he had seen along the Oregon coast, he sketched out a truss with two concave curves forming the top chords and a single convex bottom chord (top drawing, p. 132). Arching the bottom chord would provide strong support at the mid-points of the curved ceilings, along with maximum headroom. And

The gently curving roof atop this bungalow on the Olympic Peninsula (above) follows the profile of six laminated trusses that are left exposed on the interior. Facing page: Arched trusses clear-span the 30-ft. wide house, allowing an open plan without bearing walls and a ceiling nearly 16 ft. high. The trusses are varnished Sitka spruce, and the T&G ceiling boards are the same wood, left unfinished.

perhaps most important of all, the arched bottom chord would enhance the effect of the generous curved roof (photo facing page). "I wasn't sure this would work, but I loved the look of it and something like builder's intuition told me it was structurally sound," Rhoades recalls.

To verify his intuition, Rhoades hired a structural engineer to calculate whether six of these trusses would support the roof. The answer came back yes. The next problem became how to build the trusses within the budget.

To keep construction costs down, Rhoades and Stadshaug first purchased rough-cut 6x6 cants of Sitka spruce from a lumber mill on the Washington coast. Sitka spruce is used chiefly by builders of boats and small aircraft; it's lighter than Douglas fir, but it has greater tensile strength and bends more easily. Stadshaug also found that the spruce had more pitch in it than fir. As he resawed the 16-ft. to 24-ft. cants into 2x6s with a bandsaw, he had to wax the saw table and spray the blade with silicone to prevent pitch buildup. It still turned out to be cheaper to buy the spruce this way, even though

From *Fine Homebuilding* magazine (April 1987) 39:66-69

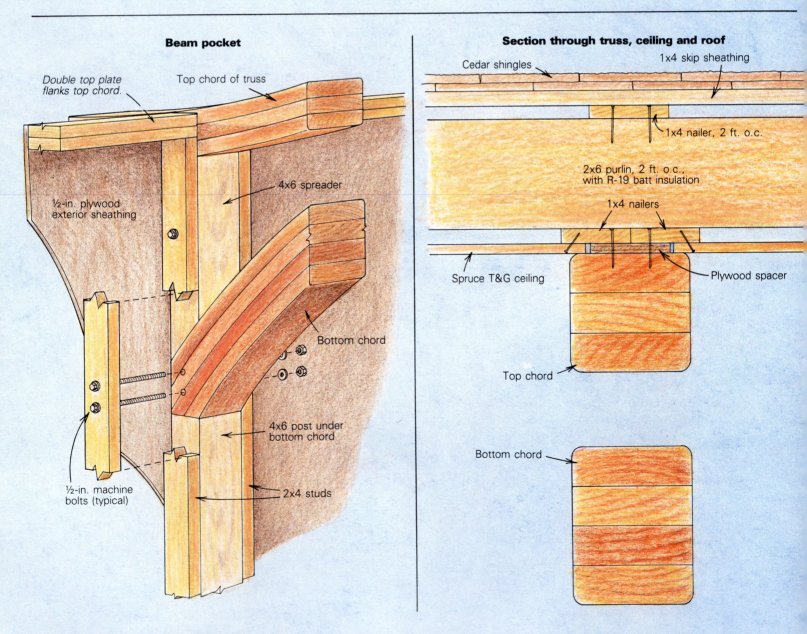

Top chords are lag-bolted from both sides at peak.

Three ½-in. lag bolts, 9 in. long (typical), at each tangent

Web members are secured with a pair of lag bolts, top and bottom.

4x6 spreader

4x6 post

Arched truss
The truss designed by Rhoades and Stadshaug is composed of two concave top chords, a convex bottom chord and two web members. At the outboard ends, 4x6 spreaders keep the chords the correct distance apart. The trusses bear on 4x6 posts, which are flanked by studs in the stick-framed walls, as shown in the detail, below left.

Bottom of chord is flattened to bear on post.

Beam pocket

Double top plate flanks top chord.

Top chord of truss

½-in. plywood exterior sheathing

4x6 spreader

Bottom chord

½-in. machine bolts (typical)

4x6 post under bottom chord

2x4 studs

Section through truss, ceiling and roof

Cedar shingles

1x4 skip sheathing

1x4 nailer, 2 ft. o.c.

2x6 purlin, 2 ft. o.c., with R-19 batt insulation

1x4 nailers

Spruce T&G ceiling

Plywood spacer

Top chord

Bottom chord

they had to add on the handling for drying, re-sawing and planing it.

The builders decided to subcontract the bending and gluing of the truss components to Port Townsend Boatworks. These wooden-boat builders are experts in these techniques, and they had the space and equipment necessary for fabricating 32-ft. arches.

At the boatworks, the 2x6s were scarf-jointed and glued together into long boards. The scarf joints were rough-cut on a bandsaw, then dressed on the jointer. Held secure by a jig at the proper angle, each scarf joint was passed over the jointer knives until its surface was perfectly smooth, with a gluing area 18 in. long.

The Boatworks crew then laid out a diagram of one concave 18-ft. long top chord of the truss on plywood tables arranged to encompass the entire curve and secured to prevent movement. They screwed blocks at intervals along the lay-out line to create a laminating form. To laminate the top chords, three 2x6s were buttered with Weldwood wood glue and arranged so that their scarf joints were staggered. Then all three were clamped at the center point of the form, with successive clamps working outward toward the ends of the chord. Although they needed only 12 top-chord members, the Boatworks made a few extras to be cut up for web parts.

The bottom chords are nearly 30 ft. long, and they were assembled using a similar form set up on the Boatworks floor. As before, the separate laminae were buttered with glue and clamped to the form's center point. But instead of applying additional clamps, the crew attached a come-along to each end of the outer lamination. Then they secured the come-alongs to the walls of the shop, and began to crank the 2x6s against the curved form. Unfortunately, this first setup began to pull the shop walls out from under the roof. So the crew anchored the come-alongs to the roof supports, and then all bent well.

Truss assembly—Before they left the shop, the truss parts were laid on their sides and put through a thickness planer to remove excess glue and to even their surfaces. Then the pieces were trucked to the site, where the housebuilders took over. The crew used routers with ½-in. roundover bits to finish the edges of each truss member, then sanded them thoroughly.

The plywood subfloor then became a truss workbench. Rhoades and Stadshaug drew the exact outline of an assembled truss on the floor. This gave them the angle and placement of the top and bottom chord plumb cuts and the position of the web members (top drawing, facing page). To assemble a truss, they first made the plumb cuts on a pair of top chords and cross-bolted them at the ridge with two ½-in. lag bolts, 9 in. long. Then, with spreaders tacked in place at both outboard ends to ensure correct alignment, the top chords were lag-bolted to the bottom chords at the tangent points.

The last members to be fitted were the two webs at the top of the truss. Cut from the extra top-chord members, the webs engaged the top and bottom chords with angled butt joints. They too were anchored with ½-in. by 9-in. lag bolts.

Finally, the crew sawed off the acute angles at the ends of the bottom chord, creating flats that bear on posts buried in the stud wall. The posts are straddled by 2x4s and covered with ply-wood on the exterior, creating beam pockets to receive the ends of the trusses (bottom left drawing, facing page).

Raising the trusses proved to be the most ex-citing part of the job. Since the site was relative-ly inaccessible, Rhoades and Stadshaug decided it would be cheaper to raise each truss in pieces and reassemble them in place than to hire a crane to hoist the assembled units into position. Before disassembling a truss, the crew made registration marks on the various components, documenting their exact alignment. Then they angled and braced the walls inward about ⅜ in. in anticipation of the outward thrust that the trusses would generate.

Stadshaug was in charge of the raising oper-ation. When asked how it was done he replied, "I guess you could say we just muscled it up. We had six guys stretched along the truss. We lifted the bottom chord, raised one end of it over the wall, and guided the other end into the beam pocket. After bracing it, we maneuvered the free end into its pocket and bolted both ends to the stud walls. Once we were sure this big arc wasn't going anywhere, we set up steel scaffolding under the tangent points, and clamped the top chords into place according to the registration marks. Finally we put in the web members and spreaders, and bolted everything back together."

Ceiling and roof—The T&G ceiling sheathing runs perpendicular to the trusses (photo, p. 131). Because it would have been tedious and time-consuming to butt the ceiling boards to the trusses, Rhoades and Stadshaug decided to run the ceiling boards a bit past the top edges of the trusses, concealing their ends. To do so, they nailed ½-in. thick plywood spacers to the tops of the trusses, followed by a pair of 1x4 nailers (bottom right drawing, facing page). This cre-ated a pocket about 1 in. deep on both sides of the truss to accept the ½-in. thick Sitka spruce sheathing. When it came time to install the ceil-ing boards, they were quickly cut to approxi-mate oversize lengths, and sprung into their awaiting slots.

Atop the ceiling nailers, rows of 2x6 purlins placed 2 ft. on center bear on the trusses (photo above). Perpendicular to the purlins are more 1x4 nailers—both inside and out. The nailers on the outside anchor the skip sheathing and cedar shingles, while the interior nailers act as inter-mediate supports for the T&G ceiling boards.

After the roof was on, the gable walls were laboriously framed by plumbing and measuring every 2 ft. along the wall plate. The tops of the studs were bevel cut, each one requiring a few more degrees of angle as they progressed toward the ridge. Rhoades and Stadshaug made gable-end fascia by cutting 7-in. wide curved segments from 1x12 cedar boards. It took three scarf-jointed segments to make each side of a gable end. These in turn were glued to pieces of ¾-in. plywood cut with the same outside radius, but 6⅝ in. wide. The ⅜-in. difference creates a rab-beted edge against which the ⅜-in. plywood sof-fit bears.

In the end, the trusses cost slightly under $4,000 (in 1982). Modifying the roof into a curved surface and building the gable walls added another $800 to the total. To make sure the top chords wouldn't separate, Rhoades and Stadshaug had some ¼-in. steel brackets made that follow the profile of the peak of the trusses. Although they didn't want to interrupt the un-adorned look of the wood, the builders and the clients were ready to bolt the brackets in place if any separation occurred between the top chords at the ridge. Happily, the brackets are still in their boxes. □

The trusses are 10 ft. on center, and support 2x6 purlins that in turn carry the roof. The 1x4s attached to the bottoms of the purlins are nailers for the T&G ceiling boards.

Freelance writer Bonnie Cullen lives in Ibiza, Spain. Before moving, she helped to build a timber-frame house in Port Townsend, Wash.

A Timbered Ceiling

Combining stick-framed walls with a timber-framed ceiling

by George Nash

Traditional timber frames have an undeniable aesthetic appeal. And coupled with high-tech materials like stress-skin panels, they're energy-efficient. But modern milling and assembly systems notwithstanding, timber framing is still more labor-intensive than stick framing and imposes severe constraints on the layout of mechanical systems. Whatever the merits or disadvantages, no one can claim that timber framing is inexpensive. As a builder living and working in a relatively poor rural area, my typical clients are well educated, seriously underpaid urban refugees—people with timber-frame tastes and stick-frame budgets.

Probably because I enjoyed the sheer sensuality of timber joinery so much myself, I tried to find a satisfying compromise between the absurdity of appliqued wood-grain plastic beams and the expense of genuine mortise-and-tenon joinery. Some builders attempt to create a timber-frame effect by notching a center beam to receive one end of the joists while carrying the other end on standard exterior wall plates. With this construction, it's impossible to finish off the junction of the interior

Exposed ceiling joists are among the most prominent and appealing features of a timber-frame home. As shown in the photo above, the system of joists, rim beams and summer beams is supported on conventionally framed walls in order to minimize cost and ease the placement of mechanical systems.

wall and the joist penetrations in a way that doesn't look clumsy or forced.

Ceiling treatment is also problematic with a timbered ceiling. Although V-grooved 2x6 decking installed over the joists has the advantage of providing finish ceiling and floor (or subfloor) simultaneously, it restricts mechanical systems to exterior walls, partitions, dropped ceilings and chases routed into beams. And even with sound-deadening board between the decking and a wood finish floor, people downstairs will experience the pitter patter of little feet as a jackboot fandango.

Grappling with these and other difficulties within the framework of tight budgets, I devised a framing system using heavy timber ceiling joists that combines the speed and

flexibility of conventional stick framing with the aesthetic and structural benefits of timber framing (photo above).

Pine woodworking—I use native eastern white pine for all my timbers. Pine is more stable than hemlock and white spruce, the two other readily available timber species in our area. It shrinks, checks and twists much less as it dries in place. Also, pine works easily. It has a uniform grain, so there is less danger of splitting the wood when cutting joints.

Timbers are best worked when green, before they've had a chance to bow or warp. You can't force a crooked timber into true, at least not without a come-along and some means of permanently maintaining the pressure.

Some builders might wonder if pine is suitable for structural use. In general, timber framing has an inherently greater margin of safety than conventional framing. In particular, with the relatively light loads typical of residential construction, and with short spans and oversize timber cross-sections, timber strength has never been a problem. With this particular system, only the central girder, or summer beam (from the Old English term "sumpter," a pack mule bred for shouldering heavy loads) carries a significant load unassisted, and is therefore greatly oversized.

All my timbers are planed on four sides to match standard dimension lumber. This lets me combine timbers with standard framing, as the design may require. Planing also speeds joinery and ensures tight fits because all timbers have the same dimensions. I typically use 4x8s, 6x8s and 8x8s milled to 3½ in. by 7¼ in., 5½ in. by 7¼ in. and 7¼ in. by 7¼ in. respectively. The summer beams, nominally 8x10s or 8x12s, are an exception. The single-side planer at my local mill has a maximum capacity of 8 in., so these timbers come through planed two sides only. The top surface will not be exposed, so I leave that rough and plane the bottom smooth with a power plane. I prefer smooth, oiled wood to roughsawn. Most clients appreciate how much less dust planed timbers collect.

Rim beams—I frame exterior walls conventionally, using 2x4 stock at 16 in. o. c., except that I eliminate window and door headers. Here the framing is the same as a nonbearing interior partition, which saves time and trouble running wiring and allows for better insulation.

In place of the rim (or band) joist of conventional platform framing, I set a 6x8 rim beam on top of the exterior walls (bottom photo). Using continuous rim beams resolves the problem of detailing the interior finishes and eliminates the need for fake beams between the joists and at the gable-end walls.

A 6x8 rim beam used over a 2x4 wall exposes 2 in. of beam on the interior. With drywall or ¾-in. wood paneling, there is still a satisfying amount of reveal. I use 1-in. foam sheathing on the outside, which along with 3½-in. fiberglass batts, gives me R-19 walls. But if a client wished to increase the R-value of the walls by going to 2x6 framing, 8x8s would maintain the same or a slightly deeper interior reveal.

Simple notches—While my crew is framing and erecting the exterior walls, I lay out and cut notches in the summer beams and the rim beams. Because the notches themselves are quite simple, I can usually have all the beams finished by the time the walls are up, plumbed, lined and braced.

Notches are laid out from the same end of the building as all other framing measurements. I use 32-in. o. c. spacing, which I feel strikes the best balance between pleasing appearance, adequate structural strength (using 4x8 joists) and efficient use of standard-length flooring and lumber lengths. Four-ft. spacing can be used with 2x6 decking, but will result in a bouncier floor and fewer beams exposed.

With a circular saw set to a depth of 3½ in., I cut 3½-in. wide notches for 4x8 joists all the way across the face of the rim joists (photo above). This depth is critical because it allows the joist to bear a full 1½ in. on the stud wall itself. The notches require only a series of circular-saw cuts and then a chisel to remove the

Notching the rim joist. Because the joists will actually bear on the stud wall, they don't have to be mortise-and-tenoned into the rim joist, but can engage simple notches cut across the face of the timber. Here the notches are being cut with a 12-in. gas-powered circular saw that the author bought at a yard sale.

Rim and summer beams. In place of the rim joists of conventional platform framing, 6x8 rim beams are set on the exterior walls, with 8x10 summer beams supporting the joists at midspan.

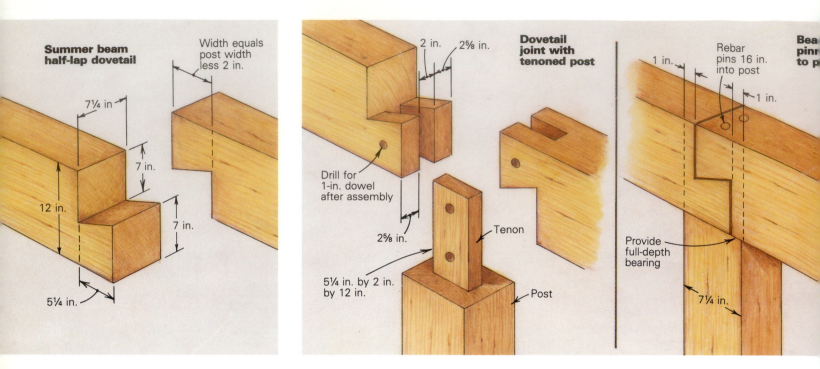

Summer beam half-lap dovetail

7¼ in
Width equals post width less 2 in.
7 in.
12 in.
7 in.
5¼ in.

Dovetail joint with tenoned post

2 in. 2⅝ in.
Drill for 1-in. dowel after assembly
2⅝ in.
5¼ in. by 2 in. by 12 in.
Tenon
Post

Bea pinn to p

Rebar pins 16 in. into post
1 in.
1 in.
Provide full-depth bearing
7¼ in.

Joists in place. Four-by-eight joists are set in their notches and secured with 12-in. spikes driven through the outside of the rim beams and with 20d nails toenailed down into the summer beams. The framing will also be tied together by a floor system above.

scrap. The back of the notch need not be perfectly smooth or uniform because it will be completely hidden.

The other end of the joist is set into a notch cut 1½ in. deep by 7¼ in. high into the face of an 8x12 or 8x10 summer beam. (I use the deeper beam for unsupported spans over 14 ft. and the shallower beam for shorter spans.) These notches demand a bit more attention, but are hardly difficult. I begin by setting the beam on extra-heavy sawhorses (a 16-ft. 8x12 of green pine can weigh nearly 400 lb.). I carefully draw the notch on the face of the beam in pencil (keep a sharp point—16ths are important). Then, I use a 2-in. Forstner bit in a ½-in. drill and drill a series of holes along the bottom end of the notch. Forstner bits cut cleanly and leave a flat-bottomed hole. Next, I make saw cuts along the pencil lines, and several more in between them. I square up the bottom corners of the notch with a sharp 2-in. framing chisel and clean the notch itself.

I try to cut the notches just a hair under the actual joist width for a snug fit. If I've done it right, the joists must be pounded into their notches, but the fit should not be so tight that the joist crushes the edges of the notch. I undercut joist lengths ⅛ in. or so. Otherwise, the joists tend to push the rim beams out of line. Chamfering the edges of the joists will also ease initial fitting.

Big beams, big nails—At corners where the rim beams intersect each other I use a simple vertical half-lap joint, with one beam let into the other to make a cleaner joint (drawing facing page). The corners are pinned with ½-in. rebar. Because these rim beams are not entirely structural, rebar and nails can substitute for complicated mortises and tenons.

The rim beams are secured to the wall plates with toenailed 20d spikes every 2 ft. This corrects any slight bowing in the timbers. Sometimes a timber bows upward instead of out-

ward or inward, causing a gap at the wall plate. Nails alone cannot close the gap, but pipe clamps will. In addition to the toenails, I drive 6-in. pole-barn nails up through the wall plate into the beams, spacing them about 6 ft. apart, with one about 3 ft. from each corner. It's a good thing that these ring-shank spikes hold so well—nailing more than a few upside down or over your head is definitely aerobic exercise.

The joists are fastened to the rim beams with two 12-in. log-cabin spikes driven through the outside face of the beam. (Around here, 80d to 100d spikes are called log-cabin spikes. I get these from the lumberyard.) I have also used 12-in. lengths of ½-in. rebar for this purpose. But cabin spikes do not require predrilling and seem even stronger than necessary. At the summer-beam notch, I toenail two 20d nails down through the top of the joist (photo left). There is little chance of the framing pulling apart because either solid decking or some other floor system will tie everything together from above.

Splicing and setting summer beams—In most cases, the summer beam has to run the entire length of the house, which often means two beams are required for the necessary length. They either terminate at opposite sides of a stairwell opening, or more likely, are spliced together over a post. This splice joint is literally the centerpoint of the ceiling frame and deserves special treatment.

I usually use a dovetailed half-lap for solid bearing on the post below (drawings above). This is fairly simple to cut and yet is pleasingly complex in appearance. An alternative would be to use a longer scarf joint or a bolster. These joints are pegged or bolted together (I countersink the bolts and plug the holes with dowels). The dovetailed joint can also be secured to the post with hardwood pegs driven through the beam and an internal tenon. Otherwise I simply pin the beams to the post with rebar.

Drawings: Michael Mandarano

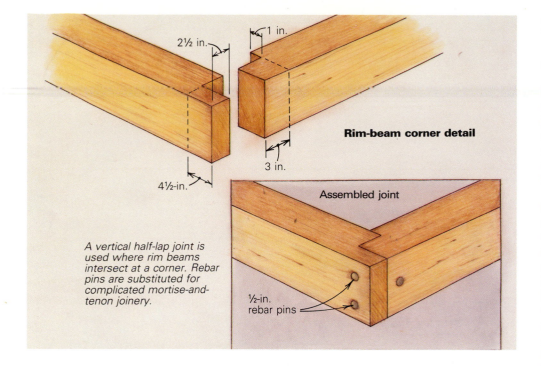

Rim-beam corner detail

2½ in.

1 in.

3 in.

4½-in.

A vertical half-lap joint is used where rim beams intersect at a corner. Rebar pins are substituted for complicated mortise-and-tenon joinery.

Assembled joint

½-in. rebar pins

Making room for pipes and wires. **When the downstairs ceiling is the upstairs floor, it complicates the routing of wires, pipes and ducts. Nash solves the problem by installing 2x4s on edge across the tops of the timbered ceiling, leaving room for mechanicals, then covers the 2x4s with plywood.**

I use a 12-in. gas-powered Homelite circular saw to make the 5-in. deep cut this joint calls for (with a maximum depth of 4⅝ in., only two cuts are needed to saw through an 8x8). Frankly, I'd prefer a 14-in. electric circular saw, for quieter working conditions, but I happened to buy the Homelite cheaply at a yard sale. Using a handsaw, I finish the cut to full depth, and then saw along the slope of the dovetail with an 8-in. circular saw and remove the waste with a chisel.

I check the face of the joint against a template, then smooth it flat with a slick. This tool is used like a plane, not like a chisel: one hand holds the flat of the blade against the work, the other hand pushes against the butt of the handle. If it's sharp, the slick puts a mirror-smooth finish on the face of a joint. It is especially useful working across the grain and should be part of every timber joiner's toolkit.

Despite the care I take to make accurate cuts, the joint seldom fits perfectly the first time. Sometimes the face is open on one side and tight on the other. With the pieces together, I can saw down the vertical face of the joint with a handsaw and remove enough stock to allow the joint to pull or slide tightly together. I'm satisfied if the finished joint barely admits a matchbook cover (a matchbook = ¹⁄₃₂ in.).

I've learned to test fit this critical joint *before* lifting the beams into place. I set them on the floor deck, resting them on doubled 2x blocking (so their ends can protrude over the sole plates at the exterior walls) and make any necessary corrections. Because this often requires several tries, the advantages of working at floor level are obvious.

The summer beams are supported at the end walls on a built-up 2x4 post. Five 2x4s nailed together make a 7½-in. wide post. I like to nail a 2x4 block flat across all the ends of the post members for better bearing. A full-length stud nailed to each side of the post forms a beam pocket and nailing surface. Be-

cause the summer beam is usually planed to 7¼ in., the ¼-in. gap allows easy placement (and removal if needed). Before the beam is secured, I fill the space with cedar shims.

A string stretched across the run of the beam determines center-post height and lines the beams after they are in place. The summer beams should be diagonally braced to the outside walls or to convenient interior partitions until after the joists are installed. Otherwise, an excessively tight-fitting joist could push the beam off line.

While beams and joists are structural timbers, they are also finish lumber. Use the same care storing and handling beams as you would your casing stock. Keep them out of the mud and don't slide them across gritty floor decks. Wash your hands and clean your tools before working on them (a dirty beam cannot be spot-sanded; the entire face must be cleaned). Never pound a joint together without protective blocking; pine is soft and easily dented, and heavy summer beams are especially awkward and prone to denting when handled. It takes four of us, two at each end, to carry a summer beam, cradled on hardwood 2x4s. I use rollers cut from 1½-in. PVC drain pipe to move beams about on the deck.

Fake posts—When the walls are ready for interior finish, I screw 2x8 pine stock to the built-up posts and 2x2 stock under each corner to imitate structural posts. The finish wall material butts against these false posts, so the reveal and the look is exactly the same as that of a true post. I sometimes add 2x4 knee braces if the client desires. Unlike a true timber frame, these are not structural and fit over the wall studding. Four-by-four knee braces can also be installed at the summer-beam posts. The faces of the rim beams, false posts, etc., would have to be notched to accept these braces when cutting the other notches. So far, most clients have preferred the simplicity of unbraced corners.

Room for mechanicals—Until recently, I used V-groove 2x6 spruce decking over the beams for flooring. Considerable time was spent designing wiring and other mechanical runs, because unlike an ordinary joisted ceiling, there were no bays between the beams to conceal utilities. My solution is to nail 2x4s on edge, 16 in. o. c. across the joists (photo above). I glue and nail T&G ¾-in. plywood on top of the 2x4s. This subfloor reduces noise transmission, finish-floor problems, fear of water damage to the ceiling before close-in and provides a virtually unobstructed space in which to run wires, pipes and hot-air ducts. So long as floor loads are ultimately carried by the joists and summer beam, greater latitude is possible when cutting and framing for penetrations than with standard joisted ceilings. The finish ceiling, whether drywall or boards, is hung between the beams from the underside of the 2x4s. □

George Nash builds in Burlington, Vermont. Photos by author except where noted.

A Hip-Roofed Timber Frame

Maine builders erect a classic sea captain's house on an island

by Christopher Hyde

Perhaps no man is an island, as John Donne contended, but almost everyone, at one time or another, has thought about living on one. Bruce Poliquin, a Manhattan investment counselor who grew up in Waterville, Maine, did more than just think about it. In 1985, he bought a tiny island in the estuary of the Kennebec River east of Bath, Maine. Consisting of about 15 acres of granite ledge, spruce and fir, Wood Island is one of the most spectacular building sites on the Maine coast.

Soon after buying the island, Poliquin began scouting for Maine contractors, soliciting bids on a relatively standard timber-framed Cape Cod house. After awarding the contract to Farrell and Thurrell Joiners of Freeport, Poliquin called up Charlie Farrell and described the house he *really* wanted to build—a Federal-style house with a hip roof. It would be, Farrell knew, one of the first hip-roofed timber frames built in the United States since the popular revival of the art about 20 years ago.

Plans by the WPA—Farrell and Thurrell have FDR's Works Progress Administration (WPA) to thank for the plans. During the depression, the WPA surveyed and drew up detailed blueprints of historic houses all over the country. The project was called the Historic American Building Survey. In Maine alone, over 200 of these houses were surveyed. Looking through a collection of them called the *His-*

torical Architecture of Maine: Historic American Building Survey (Maine State Museum, State House Station 83, Augusta, Me. 04333, 1985), Farrell discovered the Bowman-Carney House of Cedar Grove, built in 1761. It was a classic, hipped-roofed sea captain's house, and it represented New England architecture at its best.

Farrell contacted the Library of Congress (Prints and Photographs, Library of Congress, Washington, D. C. 20540) and ordered a copy of the plans. They cost him $160. The 15 pages of blueprints were fabulous, with beautiful elevations and floor plans, as well as lots of detailed drawings of window and door trim, wainscotting, fireplace mantels and more. Unfortunately, the one thing the plans didn't have was the one thing Farrell and Thurrell needed most—details of the hip-roof joinery.

Lacking detailed drawings, the builders searched out 18th-century hipped-roofed houses to study the joinery involved in bringing together seven roof members at a single point. But even with the abundance of timber-frame houses still standing in Maine, including the original Bowman-Carney House, their research was disappointing. The joinery in the houses they visited was sound but not pretty. Most of it appeared to have been done by eye. "The old-timers expected these joints, especially those at roof level, to be covered," Farrell said. "A few gaps here and there didn't

make much difference in strength, when all the members were in compression." All of the timbers and joinery in the Poliquin house, however, would be exposed—part of the interior decoration—with the hip joint a focus of the second floor (top photo, p. 140).

Cutting the frame—A four-man crew cut the entire white pine frame in Farrell and Thurrell's shop. Exterior posts were cut from 8-in. by 10-in. timbers. Larger timbers (8-in. by 12-in.) were used for the interior posts, so that gunstocks could be cut below each joint. This work, along with the curved knee braces, was done with a Mafell portable bandsaw.

Mortises were cut with a chain mortiser and tenons with a Mafell circular saw capable of cutting at a 60° angle. "But we don't cut anything all the way with a saw," said Farrell. "Every joint is finished with a chisel."

The bottom edges of the first-floor ceiling beams were beaded with a router. Then cabinetmaker Kevin Rodel used a template and a chisel to hand cut lamb's tongues at the end of each bead (bottom photo, p. 140). This provides a decorative finish to the bead, which stops short of the beam's end. The second-floor ceiling beams were chamfered, and the roof purlins and rafters were stop-chamfered at 45° angles. The crew finish sanded each member and treated it with tung oil.

From *Fine Homebuilding* magazine (June 1988) 47:44-47

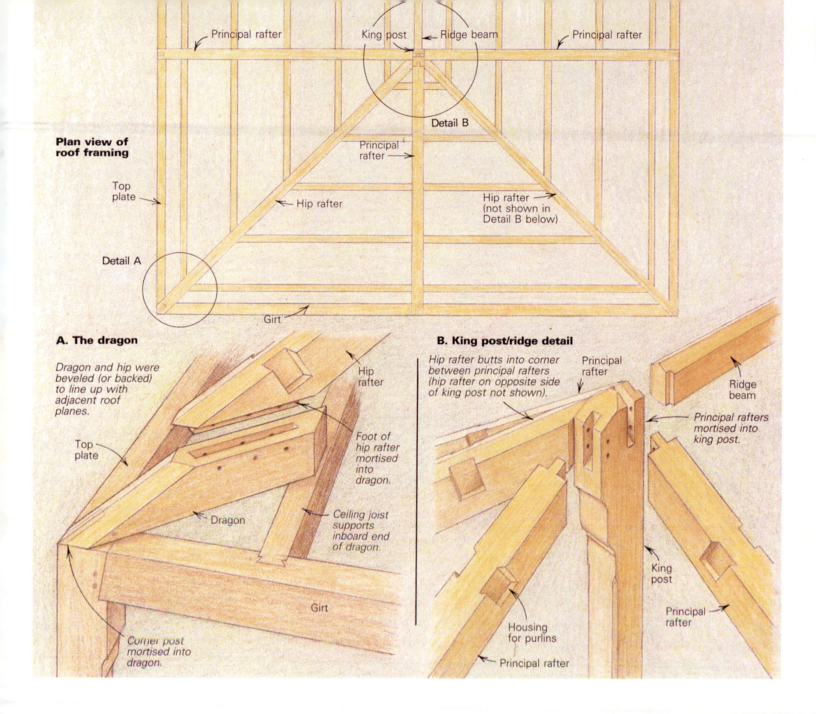

Plan view of roof framing

Principal rafter — King post — Ridge beam — Principal rafter

Detail B

Top plate

Principal rafter →

← Hip rafter

Hip rafter → (not shown in Detail B below)

Detail A

Girt

A. The dragon

Dragon and hip were beveled (or backed) to line up with adjacent roof planes.

Hip rafter

Top plate

Foot of hip rafter mortised into dragon.

Dragon

Ceiling joist supports inboard end of dragon.

Girt

Corner post mortised into dragon.

B. King post/ridge detail

Hip rafter butts into corner between principal rafters (hip rafter on opposite side of king post not shown).

Principal rafter ↓

Ridge beam

Principal rafters mortised into king post.

King post

Principal rafter

Housing for purlins

← Principal rafter

Taming the dragon—While the posts, beams and braces were being cut, Farrell and Thurrell were still speculating about the pair of hip joints in the roof, where seven members intersect—king post, ridge beam, two hip rafters and three principal rafters. The three principal rafters and the ridge beam are mortised into the top of the king post. The two hip rafters are beveled at the top and butt into the corners created by the principal rafters, held in place by compression (drawing above, detail B.). "The basic construction technique is common building experience," said Farrell. "Wanting the joint to look exactly right and working with massive 26-ft.long timbers created the challenge."

At the bottom end of the hip rafter, Farrell and Thurrell faced another problem characteristic of hip-roofed timber frames. The 90° intersection of two beams at an outside corner doesn't provide enough area to support the long foot of a hip rafter. On the Poliquin house, that foot, after being cut to the level angle for a 7-in-12 roof, measured 8 in. wide

by 32 in. long. In the book *Discovering Timber Frame Buildings* (Richard Harris, Shire Publications Ltd., Cromwell House, Church St., Princes Risborough, Aylesbury, Buckinghamshire HP17 9AJ, England, 1978), they found the answer—the medieval timber-framing technique of a dragon and cross.

The dragon is a short level beam that is mortised into the intersecting plate beams, bisecting the angle between them and projecting into the building. Traditionally the interior end of the dragon was joined at right angles to a cross—a short diagonal beam that ties the plate beams together at a corner. Instead of using crosses on the Poliquin house, the builders simply supported the inboard end of each dragon on a ceiling joist (drawing above, detail A.).

The dragon, which has an 18-inch long mortise to accept a tenon on the bottom of the hip rafter, helped Farrell and Thurrell find the backing angle of the hip rafter, because the bottom of the dragon sits on a level plane. After the hips were beveled (or backed) along

their top edge, they were cut to length. The hypotenuse of a 12-in. by 12-in. triangle is 16.97 in. and is used to calculate the length of hip rafters. When making calculations, this figure is usually rounded off to 17. But according to Farrell, "A problem with hip roofs is the multiplication of error. A $\frac{1}{16}$-inch mistake on one plane can become $\frac{1}{4}$ inch on another. The secret is care. We calculated all dimensions to the nearest $\frac{1}{256}$ in., *then* rounded them off to the smallest increment on our rulers and scribed all the pieces before cutting."

The three principal rafters, the king post and the hip rafters were test-assembled in the shop and triple-checked for square so that the dovetail housings for the purlins could be marked and cut. Housings, 48 in. o. c., had already been cut in the principal rafters because the purlins joined these members at right angles. All that remained was to mark the locations and angles of housings where the purlins joined the hip rafters. Angles were found by the scribe method. Small 7 in. by 7 in. blocks

In the old days, timber framers knew their work would be covered, so it only had to be sound, not pretty. But in this case, the builders knew that their work would remain exposed and that the hip joint in particular would be a focus of attention on the upper story (above). After marking out the shape with a template, cabinetmaker Kevin Rodel (below) uses a chisel to cut the lamb's tongues at the end of beaded edges on the ceiling beams.

were cut, placed tight against principal rafters in typical purlin fashion and scribed to the hip. Measurements were taken using the actual model and were carefully checked. After four right-hand and four left-hand sets of purlins had been cut, the roof frame was ready to go.

Taking to the air—Connected to the mainland at low tide by a half-mile sand spit, the Wood Island shoreline is sheer granite at high tide, which made it impossible to land building supplies. No wheeled vehicles are permitted on the mainland beach because it's mostly state park land. "We had two separate barge operators lined up," said Farrell, "but each of them thought better of the situation at the last moment." Instead, everything necessary for construction, from timbers to fresh water for the masons, was flown out by a helicopter piloted by Joe Brigham of Bow, N. H. (top photo, facing page). Over a two-day period, 142 1,000-lb. loads were flown out to the island from a staging area near Fort Popham.

On deck—Work on the island began in May 1986, with three days spent clearing scrub and poison ivy. The workmen either walked out and back at low tide, which made for 12-hour days (sometimes beginning at 2:30 a.m.), or they braved choppy waters and fast currents in inflatable rubber boats.

Since there were no ready-mix plants on the island, concrete for the twenty pads supporting the first floor deck had to be mixed by hand. Four reinforcing rods extended from each pad into holes drilled in the ledge with a gas-powered rock drill.

Pressure-treated 8x8 posts were laid out, cut and plumbed on site with an old Bausch & Lomb transit (No. 1) that Thurrell inherited from his grandfather. These posts were mortised into sills and girts that had been pre-cut in the shop. The procedure was to fix the pressure-treated posts to the pads, each extending one foot above deck level, establish the grade, mark each post and cut a shoulder at grade with a tenon extending above the shoulder. The floor joists were dovetailed into the sills. Because it wouldn't be seen, Farrell and Thurrell chose hemlock for the floor frame. It is cheaper than pine or oak, but rot-resistant and quite strong.

The deck was covered with 1¼-in. T&G plywood, which is capable of spanning 48 in. In the Poliquin house, the joists are 32 in. o. c., but because of the width of the timbers, the actual span is 26 inches. The posts are mortised through the plywood.

Raising the frame—In June, a crew of four on the island—Farrell, Rodel, Baggie Thompson and Larry Cochran—raised the bents using two wall jacks that Thurrell had had custom built. The jacks consisted of 24-foot sections of 3-in. steel pipe with pulleys at the top through which ³⁄₁₆-in. steel cable could be passed. Two ½ ton "comealongs" on each jack supplied the lifting power.

The advantages of the wall jacks became apparent when, due to lack of space on the deck, the last bent had to be raised with a traditional gin pole. Roof members were lifted to the roof with a homemade crane—a vertical length of steel pipe, guyed to the frame and equipped with a pulley, a lifting cable and a gasoline winch.

Closing it in—By early September, the frame was complete. Next, the roof was covered with stress-skin panels, sealed with plastic roof cement, and the surface was strapped for shingles. The crew used the best white cedar shingles available, but still had to block plane the sides of each one to get an attractive fit. The combination of light-colored roofing material and an air space between the shingles and the stress skin will alleviate the high temperature differentials that might otherwise cause deterioration of the roof panels.

The walls were sheathed with ship-lapped white pine boards run diagonally. They resist racking and provide a very good surface to which clapboards or other siding can be nailed. Conventional stud walls were run inside between the posts. "We normally use 2x6 studs to allow for more insulation, but since this house is intended as a summer home, we used 2x4 studs," Farrell explained. "The walls were prefabricated in sections and then attached to the timberframe. The trick is to fur the studs $^9/_{16}$ in. away from the posts and beams, so that when sheathing is completed, ½-in. sheet rock can be slid behind posts, beams and knee braces. The furring reduces the tricky, time-consuming job of masking all the beams and fitting the sheetrock to close tolerances. It also eliminates a lot of taping and prevents wall cracks that might otherwise occur as timbers expand and contract. Spacers for furring should be spruce rather than plywood, as the latter tends to expand if it gets wet." The beams were wrapped with 6-mil polyethylene before the stud walls went up to give the house a complete vapor barrier.

Thurrell says that using traditional sheathing costs about 15 percent more than using stress-skin panels. But overall, considering the ease of plumbing, wiring and venting, traditional sheathing is actually less expensive. It reduces what Thurrell calls "paralysis by analysis," as different crews sit around trying to solve the latest problem of wiring chases or plumbing vents. (For more on wiring in stress-skin panels, see Jeff Arvin's article on pp. 103-105.)

Farrell and Thurrell had to shut down the island operation for the winter, but by then the exterior was finished, sided with red cedar clapboards, stained and painted (photo right). The crew was sorry to leave. "It's a great place to work," said Thompson. "Nobody bothers you, and when the hammering stops, all you can hear are the waves and seagulls." □

Christopher Hyde is a free-lance writer living in Freeport, Maine.

All the construction materials from timbers to fresh water for the masons had to be carried to the island by helicopter (above). The crew either walked across at low tide or braved the choppy waters in a rubber boat. By the end of 1987, they had finished the exterior (below). With clapboard siding and a cedar-shingled roof, the island timber frame looks like the classic sea captain's house that inspired its design. *Photo by Andy Greif.*

Woodstock House

A blending of styles in a New England villa that's both rustic and refined

by Peter S. Brock

One of the most satisfying things for me about this house is the difficulty people have classifying it. Without overtly borrowing from any particular architectural style, the building possesses qualities of many periods and places. It presents very different faces to different approaches, and shapes within and around itself a diversity of spaces, all formed with a relatively simple and familiar set of architectural pieces.

Our clients, my parents, requested a house that would feel simple, sensible and old—like the 350-year-old English cottage where they had been living. Valerio Simini and I were launching our architecture practice together and were ready to pour into the project all the exploratory

A house with two wings. In form and detail, this Vermont house borrows from several traditional and vernacular styles. Slate roofs and integral, copper-lined gutters are used throughout. Dormers reach up as extensions of the wall plane, and are visually anchored by downspouts. In this view from the northeast, above, the guest wing is on the left. The hip-roofed extension on the right contains the master bedroom on the second floor and the kitchen below. On the facing page, the intersection of the two wings creates a south-facing courtyard. The windows are custom casements.

energy that our previous jobs had stifled. The typical English cottage possesses such richness because it is the product of many hands over many years. To approach this quality we sought to exploit each construction component to lend subtlety and intensity to the appearance and function of the house.

We aggressively plumbed the site and program for all the many design directions they might yield, and came to understand the design problem in terms of a series of dualities. The owners are worldly people with very simple tastes. The site is in Woodstock, Vt., a small country town bustling with cosmopolites. The house would be home for just two people, but

Photos, except where noted: Peter Brock

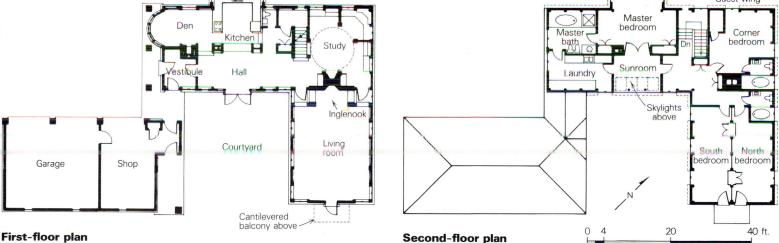

First-floor plan

Den

Kitchen

Study

Vestibule

Hall

Inglenook

Courtyard

Living room

Garage

Shop

Cantilevered balcony above

Second-floor plan

Guest wing

Master bedroom

Master bath

Corner bedroom

Dn

Laundry

Sunroom

Skylights above

South bedroom

North bedroom

N

0 4   20   40 ft.

should lure children and grandchildren to visit often and in numbers.

Valerio and I sought architectural counterparts for these opposites. The house should be rustic and refined, traditional and modern. It should take advantage of forms that are both regional and universal. And it should be energy efficient, with state-of-the-art appliances. Much of this would have remained theory without the generosity of the owners, the care of general contractor Paul Kristensen and the collaboration of several exceptional craftspeople.

Planning strategies—The site is a gentle plateau between hilly meadows, nestled among mature maples and commanding a dramatic view of the mountains to the southeast. Initially we almost put the house on an old foundation (the previous house collapsed 20 years ago), but then we remembered SITE REPAIR—the pattern formulated by Christopher Alexander which instructs: don't ruin the best part of the site by building there; put the house where the work of construction will make the greatest overall improvement to the land. So we moved the house to the north, where both sunlight and view improved. Then we turned our attention to the shaping of exterior spaces. By reaching out in two wings and connecting to the garage by a covered breezeway, the house would enclose two courtyards—one for arrival and entry, the other (photo above) a sheltered extension of the private interior spaces. One wing would be a central core of living space for the owners; the other would be for the guests.

We organized the floor plans on both levels to allow for ease of movement and expansive vistas through large windows. Masonry hearths at critical centers literally and figuratively anchor the house. By wrapping the building around the courtyard, we created views out of one set of windows into another, giving an almost urban feel to the house.

The downstairs rooms, though generally small and cozy, are open to each other and axially ar-

A few steps from the entry, the dining table fills a broad hallway. To the left, a wide pass-through connects this space to the kitchen. Stenciled white walls and a light-stained ceiling accent the cedar timber frame that is the structural and aesthetic heart of the house. The large French doors on the right open out to the courtyard.

ranged. From a tile-floored airlock entry, you step into a broad hallway that holds the dining table (photo above). To the right, tall French doors open out to the courtyard. To the left, you step up to the kitchen, which commands the entire area. Connected to the kitchen is a small den, which has a bay of windows overlooking the driveway. Here there's a Finnish style masonry heater built by Peter Moore that is the thermal heart of this entire wing.

Where the wings intersect, a highly geometric study with a circle of revealed ceiling beams eases the transition as you move toward the open living room, with its massive hearth and surrounding brick inglenook (photos facing page). This is a formal entertaining space.

Upstairs the master bedroom suite and one guest bedroom hug close to the house's core, while the guest wing affords dormitory-style sleeping accommodations (photos, p. 147).

A timber frame—Very early, a timber frame presented itself as an ideal means to give pattern and texture to the interior while affording the exceptional weathertightness of a stress-skin envelope. Stress-skin panels are laminated sand-

wiches of interior drywall, rigid insulation and exterior sheathing. When caulked and spiked to the outside face of a timber frame, they form a continuous insulative layer uninterrupted by studs or blocking. The panels used on this house were supplied by the Winter Panel Corp. (RR 5, Box 168B, Glen Orne Drive, Brattleboro, Vt. 05301). For technical details on stress-skin construction, see pp. 98-101 and *FHB* No. 25, pp. 42-46).

As we began to add functions to the timber frame, the bent spacing began to narrow. Ideally the bents would coincide with all major partitions and reinforce the geometry of rooms. The timber spacing should also coincide with the spacing between windows, and readily accept the insertion of doors, cabinets, fireplaces, stairs and closets. We hoped that closely spaced posts could be fairly slender and, if timbers coincided with panel modules, we might be able to avoid interior taped joints altogether. Our final design had 26 bents spaced on 4-ft. centers. This is five or six times the usual number of bents, a fact that earned us some strange looks from timber framers until we met Tedd Benson. He saw a positive challenge in the house's unusual complexity, and further enriched our design.

Enter Benson—In Benson and his crew we found a keen vision of how a timber frame could be an integral part of all one experiences in a house. It was his idea to rabbet the window units directly into the timbers to eliminate interior trim. His knowledge of Japanese framing came into play in making a panelized screen of the exterior walls. At the time that this frame was designed and cut, Masahiko Ishikawa, a Japanese temple builder, was working with Benson, and helped to conquer the unimagined complexity of the hips and valleys.

For the framing members, we chose Port Orford cedar for its straight grain, stability and light color. Except for the living room, where the second-floor girts are partially supported by king posts, most spans were fairly short. But in sizing the timbers, the joinery often called for larger sizes than were structurally necessary. At points where several timbers meet, there had to be enough room in the largest or principal member for all the pegged mortise-and-tenon joints.

Benson's crew efficiently coordinated the cutting and raising of over 200 timbers, each containing an average of six joints. With the aid of a crane, the frame was raised one bent at a time;

each bent subassembly usually contained two exterior posts, a horizontal girt or floor joist, a pair of rafters, a king post and two struts. In some parts of the frame, as many as eleven joints had to mate when a bent was erected. At the intersection of the wings, the joinery was especially complex, and fully assembled hip and valley rafter sections had to be dropped into place from above (bottom left photo, p. 147).

Mahogany windows—We shopped around for energy-efficient divided-lite windows and found Lawrence Berndt of Yankee Windows (P.O. Box 110, Cornish, N. H. 03746). Berndt designed a mahogany divided-lite casement with Heat Mirror glazing (Southwall Corp., 3961 East Bayshore Rd., Palo Alto, Calif. 94303) and his own system of double weatherstripping. He also developed a roll-down insect screen that's built into the head of each window unit.

The mahogany stock cost only slightly more than pine and is a handsome complement to the cedar frame. It's also stronger and more rot resistant, important factors considering the size of the windows (the average unit is 3½ ft. by 5 ft.) and the fact that they open outward.

Gutters in Vermont?—Out of stubborn belief in the power of invention and against all local opinion, we attempted the unthinkable—gutters on a Vermont house. Our roof forms concentrated a lot of runoff into the courtyard and other areas where heavy showers threatened serious erosion problems. Also, our detail for the intersection of stress-skin panels at the eaves gave a very flat profile where we felt some depth would be an important enhancement. The gutters are simple boxes of roughsawn 1x cedar lined with 16-oz. copper sheet. Though they're built into the eave, the gutters are separate enough to pose no threat of thermal or moisture leak even if they should flood or be ripped off entirely. The gutters are interrupted frequently by the dormers and feed into 3-in. dia. copper downspouts. These are an important vertical element on the facades, coinciding with the otherwise invisible timber posts, and reinforce the tower-like quality of the dormers. The system proved expensive and labor-intensive to install, and failures are keenly awaited by local skeptics. There were only minor backups in the first winter, but we've probably got to endure a good 20 years of ice, snowdrifts and snap-thaws before anyone is satisfied.

Radiant wood floors—We were well into figuring out how to lace hot-water heat pipes through the timber frame before Valerio and I realized that hydronic radiant floors were by far the best way to heat this house. In exchange for extra floor sleepers, a little insulation and the hassle of working out yet another system that nobody else seemed to be doing, we could have

Top right, in this view toward the study, a circular ceiling cutout brings joists into view. The floors and stairways are cherry. The living room, right, is the largest room in the house, and has a brick fireplace and inglenook as its focal point.

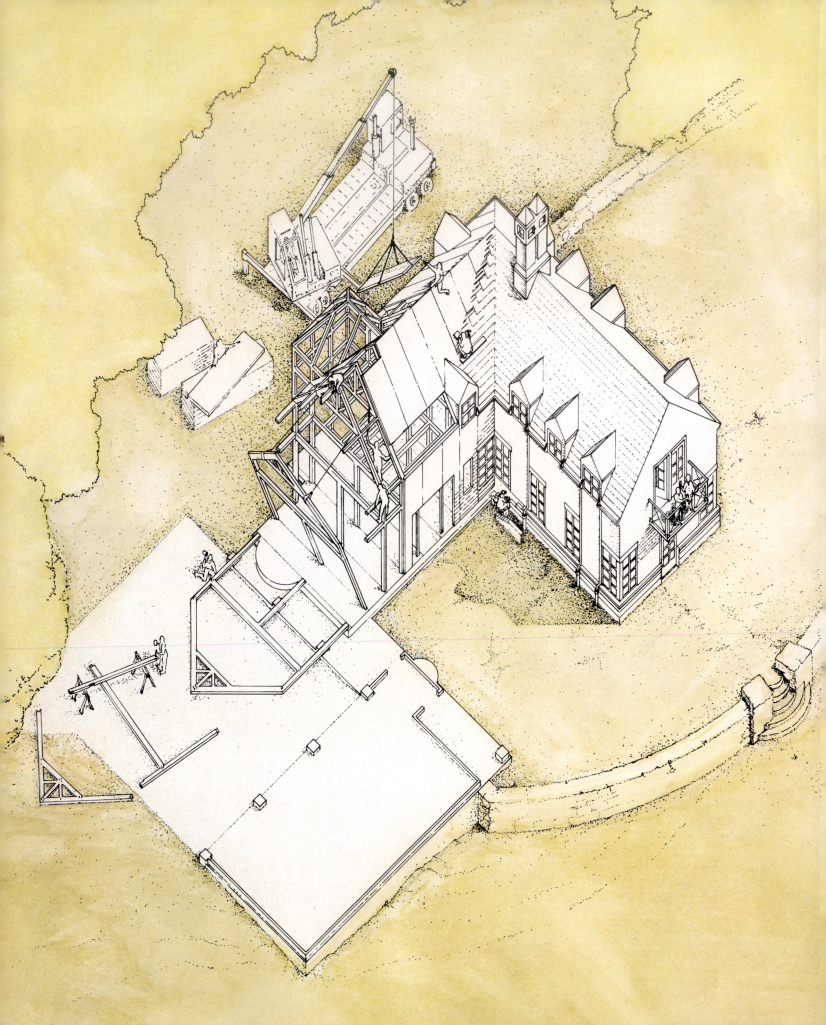

Construction axonometric

The author's axonometric drawing presents a fantasized bird's-eye view of the construction process. Here, a lengthy and complex sequence of operations is compressed into a single image. While the owners enjoy the view from the balcony of the finished guest wing, a crane aids in the installation of stress-skin panels and roofing slate near the valley where roof planes intersect. Nearer the driveway, timber-frame bents are assembled on the ground and then hoisted into position. Pegged mortise-and-tenon joints hold the frame together.

even radiant heat without ducts, radiators or baseboards and their attendant loss of wall and floor space. The house was already tight enough to require only a fairly modest system. We had the concept worked out but no qualified subcontractor until we found Matthew Friedlander of Solar Alternatives in Brattleboro, Vt. He had done quite a few radiant slabs and couldn't see why it wouldn't work in wood if we could be sure the hardwood flooring could take the heat.

For this radiant floor, the basic design procedure was to work backwards, starting from a design temperature of 87°F for the surface of the floor. Heat-exchange factors between elements of the floor assembly then dictated an air-cavity temperature of 100°F and a water temperature of 145°F. The flow rate was then set to offset the rate of heat loss under peak conditions (an outdoor temperature of −10°F). The boiler controller anticipates heating need by means of an outdoor temperature sensor and makes the appropriate amount of heat available. Four circulator pumps respond individually to the thermostats in each zone.

Thanks to Kristensen's care in installing the 1x6 T&G cherry flooring, it has shown only minor shrinkage gaps. The subtle warmth that emanates from the floor is complemented by the lustrous figure of the boards.

Hindsight—This was a difficult house to build. The design and construction spanned three full years. The project involved an unusually large number of tradespeople, none of whom had ever worked together before. The precise relationship of pieces that we sought in the finished house created an unusually intricate interdependence of effort as construction proceeded. Great amounts of time and effort were required

to coordinate things, and some mixed signals were inevitable. The 500-mile distance between our Washington, D. C., office and the site was a definite disadvantage.

Valerio and I know that architects, when proposing novel solutions, can evoke the kind of disenchanted reaction of "Sure, I'll build it upside down if that's the way you want it." So we gave extensive explanations and rationales, and did quite a few extra drawings in an effort to clarify details. Sometimes, we succeeded in drawing craftspeople into the solution of the

problem; other times, our efforts only convinced them that anything needing this much explaining is probably wrong.

Almost every aspect of the work was contracted on a time-and-materials basis. I would not do this again. Without having to make a solid bid on the work, some tradesmen never bothered to come to a really thorough understanding of the work ahead of time. They were not always fully prepared for the unfamiliar work and the final prices varied widely from initial estimates. Without reliable figures ahead of time it was very hard for us to guide our clients to appropriate value assessments, or to know how long anything would take.

In addition to a long construction process, our building methods called for some awkward sequencing. The timber frame went up first and afforded a useful staging for subsequent work, but its many members were also to serve as finished trim. It's a tribute to the care of the crews that this trim suffered as little as it did from ten months of foot traffic, water and miscellaneous wear and tear. The radiant floor produced a similar situation. If we sheetrocked before installing the heating system, we would have to punch holes through it for the pipes, or hold it off the framing. If we installed the pipes ahead of time then we would have to install sleepers and finish flooring in order to have a platform for the drywall crew. This would mean mud flying with finished cherry underneath. The drywall crew was tied up on another job anyway, so this was the route we went.

This house stands at the cornerstone of much that we hope to achieve as architects. Its design and construction drew momentum from its many participants and grew to be much more than any of us had initially set out to make. □

Upstairs. Masterful timber-frame joinery predominates on the second floor as the intricate geometry of the roof system reveals itself in every room. As is the case throughout the house, exposed framing members also serve as interior trim for windows and doors. The hip roof in the master bedroom, above, was one of the most difficult parts of the timber frame to erect. At left, workers maneuver a hip-roof subassembly above its corner. In the guest wing, top, rafters, collar ties and dormers flank twin beds. The door at the end of the room opens onto a cantilevered balcony.

Photo above left: Tafi Brown

San Juan Island Cabin

Simplicity and comfort in the same package

by Jeffrey Prentiss

Is it possible for three brothers, each with a different dream and an independent nature, to build a shared family retreat? It didn't seem likely to me at first. Each of us lives far from the others (Rhode Island, Texas and Washington), and each has a very different lifestyle. What we did have in common was the wish to maintain a strong connection with the area that nurtured us as children, the San Juan Islands, by establishing a vacation home for our families and our friends to share.

Back to the homestead—The 176 San Juan Islands make up an archipelago in northwest Washington. The waterborne U. S.-Canada boundary snakes around the islands on the north and west, with British Columbia's capital city Victoria located a few miles to the southwest. Our family link to this area goes back to the 1860s, when our great-grandfather and his brother homesteaded several hundred acres on one of the largest islands of the group, San Juan Island. The brothers and their children prospered on the island, but in the 1940s, the glamour of burgeoning Tacoma and Seattle to the south lured our mother and many of her generation to a different sort of prosperity. It was our generation that was the first to be raised off-island and to be taught the lessons of urban life.

Our urge to establish a family enclave was largely a refusal to be parted from our family ties to this place, to the island cemetery that marks the lives of innumerable kinfolk and to the still-existing trails where our mother, as a young girl, drove sheep from one pasture to another. By 1984, the acres that had been acquired since the original homestead had dwindled, until only a small stretch of waterfront land, purchased in 1918, was left. As children we had traveled from the mainland each summer to visit our grandmother and play with our cousins. An aunt still lives on the property, and an uncle and aunt have built a retirement home on an adjoining parcel. When our mother decided to sell her 2½-acre portion of the waterfront property, my brothers and I quickly conferred and decided that we would have to be the buyers.

We bought the land without intending to build on it for several years, but two events prompted us to earlier action. I was already liv-

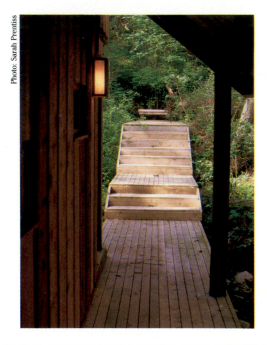

Photo: Sarah Prentiss

ing on the island, but my two brothers weren't satisfied with the houses they'd rented during annual visits and decided to build a vacation house for privacy and independence. The sudden death of our father finally prompted us to cement our fraternity by building a place in which to rendezvous. I didn't need another retreat on the island, but I was committed to our goal—and, as an architect, I was intrigued by the chance to design something for such precious land.

Defining a cabin—All three of us agreed that our family retreat should have the feeling of a cabin, so my first step was to define the cabin as a building type. I pored over books and magazines that illustrated second homes, vacation houses, retreats, cabins and lodges. I photocopied images that looked to have some semblance of cabin-ness and sent these to my brothers for comment. Each sorted through his stack and returned some of the images to me, along with comments about what was appealing and what wasn't. I gathered their responses and came up with a first attempt at describing what our cabin should be like.

A cabin, we agreed, is a shelter that is removed from human and technological con-gestion. A cabin is basic, functional and sympathetic to its surroundings, and it avoids excess convenience. Some measure of effort is required to accomplish day-to-day existence: ladders are used instead of stairs; the bath and toilet are necessities, not luxuries; and the location is at the end of a long journey that clearly separates the world of the cabin from the world outside. You have to pack it in, so to speak. Life in a cabin pivots around key functional elements: the kitchen and the fireplace. And at least some rooms of the cabin connect directly to the out-of-doors.

A cabin is built from local materials, either available on site or easily transported there. A mountain cabin, for example, could be built from logs felled from the surrounding forest and could have shake roofing if cedar trees were indigenous. The materials of a cabin are simple, clearly recognizable and honestly applied.

We work out a program—The next task was to agree on a program for the cabin. *The Place of Houses* (by Charles Moore, Gerald Allen and Donlyn Lyndon. Holt, Rinehart & Winston, 521 5th Ave., New York, N. Y. 10175, 1977), includes a useful and detailed checklist for people who are building a home. I tailored this list to our cabin project. Here are two examples of my questions:

Question #5: How are the dishes going to be washed?
  a. In a bucket, waterside.
  b. In a sink.
  c. In a double sink.
  d. In a dishwasher.
  e. You don't care; the maid does them.

A boardwalk ties the three-family cabin to the parking area by way of a footpath through the woods (photo above). The author designed the outdoor light fixture of fir and translucent glass. Several species of native northwest woods provide structure and finish inside the cabin (photo facing page). Posts and beams are Douglas fir, the roof decking is T&G spruce, and fir is used for trim, balustrades, flooring and the stiles and rails of the pine-paneled door to an upstairs bedroom. A cast-in-place concrete fireplace and metal bar-stock bookshelf supports give the rustic cabin some modern detail.

Photo facing page: Tom Collicott

Site plan

Firewood storage

Boardwalk to parking

W D

Kitchen

Up

Entry

Sleeping

Dn

Loft

Dn

Sundeck

Dining/ living

Dn

Open to below

North

Dn

Up

Loft

Fireplace

Dn

Outdoor fireplace

Sleeping porch

Sleeping

0 2 4 8 ft.

First floor

Second floor

Question #25: How accessible should the cabin be?

a. Vehicles will park on the county road with a footpath to the cabin.

b. Vehicles will park on the property but away from the cabin, within a short walk.

c. Parking is out of sight.

d. Parking is within sight of cabin.

e. Vehicles will have access to the cabin for moving purposes only.

f. Vehicles will park adjacent to the cabin.

This questionnaire was a big help in clarifying and quantifying what each of us expected. It also made it clear to me that it was far simpler to agree on the nature of what we were after than it was to agree on specifics.

Brother #1 wanted a tiny two- or three-room cabin that would have minimal impact on the land, cold running water, a wash bucket, an outhouse and no electricity. His cabin would be set deep in the woods at the end of a footpath, away from the shore and far from parking. Brother #2 wanted a small but comfortable cabin with indoor plumbing, electricity and some (but not all) of the amenities of home. He would forego a dishwasher, but would be near his car and close to the shore. Brother #3 wanted a cabin offering all the amenities of a luxury home, with several bathrooms, space for guests and a room for a governess. He would live on the shoreline.

After completing the checklists, we used the telephone and the mail to orchestrate what seemed like endless rounds of compromising. As the designer, I controlled the process, and that made me an obvious target for any disgruntlement my two brothers felt. It would

have been better if we'd sat down together to work out the program without the pressures of time, and if we'd studied and accepted all the details before construction began.

Each of us compromised our original definitions of a cabin. We agreed on a full bath and a half-bath, both indoors, located side-by-side away from the bedrooms. Similarly, we agreed (in answer to Question #5) that the dishes should not have to be hauled down to the shore and washed in a bucket. Instead, there is a double-bowl sink—but no dishwasher. Negotiations over Question #25, the placement of the cabin, led one brother to agree reluctantly to locate the cabin away from the shoreline, but only if the cabin's square footage was substantially increased.

The cabin plan—We finally came to a consensus about how the cabin should be laid out. The cabin has an obvious lack of formality, both in form and use. It contains a large central space, with a hearth that dominates activity in the way that a campfire focuses attention (photo previous page). Backing up to the indoor fireplace is an outdoor fireplace for barbecuing. At times the cabin holds only two people, but on special occasions, it has to fit all three families, or up to 14 people.

All interior spaces and exterior activity zones open directly into the central space. This eliminates hallways and maintains contact between the cabin's occupants. The only room with a separate entrance is a playroom for the children, located on the ground floor under the central room, out of sight of parents and out of earshot of adults seeking tranquility.

We wanted to emphasize the number three—three sets of French doors onto the deck, three main sleeping areas (one is the covered porch for the brother who prefers to sleep outside). We would cluster plumbing fixtures and piping at one end of the cabin, opposite the fireplace. Consolidating the plumbing would keep the cost down and reinforce the concept of simplicity, and would maintain a polarity between the wet zone and the fire zone in the central space. Finally, we agreed that despite the cabin's east-facing site, the long axis of the cabin should be aligned close to east-west to take advantage of solar gain along a long south face.

Siting concerns—It is tempting to build on the most dramatic part of a site, to conquer a hill or a shoreline with a house. But by building on a duller part of the site, the best spots are preserved in their natural beauty. The unobtrusive building site we chose became an additional focus that would have gone unnoticed otherwise. And, for us, avoiding the shoreline kept us from the throng of summer boaters who make the local waters look like the interstate on a Sunday afternoon. Building behind the tree line not only gave us privacy but, more important, it maintained a small part of the rapidly disintegrating natural shoreline (drawing above). We still have a view of the water and can hear the sound of seals on the rocks below.

We tried hard to keep site disturbance to a minimum during construction, although we had to blast out a corner of the rocky site to fit the house into the hill. Heavy equipment operators were instructed to stay within the

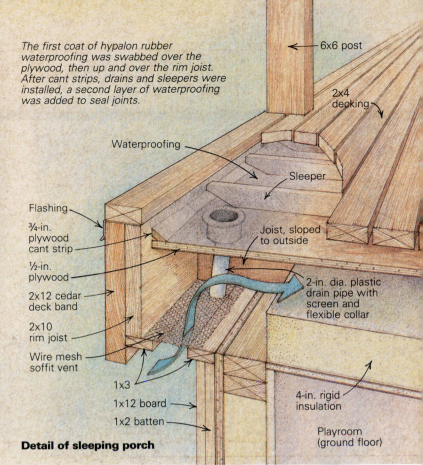

Photo: Sarah Prentiss

The first coat of hypalon rubber waterproofing was swabbed over the plywood, then up and over the rim joist. After cant strips, drains and sleepers were installed, a second layer of waterproofing was added to seal joints.

6x6 post

2x4 decking

Waterproofing

Sleeper

Flashing

¾-in. plywood cant strip

½-in. plywood

2x12 cedar deck band

2x10 rim joist

Wire mesh soffit vent

Joist, sloped to outside

2-in. dia. plastic drain pipe with screen and flexible collar

1x3

1x12 board

1x2 batten

4-in. rigid insulation

Playroom (ground floor)

Detail of sleeping porch

The board-on-batten siding establishes the location of window mullions to repeat the pattern of surrounding trees. The deck of the sleeping porch at the right is waterproofed to protect the playroom below it.

building's footprint. Trees and boundaries were marked with precision and watched with vigilance. Storage of construction materials and debris was limited to three spots: the building footprint, a temporary construction access road and the parking area. When construction was complete, the natural landscape remained intact. The county requires that septic systems be kept away from the shoreline so we pump waste to a septic system uphill.

Building trust—We had intended to build the shell of the cabin for $45,000. We figured that during joint vacations over the next few years, we could build the interior piece by piece. But as we worked out the program, we were tempted by the thought of building the complete cabin. A generous loan and unrelenting pressure from the wealthiest partner caused us to enlarge the scope of the project. By this time, I was in Japan on a research grant, but I spent a brief stint in the U. S. hustling to come up with details of the interior to complete the drawings.

The only contractor we interviewed was Peter Kilpatrick. He and his oft-times partner Tim Eslick had established a good reputation on the island by building several well-crafted houses. Kilpatrick's first estimates ranged from $50 to $55 per sq. ft. Despite the fact that we added several items that weren't on the original drawings, final costs worked out to be $51 per sq. ft.

One of the biggest blessings of building this cabin was working with Kilpatrick. The trust I had in him was especially important because I was back in Japan during much of the construction. The drawings were carefully

detailed and I conferred with him weekly by telephone, but he still had to make many of the design decisions that I would have made during site visits. When I returned home, I saw the results of the work and agreed with most of the decisions. Some of the choices were definite improvements to what I had drawn. For example, I detailed the 4x4 rough-sawn fir-top rail of the exterior balustrade to rest on 6x6 rough-sawn fir posts. Instead, Kilpatrick notched the posts into the rail—a stronger and more attractive solution than mine.

A post-and-beam structure—The characteristics we wanted in the cabin demanded that we build it of wood and expose its structure. Post-and-beam construction is straightforward, simple and fairly common on the islands. But San Juan's several mills didn't have enough Douglas fir timbers when we needed them so we had to order timber from a mill in Oregon.

The structural plan is simple. Starting with a 16-ft. by 60-ft. rectangle, I laid out a grid of 8-ft. square bays, with a half-bay at one end. The narrower 4-ft. bay accommodates wood storage on the main level and adds space to the bedroom above. Adding space to this bedroom compensates for it not having the water view. Along the north side of the rectangle, I added 4 ft. onto five of the bays for a covered porch and entry and on the south side, I added 8 ft. to five of the bays to provide a sundeck (drawing facing page). The site slopes steeply, so individual 8-in. by 16-in. concrete piers step downhill, following the grid. Six-by-six posts bear on the piers and support the rough-sawn 6x10 beams. At the first level, 2x10 floor joists hang from the

beams, and spaces between joists are filled with R-30 batt insulation.

The second-floor sleeping porch is open to the weather on three sides, so we had to waterproof its deck to keep water from leaking into the playroom beneath (drawing above). The system we devised relies on layers of Spantex, a hypalon rubber topping that provides a tough, flexible and waterproof coating (Tex Enterprises, P. O. Box 1192, Auburn, Wash. 98071). The top of each 2x10 joist was sawn to provide a slope toward the outside of the building, then decked with plywood. A layer of hypalon was swabbed over the plywood and up the inside of the rim joist. Once this layer cured we installed cant strips, drains and sleepers for the decking and a second layer of hypalon was swabbed on. A continuous soffit vent allows air to circulate in the joist spaces.

Each end of the cabin contains sleeping areas on a second level, but the center of the cabin is open to a gabled roof structure of 6x8 rough-sawn rafters, 4x4 rough-sawn purlins and 2x6 T&G spruce decking. In order to expose beams supporting each second level while allowing space for wiring and plumbing, the second-level joists bear on the tops of the beams, and 1x4 T&G decking was applied to the underside of the joists. We used standard 2x6 T&G fir decking for the finished floors at the second level, but it would have looked too busy if we had also used it in the central room. Instead, we had 2x12 fir planking specially milled for the first-level floors.

Simple materials—In keeping with the simplicity and honesty of a cabin's materials, we

Photos: Tom Collicott

Metal bar stock ground to a sheen supports shelving and dish racks (top photo). Ceiling fixtures are porcelain sockets with spun-aluminum shades taken from painter's lights. The chimney is a puzzle made up of back-to-back fireplaces, two flues and a flight of stairs (bottom photo). First, fireboxes were laid up with brick and block, then flues were built of tile. To bypass the beam and the indentations made by the stair, the exterior flue was twisted right, then angled sharply into the room. The flue for the interior fireplace was angled just enough to avoid a step. Both flues rise vertically from the ceiling to the roof. Forms for stairs and surround were oiled and reinforced, and a high-slump concrete was poured, filling even the tightest spots. The concrete was belt-sanded to give it a light polish.

chose the least expensive but most appropriate materials. The roof is metal, a material traditionally used on cabins. The siding is Western red cedar reverse board-on-batten, with 1x12 rough-sawn boards and 1x2 battens (photo, front cover). Both inside and out, there's an interplay of colors and figure between spruce, fir, cedar and pine.

Not all of the materials are conventional, however. We used ¾-in. by ⅜-in. metal bar stock to suspend shelves from the ceiling, to make bookshelves and to make the firescreen. Its light appearance makes the shelving for dishes appear to float between the cooking and eating areas (photo top). Slats in the bot-

tom shelf over the sink enable the shelf unit to function as a dish-drying rack.

The light fixtures in the kitchen are as simple and economical as we could find (photo left). These $3 lights are made from off-the-shelf porcelain fixtures, and the spun-aluminum shades are made from painter's lights. I designed exterior wall-mounted lighting fixtures to echo the materials and proportions of the cabin, with a rectangular fir frame and translucent glass panels (photo, p. 148). The fixtures have the diffusive character of paper lanterns.

The more romantic notions of "cabin" made us think of a huge stone fireplace for the main living area, but cost and the fact that the site is less than a mile from a gravel pit indicated cast-in-place concrete as the more economical solution. The mass of the fireplace became a real design puzzle, particularly because I wanted to include a stairway in the same area and a second fireplace for the sleeping porch. My solution was to cast steps into the side of the chimney. The concrete was later belt-sanded to a satin-smooth finish (photo lower left).

The chain-mesh firescreen was designed to work with the Rumford fireplace. The screen prevents sparks from shooting out but doesn't reduce the radiating heat from the upper third. Keeping this part of the opening free of mesh also allows easy access to the fire with wood or poker.

Transitions—My studies in Japan were the continuation of a long interest in how transitional devices heighten the experience of moving through space, something that the Japanese do well in both architecture and landscape design. I'm especially interested in transitions between inside and outside. So I tried to emphasize the experience of travelling by turning the gravel drive at an angle to the house in order to lengthen the approach and obscure the view of the drive from the house. Once you arrive at the parking area, you turn 90° onto a narrow woodland footpath, covered with sawdust, which suddenly meets a boardwalk. Only when you step onto the boardwalk and turn to follow it do you see the cabin. Materials underfoot change, angles of the path change and dimensions of the route change, each contributing to the experience of taking a journey.

My first design sketch of the house itself showed a static arrangement of windows, which was fine for light and observation but which did little to enliven the transition between inside and out. Then I thought about what someone sees while moving through the woods, catching glimpses of objects through the random openings between trunks and branches. It took no small amount of convincing to get my brothers to accept small windows with many mullions instead of larger plates of glass. Fortunately, no one seems to mind despite the occasional chore of having to wash 360 panes of glass. □

_____

Jeffrey Prentiss is an architect and landscape designer in Seattle and Friday Harbor, Wash.

The Tidewater Timber Frame

Three builders revive a vernacular form with modern shop equipment and production methods

by Gary Revel, Ryan Revel and Brent Clark

Like many timber framers, our introduction to this method of building began with the dismantling of old houses, barns and outbuildings. In the restoration work that we did with architect and historian George Fletcher Bennett, we came to appreciate the modular nature of early timber frames on the Delaware Peninsula. In fact, the new frames that we design and build have a similar selection of components.

The traditional Tidewater timber frame was a single-bay, single-story Cape Cod style house. A size of 16 ft. by 20 ft. was common, and the structural members typically were closely spaced and small in dimension (4x6 corner posts, 3x6 studs, 3x8 rafters). Stud spacing was usually determined by window and door location, with studs framing the opening. Otherwise, rough 32-in. centers were used. Chimneys were always on the gable ends; never in the center of the house, as with many traditional New England homes.

Nails were used in many later timber frames, but sparingly. On many of the old frames we examined, some joints were held with a single nail and one or more wooden pegs. Perhaps the nail

The authors are the owners of Timber Frame Systems, based in Frankford, Del.

was used simply to secure the joint until the joint could be bored and pegged. The earliest Tidewater timber-frame homes were built with oak. In the late 17th and early 18th centuries, colonists switched to red gum or poplar. Still later, pine framing members were used.

The basic 16-ft. by 20-ft. timber frame often formed the first section or core of a house that "telescoped" over generations with various additions. There are hundreds of these frames in the tidewater regions of Delaware, Maryland and Virginia. In 1983, we built the replica shown above as part of "Old Dover Days," a fair celebrating history and tradition in Dover, Del.

Combining tradition and technology—We soon became involved in new construction using timber-frame joinery. With the advent of stress-skin panels, modern timber-frame building became competitive with conventional stick-frame construction. In fact, enclosing a timber frame with stress-skin panels yields a structure whose energy performance will exceed that of a conventionally built home of similar wall thickness (see *FHB* #24, pp. 55-59).

The combination of tradition and current technology has been very exciting for us. The standard 4x8 size of the stress-skin panel lends itself well to the modular spacing of posts, plates and rafters in a typical residential timber frame (photos facing page). What we've done is to adapt our frame design to panel characteristics and modify the joinery somewhat so all this precise cutting can be done by shop equipment. The result, which we continue to refine, enables us to build structures that should last at least as long as those we've restored.

We use Southern yellow pine as our primary framing material. It is commercially available in a #1 dense grade, kiln dried, cut and thickness-planed to whatever dimensions we specify. This type of pine has a very high strength-to-weight ratio, as well as an attractive grain, and it's available in lengths up to 34 ft.

Joinery—The principal joints that we use in a typical frame are shown on p. 155. Many of these joints are identical to those we found in old Tidewater frames, while others are based on Japanese-style timber framing. Where we've departed from traditional joinery, it's because in a modern timber frame, all timbers and joints remain exposed in the finished house, so they have to look good. In the old days before stress-

Old and new. Found throughout the maritime regions of Delaware, Maryland and Virginia, the traditional Tidewater timber frame (photo facing page) is small, simple and symmetrical. After disassembling and restoring a number of these historic structures, the authors became involved in new timber-frame construction. Though their frames are larger and more complex (photos this page), they rely on similar joinery and structural members. Once erected, new timber-frames are enclosed with stress-skin panels (below left). These rigid sandwiches of foam insulation, interior drywall and exterior sheathing are spiked to the outside of the frame, giving great shear strength to the structure and creating a highly insulated building envelope. Openings in the panels are for doors and windows. Below right: This view of an enclosed timber frame shows how structural posts can be used as interior trim elements for doors and windows. Precise joinery and careful planning make this kind of integral design possible.

Photos: Michael Halminski (top and bottom left); Timber Frame Systems (bottom right)

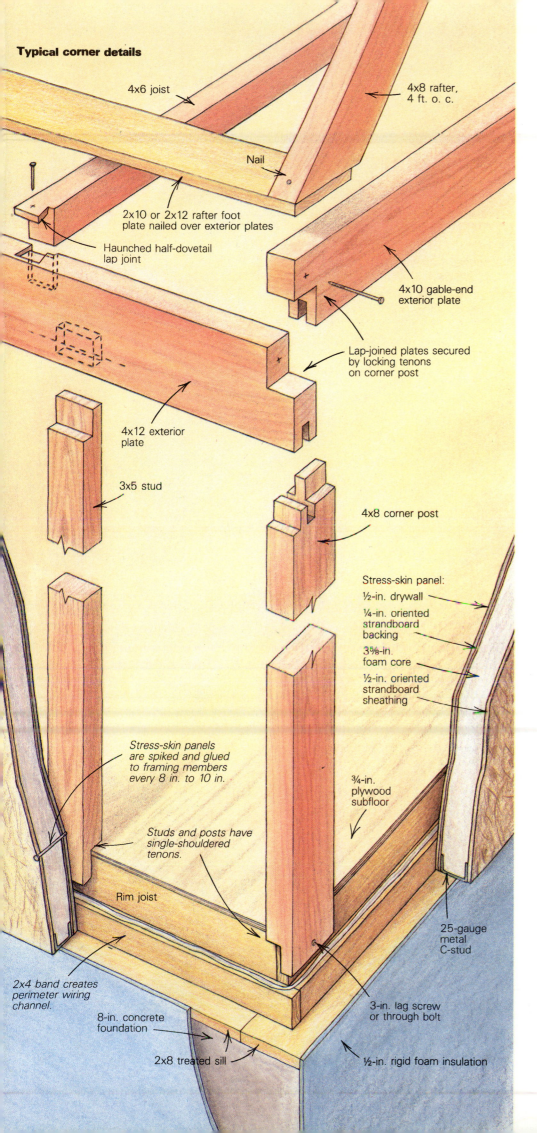

Typical corner details

4x6 joist

4x8 rafter, 4 ft. o. c.

Nail

2x10 or 2x12 rafter foot plate nailed over exterior plates

Haunched half-dovetail lap joint

4x10 gable-end exterior plate

Lap-joined plates secured by locking tenons on corner post

4x12 exterior plate

3x5 stud

4x8 corner post

Stress-skin panel:
½-in. drywall

¼-in. oriented strandboard backing

3⅝-in. foam core

½-in. oriented strandboard sheathing

Stress-skin panels are spiked and glued to framing members every 8 in. to 10 in.

¾-in. plywood subfloor

Studs and posts have single-shouldered tenons.

Rim joist

25-gauge metal C-stud

2x4 band creates perimeter wiring channel.

8-in. concrete foundation

2x8 treated sill

3-in. lag screw or through bolt

½-in. rigid foam insulation

Drawing: Chuck Lockhart

---

skin panels, structural members were usually hidden behind wood paneling or plaster.

To maximize strength and to help resist racking and withdrawal forces, vertical members (posts and studs) are tenoned on both ends, with either a nail or a wood peg securing the joint. Early Tidewater frames had solitary nails used in this way, but when we use nails, they are not exposed in the finished house. Horizontal members (plates, joists and summer beams) are joined with fully haunched, half-dovetail laps. Where plates join over a corner post, tenons in the post key into the plates, and the plates always overlap as well for added stability.

Collar ties are joined to rafters with a half-dovetail lap. We normally use a tongue-and-fork joint where rafter pairs meet at the roof peak. Both these joints are pegged.

Sizing and layout—Usually, corner posts are 4x6s or 4x8s. These support 4x10 and 4x12 wall plates that meet in a tenoned lap joint. Intermediate posts in an exterior wall are usually 3x5 studs. These are let into mortises in the plates with a single-shouldered tenon.

The widest spacing between posts is 16 ft. But we often use more closely spaced studs as interior trim for windows and doors. By adjusting stud layout, we can design a house whose window and door trim is integral to the frame.

Interior posts, horizontal members, floor joists and summer beams are sized and laid out according to the floor plan, spans and aesthetics. For spans up to 12 ft., we typically use 4x6 floor joists, spaced 32 in. o. c. Summer beams are at least 6x8 in section.

Rafters are generally 4x6 and/or 4x8, depending on run, span and roof load. On simple roofs, we join rafters to wall plates by making a level cut at the rafter end and nailing the end to a rafter foot plate that has been nailed to the top plate of the wall, as shown in the drawing. Where roof spans are long, rafter sections are haunched into intermediate rafter plates. These are simply kneewalls that run parallel to the main wall but inside it. We take care to space these intermediate plates so that they fall beneath a roof panel joint.

Shop techniques—Once a frame has been designed and the drawings are complete, we cut all the parts in our shop. Members are grouped into sets, and like components are cut together. Studs, plates, summer beams, joists, rafters and collar ties all lend themselves to repetitive processing at one of several work stations.

Some timbers have to be straightened and thicknessed before any cutting can happen. We do this at our first work station, which is a Hitachi 18-in. jointer/planer (model #F-1500).

The second work station consists of paired cutoff saws. One sits on a fixed table, while the other table is adjustable left to right along a straight track that runs the entire length of the shop (top left photo, p.157). Here studs and smaller posts are cut to final length.

Farther down the track, paired radial-arm saws (bottom photo, p.157) make up the third work station. As with the cutoff saws, there's one fixed radial-arm saw and one adjustable

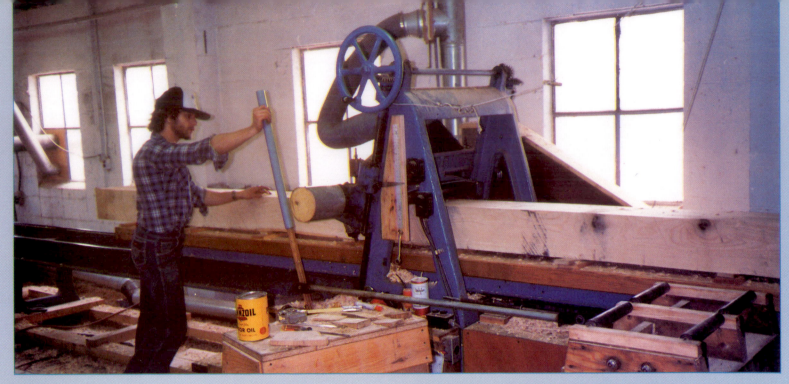

Another framer turns to power tools

by Stan Lesser

Bob Donahoe of Atlantic Boatworks likes to describe himself as "a lazy person looking for an easier way." This is a simplification, but it rings true if you look at the mechanization that Donahoe has brought to the craft of timber framing. Like other framers in different parts of the country, Donahoe has sought to replace labor-intensive handwork with specially designed power tools. Thanks to carefully thought-out equipment, Donahoe can achieve the tightness of traditional hand-cut joinery in far less time, and with less chance of error.

Atlantic Boatworks is located in Hartstown, a small town in northwestern Pennsylvania. Donahoe originally started the company in nearby Atlantic, Pa., intending to produce wooden boats. While a few steel boats were fabricated, the timber-framing business evolved when Donahoe built his house.

The heart of the Atlantic Boatworks shop is a huge timber facer that is used to surface and true all stock before actual joint cutting begins. Donahoe bought this 1893-vintage machine from the Bessemer and Lake Erie Railroad, where it had been used in manufacturing railroad cars. To resurrect the derelict collection of cast iron, Donahoe had to pour new babbitt bearings, devise a V-belt drive system and fabricate numerous missing parts. The work took a year. Timbers up to 24 in. wide and 18 in. high

move beneath the cutterhead on a sliding carriage, as shown in the photo above.

Once the timbers are surfaced, layout marks are made. Then all members are cut to length on a 24-in. DeWalt radial-arm saw. Donahoe works primarily in native red oak, and a 15-ft. 8x8 weighs about 1,000 lb. So he and his crew use an overhead hoist and trolley to maneuver timbers from one work station to another.

Tenons are cut on a Boice-Crane radial-arm saw that has been modified to accept two blades that are spaced apart the thickness of the tenon (middle photo). With adjustable stops in place, the operator needs only to check that the timber is against the fence to get a precise cut. The shoulders are cut on a Walker-Turner radial-arm saw.

Peg holes are drilled using an old radial-arm drill press with a 9-in. stroke. Because of the large size and type of drill, multiple holes can often be bored without moving the timber. To avoid tearout, the holes are finished from the opposite side after the pilot has punched through to act as a guide.

To cut mortises, Donahoe uses a Greenlee model 207 hollow-chisel horizontal mortiser with a 1½-in. bit capacity (bottom photo). Each timber is locked into a vise that's integral to the machine, and the operator uses compressed air to clear the waste from the mortise as it's cut.

Sanding, edge chamfering, test-fitting and sealing are the final operations before shipping the frame to the site. □

Stan Lesser is a furniture maker in Chicora, Pa.

To plane and dimension roughsawn red oak, Atlantic Boatworks uses an old timber surfacer rescued from a railroad company scrapyard (top). Timbers up to 24 in. wide and 18 in. high pass beneath the cutterhead on a sliding carriage. Tenon cheeks are cut on a radial-arm saw modified to accept two blades (middle photo), and mortising is done on a Greenlee horizontal mortiser (above) that can handle bits up to 1½ in. thick.

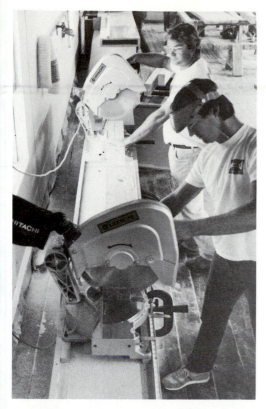

A well-equipped shop. Systematic cutting of all frame members happens at a series of work stations. Paired cutoff saws, top left, are used for repetitive cutting to length. One of these saws is fixed, while the other can be adjusted along a straight track to change the distance between blades. Below, a pair of radial-arm saws —one fixed and the other adjustable—form the work station for cutting tenon shoulders and miters. Mortises are cut with a portable chain mortiser, left, that is set up over layout lines and plunged into the wood. With a pair of routers and a plywood template, above, 1-in. deep haunches for joists are cut in wall plates. A straight bit in the first router removes the first ½ in. of the haunch; then a dovetail bit in the second router removes the final ½ in., relieving the back of the joint to ease assembly.

one. We use these saws for repetitive cutoff work, and also to cut tenons and miters.

The last work station consists of three portable power tools: a chain mortiser and two routers. The chain mortiser (a Makita model #7104) is set up on plates and summer beams, aligned with layout lines, and plunged to dig the mortise, as shown in the middle photo at left. Normally, no cleanup work with a chisel is required.

The routers are used in conjunction with templates to cut haunches in plates, rafters and summer beams. The plywood template is temporarily fastened to the plate with drywall screws (photo top right). The haunch is 1 in. deep. The first ½ in. is cut with a spiral-flute bit. A dovetail bit is chucked in a second router, and this is used to cut the second ½ in. of the haunch. The dovetail bit relieves the insides of the joint slightly, easing the assembly process.

Very little hand cutting or chiseling is required when we do a frame. This is the way we want it. With carefully thought-out production techniques and good power tools, we can confidently and quickly produce the groups of identical components that go into a timber frame.

Raising—Putting the house up is basically a three-phase operation: foundation and deck construction; frame erection; and panel application and window and door installation.

Decks are designed by us and built to our specifications. Except for the perimeter wiring channel and a setback that creates a ledge for the stress-skin panels, deck and subfloor construction is conventional. Because of the precision of the joinery, it's crucial to start with a deck that is perfectly square. All rectangles are squared by checking the diagonals, then horizontal members are leveled.

At their bottoms, exterior-wall posts and studs have single-shouldered tenons that fit into a perimeter wiring slot (drawing, p. 155). Where an interior post is mortised into the deck, we use solid wood blocking beneath the post to provide the meat for its mortise. Wood or steel columns transfer the load from interior posts down to concrete footings in the basement.

Perimeter walls are erected first. Posts are set and braced plumb, then plates are dropped onto them. Temporary braces nailed in place during the frame raising will remain until the frame and stress-skin panel shell is complete.

Rafter pairs are usually assembled with collar ties on the ground, and then hoisted into position by crane. Gable ends are also preassembled, and can even be paneled, with windows installed before the wall is raised.

Before panels are caulked and spiked to the frame, we recheck all posts and studs for plumb, and make sure that the outside faces of the timbers are flush so that panel attachment can go smoothly. Wall panels are attached first to provide shear strength. Generally, we install most full-size panels first, then fill in leftover areas. Any remaining voids that are too small to seal with panels are filled with insulating foam.

Finally, overhang, soffit and exterior trim details are completed, and tar paper is nailed down over the roof to keep the weather out until the shingles can go on. □

A Day at the Raisings

It had rained for two weeks straight, but on May 18th the skies around Hanover, Pennsylvania, were as clear as the motives of the people who assembled there. Like the guests at a potluck supper, timber framers from all over the country got together, not to eat, but to help Habitat for Humanity build a pair of houses for two local families. Instead of tuna-noodle casseroles and Jello salads, each framer brought a fully dressed timber, hoping it would fit with everyone else's. I suspect that over the years a lot of grandchildren will hear about "the time we raised two frames in one day."

—*Kevin Ireton*

Index